return
to Margo Ga

MW00714760

And So I Did

A Northern Irish Memoir

By

Patricia Sheehan

Copyright © 2004 by Patricia M. Sheehan

ISBN 0-7414-1725-1

Published by:

519 West Lancaster Avenue
Haverford, PA 19041-1413
Info@buybooksontheweb.com
www.buybooksontheweb.com
Toll-free (877) BUY BOOK
Local Phone (610) 520-2500
Fax (610) 519-0261

Printed in the United States of America

Printed on Recycled Paper

Published November 2003

DEDICATION

For my children
Terrie, Brian, Rory and Kevin
and
my grandchildren
Sean and Toby

ACKNOWLEDGMENTS

I'd like to thank my husband, Neil for putting up with half-a-wife for several years and cooking up most of the meals. My siblings, Pauline, Irene, Denis and Michael for their encouragement, and for awakening memories that lay dormant for so long. We had many laughs recalling happy times together. Many thanks to all the members of the San Dimas Writers Workshop for their welcome suggestions and critiques. To Judith Cunningham for typing the first half of my material to her computer and then onto a disk so that it could be entered into my first computer. To Deanna Hessedal Tiddle for her patience, and tireless help in my switch from typewriter to iMac. To Janice Bartholome, Dolores Cullen, Pat Feldman, Don Higgins, Susan Littlepage and Judy Vigo, for their extra help outside of the workshop. Without all these people this story would never have been written.

Chapter One

I've been standing behind the door, repeating over and over to myself. "Mammy, may I have thrupence for sweets?" After taking the plunge and asking, I drop my head and wait.

Mammy looks serious and asks, "Did you wet your knickers, Patricia?" I don't need to lift my skirt, but just squeeze my legs together in my baggy knickers and feel that awful dampness all the way down to my knees. I'm still hanging my head, and say, "I did, Mammy," in a very quiet voice.

"Pardon me?" Mammy says.

"I did, Mammy," I say again, this time a little louder.

"Ach, Patricia." She shakes her head no, and runs water over the dishes. "Didn't I tell you only an hour ago not to be wetting your knickers. Go up and change, Patricia, and don't forget to soak them in the lavatory sink." I trudge upstairs, and pull my wee stool over to the hand basin. As I run the water, I'm wishing I had taken the time to come in, instead of trying to hold it when I was dying to go. I get a fresh pair of knickers out of the hot-press and they're lovely and warm against my cold, damp cushion.

I'm dreaming of Dolly Mixtures, my favorite sweets and get a bright idea. I return to the street, and find Florence, who lives two doors down. "Do you think your mammy would give you thrupence for sweets?" I ask. "Mine is raging at me."

She disappears into their house and I wait. Mammy is always saying, "That wee girl has all her orders, so she

1

does." She's right. Florence is three years old like me, but she's an only child *and* adopted. She gets just about anything she wants! It must be great to be the only child, so it must, but I think I'd miss my older sisters.

She comes back out in no time waving a thrupenny bit in the air.

We skip down to the sweet shop and stand behind the older children, waiting for them to make up their minds. Mary Cunningham is hemming and hawing, and hopping from one foot to the other. Finally she decides on a bar of McGowan's toffee. Desi O'Connell is waiting for a slider, and we watch with mouths watering as Mr. Mullholland gets a wafer, slaps vanilla ice cream on it, then slaps another wafer on top, making a wonderful ice cream sandwich.

Desi walks out the door and we gaze at him. Florence orders two ounces of Dolly Mixtures.

We dander up the hill and Florence is more than generous as she lets me pick the ones I like. My favorites are the pink ones and she likes the yellow. Desi is standing at the top of the street licking the edges of his slider, and Florence is called in just as we reach her house.

Florence lives in a corner house, and as I go around toward home I see our Irene jumping up and down on the footpath. She seems awfully upset, and as I get closer I can see why. Right in front of our house are two dogs that seem to be stuck together. Their heads are pointing in different directions and they're doing a kind of circular dance. Round and round they spin like a merry-go-round, with their tails standing straight up in the air above the spot where they're joined. I've never seen anything like this before. Their tongues are hanging out and dripping water on the footpath. It's like they just ran a race. The big one's looking like he's ready to pass out and the wee one is making a kind of a yipping sound.

Irene is almost crying. "Someone must have vacuumed them together, Patricia. What are we going to do?"

"Maybe they used glue," I say. "Let's go ask Daddy, he'll probably know how to get them unstuck."

When we tell Daddy about the awful problem with the dogs, he opens the front door to have a look. "Don't worry about them, girls. Stay in the house now, your mammy's just after making your lunch anyhow."

We finish eating and Irene runs upstairs to look out the window. "They're unstuck!" She shouts.

"See, didn't I tell you not to worry?" Daddy yells back.

With the dog problem fixed I decide to go out to the back garden and see if our cat, Ginger, is around. I don't see her, but I can smell the wild roses that grow all over the hedge between our house and the MacCarrick's. The flowers are pale pink and smell so delicate. Irene and Pauline make perfume from their petals. They just soak them in a jam pot with water for a week or so. Pauline says that when she is grown up and has a job, she is going to buy real perfume from the chemist's shop. Pauline is already eight and Irene is six.

Mrs. MacCarrick comes out her back door and shouts, "Yoohoo, Mrs. Owens, yoohoo."

Mammy comes out. She's smiles, wipes her hands on her apron, and leans over the hedge. "What is it Mrs. MacCarrick?"

"Can the girls come to Sandra's birthday party on Saturday?" They stand facing each other across the rose covered hedge between the gardens, just like they do every day. Mammy nods her head, "Certainly, they'll be delighted to hear about it, so they will." They start chatting about how fast children grow. "How time flies."

I'm trying to imagine the clock on our mantelpiece flying though the air, and it doesn't make sense to me.

When we ask about buying something for Sandra, Mammy suggests that we walk down to the chemist's shop on the Glen Road. She hands Pauline a shilling to spend on the present. "Pauline, you hold the money. Irene, you hold Patricia's hand. On second thought, Pauline, put her in the tansad. She'd never make it walking there and back. You'd only end up having to carry her, so you would."

3

Pauline gets the tansad that we all used when we outgrew the baby pram and lifts me in. I'm feeling a wee bit embarrassed, as I haven't been in it for a long time. I think I should be able to walk like them. I'm too big to be pushed like a baby. I even know my A B C's and all.

When Saturday arrives we're scrubbed clean and dressed in our finest for the party.

Mrs. MacCarrick is just about the best baker on our street. Walking into her parlour, we see a big table set with all kinds of beautiful pastries and a scrumptious looking cake. She's been saving her sugar coupons for the party, and the cake has three layers with whipped cream and jelly between each layer. She has also baked crunchy white meringues that melt in your mouth. She told Mammy that she got the eggs from her brother's farm near Lurgan.

We go into the back garden first for a few games of Blindman's Bluff. The winner gets a wooden spinning top called a peri with a whip that is used to keep it going. Everyone loves to play this game, and the older children usually spin their tops up and down the street for ages before one hits the air-raid shelter, falls over and they're out. Our Pauline usually beats the others, but she's very modest and not the least bit full of herself.

We're called back to Sandra's house, and after singing "Happy Birthday," we dig into the most wonderful cake in the world. All our mother ever bakes are wee buns with no cream or icing, although we do love them, and her apple tarts are delicious.

When we've had our fill, Sandra opens her presents. We're thrilled that she likes the paper dolls we bought for her. Each doll has at least two different dresses, so Sandra and our Irene should be kept busy for hours on rainy days from now on.

Sandra's brother Edwin is my age and we're good friends. The MacCarricks are the only family on Andersonstown Crescent or even in our part of Belfast who don't go to St.Theresa's Church. Broadway Presbyterian is their church. Sandra goes to a different school called Rose-land. It sounds real fancy to me, so it does.

Their church is different from ours. Edwin says they have baskets of fruit around the place and I wonder if they ever get to eat any. They don't have crucifixes like we do and his mammy never says "Jesus, Mary and Joseph" the way the rest of the women on our street do. They have to take a bus all the way down to Divis Street, but we only have to walk up St. Meryl Park to the Glen Road. I ask Edwin if his minister is as frightening as our priest.

When we go to Sunday School he climbs up in the pulpit and looks down at us with fierce eyes. He bangs his fist on the pulpit, frowns at us, and calls us instruments of the devil. He keeps reminding us to go to confession. I'm very glad that I'm too young yet and I'm always relieved when it's time to sing "Hail Holy Queen." Edwin thinks his minister is almost as scary as our priest. They never sing hymns to Mary though, just ones like, "Holy God We Praise Thy Name."

He also says that Sandra gets hit with the cane at her Protestant school just like our Pauline does at her Catholic one.

When the party's over we go home and ask Mammy if we can forget about dinner tonight because we've never been so stuffed. She nods, then tells me to go up and have my forty winks. I drag myself upstairs. When I wake up I can hear Daddy singing while bathing. I love to listen to him and I think he's good enough to be on the wireless, so he is:

There are three lovely lassies in Banion,
And I am the best of them all...

I'm taking my shoes to be mended...
And my petticoat to be dyed green

And I shall be dressed like a queen
Oh...I shall be dressed like a queen

I try to imagine my daddy dressed like a queen, and it makes me giggle.

Sometimes when he falls asleep in his easy chair, we climb up on the arms, and put Mammy's curlers in the long hair on top that he usually likes to comb straight back. When he wakes up he looks at himself in the mirror and acts like he's shocked. He doesn't seem to mind the curls, but chases us around and we scream in delight.

Daddy's favorite song is "I'll Take You Home Again, Kathleen." It makes me feel happy to be living in Ireland. He sings while he's shaving, too. I love to watch him dab the lather on his face with the soft shaving brush and run the blade in neat, wee rows across his cheeks. I get him some bits of newspaper to put on the nicks.

Sometimes people take too long in the lavatory, because they're busy reading the squares of newspaper hanging on the string. You have to crumple them up before you use them, so that they're softer on your bum. usually I can hardly hold it, when Irene's in the toilet. She is just after learning how to read and can't bear to see anything in writing without taking the time to read it. I usually end up hopping up and down and begging her to please hurry up.

After listening to the last verse of Daddy's song, I hear him starting up on "Jerusalem." It has so many verses that I decide to go out and play instead of waiting to hear them all.

Irene is sitting on the doorstep adjusting the skates that she shares with our Pauline. I like to watch them when they're wearing one skate each. They spread their arms and each skate on one foot down the hill. Maybe I'll learn how when I'm older.

Before Irene can get them on, Sandra comes in the front gate and asks if Irene can go with her to Celine McGuire's house. Irene loves to go there because Celine has a playhouse in her back garden with real furniture and everything. She hands the skates to me.

"Why don't you try them, Patricia." She skips happily down the street after Sandra and I sit on the step. I can't slide the skates in far enough to fit my shoes, and the tightening key is too hard for me to twist anyhow.

"What's the matter?" I ask a few minutes later, when I see Irene coming back up the street looking sorrowful. She's having trouble keeping her bottom lip from shaking.

"Celine can only play with one person at a time, so I was sent home." I hand over the skates and tell her they're far too big for my shoes. "You could always go up and see if Mairead can play with you," I suggest. Just because Irene wears spectacles, she sometimes gets left out, and she has to listen to boys calling her "Specky four eyes." But she's very brave about it and pretends it doesn't even bother her. She asked me the other day, if I thought she might be adopted.

When we're all together, because of Irene's blonde hair and green eyes, people will look at her and say to Mammy, "She's not one of yours, is she?" and Irene is really beginning to believe it.

Chapter Two

"Will you please get out from under my feet, Patricia!" Mammy says. Material is draped over the kitchen table, and she's cutting out a school blazer for a boy who lives up the Road.

"But, Mammy, this is the only warm room in the house!"

"I know, love, but could you sit on the sofa and do some colouring or something? I've got to have this ready for a fitting tonight."

Daddy comes into the room and grabs me up into his arms. "Don't worry, Bessie, I'll take her downtown. I'm going to pick up my wages anyhow."

Daddy drives a trolley bus, and seems to really enjoy his job. I love to go with him and when we're walking over toward the docks, his hand is like toast and it keeps mine lovely and warm. I'm wearing a beautiful pale pink coat that Mammy made for me out of one of Aunt Eileen's old coats. It even has lining, and feels so cozy and warm.

Daddy gets his wages at an office near the docks. I love to lean over the railing and look down at the boats, big and small, that come and go delivering and picking up goods.

One boat has a scruffy brown and white dog on deck, and he's barking at me, as if I were going to come on board or something. The water in the quay is very dark and oily looking. I'd better watch my step because they wouldn't be able to find me if I fell in. When we reach the office, some of

Daddy's friends are also getting their wages, and they smile at me and call me "Sweetie" and "Love."

"This is my little Fairy Queen," Daddy says with a smile, and he laughs when I hide behind his legs.

When we're walking back down Royal Avenue, I'm counting the British flags flying above the shops.

"We're in Ireland and there's no reason we should have to be looking at foreign flags like Union Jacks," Daddy says. "Some day, please God, you'll be counting Irish Tri-Colours instead."

Maybe when I'm older, I'll be able to understand all about flags and foreigners.

When we get home, Mammy is already sewing the sleeves into the boy's blazer. She shows us a bandage on the end of her pointing finger. "Got me again, Danny," she says with a sigh. She's just after having the needle go right through her fingernail, and I don't know how she got it out. It's not the first time this has happened, and we hate to see her in pain. But she goes on sewing anyhow.

Pauline answers the door when the boy comes for his fitting, and shows him into the parlour. We keep this room for visitors and the sofa is really nice. There's a piano also, and a pretty lamp with a shade that has tassels hanging all around the bottom. The fireplace is hardly ever lit, as coal is too dear.

Granny Gordon's parlour is very fancy with it's soft velvety sofa and white lace curtains. It even has a wee button on the wall. When we ask about it, we are told that in the old days, rich people lived in her house and they would just push the button to call the maid. People don't live like that around here anymore.

The next morning I'm watching Daddy shining his shoes for Mass. He has an iron thing that's called a *last* in the same cupboard as his polishing kit. It's shaped like a foot, and all he has to do is buy a new heel when the old one wears down. He then puts his shoe over the last and hammers the new heel on with tiny nails.

As we walk up the road to St. Theresa's, I keep looking down to make sure that Daddy's shoes are holding their shine. I start to look at other men's feet as well but Daddy's shoes still seem to be the shiniest.

We're all sitting in Mass now and the priest is giving his usual boring sermon. As he drones on, some people are nodding off. Their heads move slowly down so that their chins are resting on their chests and in just about five seconds their heads jerk back up again and they pretend they were awake the whole time. I'm staring at the fox the lady in front of me is wearing. Its head is hanging over the back of the pew, and its wee beady eyes are looking right at me. Suddenly its mouth opens and it begins to speak.

"All I did was kill one plump chicken to feed my babies and that bleedin' farmer had to put out a trap and kill me. All that, so this rich lady could throw me over her shoulder. There's not even enough of me to do a decent job of keeping her warm and now my babies are orphans."

"I'm so sorry, Mrs. Fox. I wish you weren't dead. I'd bring you back to life if I could!"

I feel an elbow in my side and Mammy is looking down at me in exasperation. The lady wearing the fox is looking around in a huff and her nose is a mile in the air. Mammy looks embarrassed and I'm relieved when the priest says, "Please stand for the creed." *I believe in One God, the Father Almighty, Maker of heaven and earth, and of all things visible and invisible.*

The drone goes on, and I'm looking across the middle aisle now at an old woman who's starting to sway back and forth. Before you can say "Tir Na Nog; The Land of Youth" she's pitched sideways and landed on the kneeler in front of the people next to her. There's a noisy scramble to get her up, and the ushers drag her out into the fresh air. I suppose she's sitting on that wee wall outside right now, with her head between her knees. It happened to Irene once and she told me all about it.

Wintertime is definitely the most interesting time to go to Mass because all the windows are closed and the crush of

10

people makes the place real stuffy, so it does. I'm looking around to see who will be next, and the ushers open all the doors to let in the fresh air. You can hear the cows mooing in the field behind St. Theresa's School. I suppose they're wondering what we're all doing in here.

The lady wearing the fox is feeling the chill now and is starting to jerk her shoulders. She pulls the fur closer to her throat. This makes the poor wee fox sway back and forth. I'm just putting my hand out to steady it when Mammy clears her throat again and gives me a sharp look. I pull my arm back and concentrate on how to get rid of the watery discharge that the breeze has caused to run out of my nose. Daddy and his hanky are all the way down at the other end of the pew. I try sniffing it back up, but there's just too much. I'm starting to raise my sleeve towards my leaking nose, when Mammy looks over and digs me in the side again. The word finally gets to Daddy and his hanky is passed down the line to my great relief.

When it's time for Communion, Mammy, Daddy and Pauline go up to receive Jesus. Irene and I kneel down as we haven't made our First Communion yet. The lady with the fox must have forgotten to go to confession, because she's still sitting in the pew while the Pure of Heart are receiving Jesus. I'm kneeling so close now, that I can actually feel the wee fox's soft fur. I touch her nose with my finger, and it's dry and hard. I wish she could be running up the mountain loney, smelling the bluebells and primroses and licking her babies clean.

After communion and the closing prayer we all file out of the church. I try to keep up with the wee fox as she sways back and forth on the lady's back. But too many big people get in the way and I can't see her any more. Maybe next week she'll come to the nine o'clock Mass. I hope she does. I know one thing for sure, so I do. When I grow up, even if I become rich and important, I'll never wear a dead fox over my shoulder!

***

It's Christmas Eve again, and the inside of our house has been scrubbed, dusted, and polished. Mammy is baking, and it's time for us to go with Daddy to the Christmas Tree lighting at Belfast City Hall. The tree looks almost twice as high as our house and just as wide, so it does.

The crowd is standing quietly listening to Christmas carols, waiting for the big moment. I'm wondering how they could possibly have gotten those decorations all the way to the top. A cheer breaks out when the tree is finally lit and, after admiring its beauty, we have to listen to a long speech by some important man. After the speech Daddy says, "It's time to stop at the churches and look at all the lovely cribs."

"Daddy, maybe we should be going home for fear of Father Christmas missing our house," Irene whines, She is getting very fidgety and looks worried.

"Aren't I just after leaving him a note before we left to visit our house on his late run?" Daddy says with a grin, and Irene smiles.

St. Peter's crib is lovely, with the donkey and cow resting in the straw behind Mary and Joseph and an empty space in the hay for the baby Jesus. "If we came in here after midnight," Daddy whispers, "you'd see the priest putting the infant in the manger."

Back on the bus again we pass the Diamond Cinema and Daddy starts to reminisce.

"When your mammy and I were first married I was working as a projectionist in that picture house."

"You must have loved your job, Daddy." Pauline says.

"Aye, I did, but the money was a pittance. I remember I used to run the Charlie Chaplin features backwards after they came to the end, and the weeuns would hoot and whistle and enjoy every minute of it."

"I wish we could've been there," Pauline says.

"But you weren't even born yet," Daddy says and then chuckles to himself. "I used to cut out all the kissing scenes in the grown-up features."

"Do you think they noticed?" Pauline asks.

"If they did, they didn't complain. They were better off without that nonsense anyhow."

This time we've reached St. Paul's, and we hop off the bus one more time. Their crib is smaller but more colourful than the one at St. Peter's.

"That cow looks real," Pauline whispers as we kneel before the crib, and Daddy laughs.

"If it *was* real, this Church would stink something awful. It *is* a very good likeness." The crib is also missing the baby, and when we get off at St. John's it's the same story.

"We'll look at St. Theresa's crib tomorrow when we go to Mass," Daddy says, and I'm glad. Irene looks relieved too. It's been a long day. We're happy to be going home, and Irene has been worried all evening in case Father Christmas didn't get the note.

There's a lovely little tree in the parlour when we get in. Its branches are a wee bit spindly but it smells like the forest.

Mammy has the extra pillowcases ready with some paper and pins. Pauline writes our names on the paper and Irene cuts them out in neat squares. We each pin our own name on a pillowcase and Mammy tells us that she will lay them under the tree after they decorate it.

"Time for a sponge bath," Mammy says. "Then you can sit by the fire for a while."

Gazing into the flames I'm excited that this is the night we've been waiting for.

"How does Father Christmas know that our house has children?" I ask.

"He's magic," Mammy says with a smile.

"So he'll know that the parlour chimney is the one without the fire?" Irene asks.

"Indeed aye. He'll have no problem figuring that out," Mammy says, and I feel a bit better about the problem of Father Christmas getting burned.

"He also makes himself shrink and then get bigger again, to make it easier on him," Daddy assures me. "Why don't you girls go on up now. You wouldn't want him to catch you sitting here by the fire." He only has to say it once and we are climbing up the stairs with delight.

Lying in bed with lots of overcoats piled on top of the blankets, I'm finding it hard to fall asleep. I hear the door opening softly, and I bury my head under the covers. The sound of shuffling steps moves from one bed to the other and finally the door closes quietly again. I can hardly breath. It must have been Father Christmas. What will I do if he saw me lying awake? I close my eyes and the next thing I know dawn is creeping through the window.

Pauline and Irene are stirring, and I jump out of bed. We tiptoe down the stairs and shiver with excitement, as we admire the tree that Mammy and Daddy decorated with Christmas cards and balloons while we slept. Then we see the pillowcases laid out underneath, and we each find the one with our name on it.

"Here, Patricia, this is your doll, I didn't ask for one," Irene says, as she pulls a lovely doll from hers.

I feel inside my pillowcase and pull out a doll with a delft head and a cloth body. "That was *your* doll, Irene, I've got one too," I say as I hug my own doll. It has dark brown hair painted on its head and Irene's has yellow hair. We each have a colouring book and some crayons.

"Oh look, did you ever see such a beautiful schoolbag?" Pauline asks with excitement when she looks in her pillowcase. There are a few books inside it, too.

After Mammy and Daddy wake up and watch our excitement, we have to get ready for Mass. I am relieved when we arrive there and see that our priest remembered to put the baby Jesus in his little bed of straw.

When we get back home we can smell the chicken cooking in the oven. Mammy and Daddy had to pluck and clean it last night. They must be tired from all the things they had to do. The day has been wonderful so far, and tomorrow we go down to Granny's for Boxing Day. It's a holiday from work for all, the day when people go to their other relatives houses to exchange presents. Some people think it has something to do with punch boxing, but I think the real meaning has to do with the boxes that contain the presents for the extended families.

When we get to Granny's on Boxing Day, our uncles, Tom, Frank, and Freddy and aunts Lucy, Eileen, and Marjorie, are there. Granny has a turkey in the oven and all the women are helping with the meal. Granny has her usual holly tree in the parlour. It has lovely red berries all over and it feels prickly if you touch the edges of the leaves with your finger. Mammy has brought some Madeira cakes that she made while we were at the City hall with Daddy. They're just like fruit cakes, except there's no fruit in them.

Before dinner, we open our presents. Marjorie has knit cardigans for all of us. They have neat patterns and must have been hard to do. When Irene asks if she had time to do anything else, Marjorie just laughs and says, "What else is there to do on these winter evenings but sit by the fire, listen to the radio, and knit." Granny loves her gloves and scarf that Pauline and Irene helped to make. "They'll keep me right warm in the middle of the night when I'm called out to deliver a baby," she says.

The turkey is delicious and everyone eats too much. We even have to wait a long time for dessert because we're so full. Later when Granny brings out the plum pudding everyone cheers. She has poured brandy over it and set it on fire. It's so rich that you can only eat a small piece. The best part is the hot yellow custard that is poured over it and helps it slide down just right.

Months ago, Mammy and Daddy spent days preparing the plum pudding. They say the longer it sits the better. Daddy sat for ages with a big enamel bowl grating bread crumbs. Mammy mixed the suet, bread crumbs, sugar, raisins and spices together in another container. She threw in a couple of bottles of Guinness's stout and after everything was combined in the big bowl, she greased and filled some smaller ones with the ingredients. She then placed small pieces of cut up bed sheets over the bowls and tied string tightly around the sides so that they were sealed. She left enough string to make a handle across the top. Next she mixed flour and water to make a paste, and spread it over the cloth covering the pudding mixture to seal the bowls when they were dropped in a pot of boiling water. They had to be boiled for hours, so she needed to keep adding hot water to the pot whenever it boiled down. It was a lot of work but worth it, for there's nothing so delicious as plum pudding covered with Bird's custard.

On the bus going home, I have a hard time staying awake. It was a wonderful day and later as I lie in bed I can hear Pauline and Irene talking about looking forward to next Christmas.

***

It was a long, cold winter and even though spring was pleasant, I'm happy that summer is here at last. We're enjoying a weeks holiday in Bundoran on the West Coast of Donegal. We spent hours on trains and buses yesterday to get to this seaside town on the opposite side of Ireland.

We're staying in rooms above a bicycle shop on the main road, and the sea is visible from the front window. We all need the change and Daddy needs the rest.

As we make our way to the strand I'm sitting on Daddy's shoulders. Pauline and Irene have run on ahead and I have a great view of Bundoran.

"Time to feed the ducks." Daddy says, and he sets me down and walks of.

"Why can't we feed them too?" I ask.

"Ach, it's just for men, Patricia," Mammy says with a smile. When Daddy appears again we catch up to Pauline and Irene and find a nice spot on the soft sand.

The waves are really far out, and the three of us are making great sandcastles in the hard sand close to the water. Daddy and Mammy are dozing on a blanket and lots of people are doing the same. Suddenly our castles are being washed out and people are yelling and shouting at each other, and gathering up their things. The tide has come in so fast that no one expected it. There's a mad scramble and everyone is laughing at how ridiculous we all look.

"This is one of the most treacherous shores in Ireland," Daddy says. "That's why you don't see me out there swimming."

Whenever we go to Bangor for the day Daddy always makes his way straight out, and then starts swimming down along the shoreline until he is out of sight. We sometimes don't see him for more than an hour, and Mammy always gets agitated. He just loves to swim, and when he finally returns, his mouth is watering for some tomato sandwiches and hot tea cooked on our primus stove. Mammy always looks so relieved when she sees his head bobbing along the waves. I can just imagine how scared she must have been. But here in Bundoran she doesn't have to worry and I think she's relieved that Daddy won't take a chance and swim here.

A few days later I'm congested and have to stay in bed all day. Mammy leaves and comes back with a toy that makes a chiming sound. It makes me happy for a while after everyone goes out, but I soon get bored lying here all alone, while they're strolling the strand. Daddy is probably feeding the ducks right now. After about an hour the lady who owns the shop downstairs, peeks in to see if I'm all right. I smile and nod and she leaves. I snuggle under the covers trying to get warm. When they finally return they have to wake me up, and I notice Irene has been crying. I ask what happened.

"Oh, Irene's just after getting herself lost," Mammy says with a sigh. "You know how she always likes to run ahead of the rest of us? Well, a woman found her crying and brought her into one of the shops. It took us ages to find the right one. We were looking all over the place for her. Had us worried sick. Thank God she's safe and sound again."

They've brought some medicine from the chemist's shop and the next day I'm feeling much better and ready to go out. Pauline and Irene wish they could stay here forever, but we're soon on the bus back to Belfast waving goodbye to the beautiful County Donegal.

Chapter Three

The name *Patricia* and the word *tissue* sound a wee bit alike, so my friends are always calling me *Tissue Paper* for the fun of it. It's 1947 and my fifth birthday, and as I swing on my rope around the lamppost in front of our house, Maureen, Edwin, and Florence are singing, "Tissue Paper's five, Tissue Paper's five."

I don't mind because it's not a bad name or anything.

We have to keep an eye out for Tig McFeeney, the peeler who patrols this area. He puts the fear of God into everyone, except everyone fears him more than God. Maybe he doesn't like children or something, but he just can't tolerate any sort of bad behaviour, especially breaking the law by tying ropes *to*, and swinging *on* ropes *around* city owned lampposts. He's well known for cutting them into small pieces, and that could really spoil the rest of your day. People will be stopped for no reason and asked things about where they're going, and what they're going to do when they get there and all sorts of other strange questions. Constable McFeeney's mind seems to run on a suspicious track, so everyone is up to no good as far as he can see. His eyebrows are bushy and he has to lift his chin and look down his nose to see out from under them. Having big thick arms and legs, he reminds me of the gangsters in the cinema.

He lives in a Catholic area, but no one has ever seen him inside the church so they say he must be a Protestant like most of the policemen in Belfast. Daddy says that no Catholic can do any good in Tig McFeeney's eyes.

Mammy says that Aunt Mari is coming to visit us today. She's been doing her nurse's training in England. I really can't remember her, but I'm kind of excited anyhow. We're still swinging around the lamppost when I hear a strange voice behind me.

"Well, hello there, Patricia."

I turn around and see a lovely lady looking at us. She has dark hair and eyes and a beautiful smile that makes dimples appear on her cheeks.

"Happy birthday, Patricia. What's this tissue paper nonsense?"

"Oh, that's just my nickname."

"Do you remember me? I'm your Aunt Mari and I'm on a holiday from London. I was there the day you were christened. It was snowing and we had to bundle you up."

I smile at her and say shyly, "Mammy's in the house making a sponge cake for tea."

"Right, Patricia. See you inside."

She bends over and smells the flowers along our pathway, and I tell her I'll be in shortly.

Mammy and Mari are eating biscuits with their tea and reminiscing about the good old days. Tomorrow is Sunday and Aunt Mari wants to take us to Bellevue Park.

"By all means, I could use the rest," Mammy says with a big smile.

Our house faces the Divis Mountain, and Bellevue, with its zoo and hiking paths, is on the other side of the mountain near Cave Hill.

When Mari comes to collect us the next day we go down to the Falls Road, hop on a bus, and are jumpy with anticipation.

"I've really missed this place you know. I wish I could get home more often," Mari says with a sigh. "You girls have grown so much since I've been gone." She tells us about the American doctors who were stationed at Army bases in England. She worked with them during her training, and they were always trying to talk her into emigrating to America.

She talks about the blitz and the air-raid shelters in London. "The food shortages were really awful. You couldn't get butter, sugar, tea, and Lord knows what else," she says.

"It was just like that here in Belfast too!" Pauline says excitedly. "Did you see the bomb shelter on our street? The girls usually stay out of it, because the boys piddle in there and it reeks to the high heavens!"

"You know what, Mari," Irene pipes in, "we even have a couple of left-over gas masks under our stairs. We sometimes play with them, except Patricia can't stand to have them on for more than five seconds, or she'll start to panic and say she can't breathe."

"Aye, they were awful things, weren't they?" Marie says. "Let's hope we never need them again." She pats me on the knee and smiles, showing off her lovely dimples.

Pauline tells Mari about the bombs falling on Belfast. "We had black curtains to block out any light from the bombers. When the wail of the sirens started, everyone would hide under beds and tables and listen to the whistling sounds as the bombs fell from the sky. When they landed nearby and we heard the explosion our hearts would almost stop. But when they dropped at a distance, we would thank God and wait for the next one." Pauline is shaking now as she remembers that terrible time.

"Mammy says she was terrified when darkness fell," Irene says. "I'm glad I was too young to remember too much of it."

"Our house was so crowded every night during the blitz," Pauline says. "Granny Gordon, the O'Hare cousins and lots of other relatives came up to Andersonstown to get out of the city center. We had people sleeping on the floors, and even the stairs. It was really awful, so it was. A few of the houses in Granny's neighbourhood were hit, but no one was injured. They were probably hiding in a shelter. I think the big buildings downtown were the target since that's where most of the worst damage occurred."

Mari tells us the ship-building industry is what the Germans were after. "Aren't you glad you were too young to remember the war, Patricia?"

"Yes, I am lucky," I say. "I wouldn't want memories like that." The bus passes some of the bombed out buildings downtown that had to be demolished for safety's sake and are now just piles of rubble.

"Please, God, that one was the end of all wars," Mari says and we all agree.

We finally arrive at the zoo and are fascinated by the lions and the hilarious monkeys. It's too bad that they have to stay in those cages all day. The lions are pacing back and forth, back and forth like they're going crazy.

"These cages are entirely too small," Mari says. "The poor creatures should have their freedom." When we've seen all the animals, she treats us to a meal in the big restaurant on the grounds, and we get to pick whatever we want to eat. She even lets us choose our own dessert.

While having our meal, we tell Mari about the antics of her youngest sister, Aunt Marjorie.

"She minds us when Mammy and Daddy want to go to the pictures," Irene says. "She'll loosen her false teeth, and stick them out over her top lip, and make us scream when she chases us around."

"We always get Roses chocolates when Marjorie comes," I say.

"She *is* very generous," Mari says, "Roses chocolates are so dear that people usually only get them on special occasions. She must think a lot of you girls."

Mari's right. Those expensive chocolates are the mouth-watering best. We save their coloured wrappers and keep them in a wee tin with a hinged lid.

Aunt Marjorie is so much fun. When we walk down the road with her, she sings out loud and doesn't care who looks at her. If she feels like singing she does just that.

Mammy is the eldest and Mari is the second eldest of the four sisters. Mari says she would love to be able to mind us, but living in London makes it impossible. She tells us how their daddy was in hospital with typhoid fever when they were little. They were all looking forward to his homecoming on a Sunday, but on Saturday, he had a relapse and died. Granny was left a widow with seven children and was beside herself. She didn't know what to do, but heard about a training program for midwives and decided to try it. The training college was a long distance from Belfast, so the children were left to fend for themselves, with a little help from Granny's sister Rynes who lived two doors down. But Rynes had many children of her own to take care of, so she would just look in once in a while to make sure Mammy was feeding everyone and Uncle Tom was keeping up with the laundry. Tom, the eldest boy, was twelve and Mammy was ten. Granny came home once in awhile, but it was very hard on Mammy to go have to school every day and then come home and become a ten-year-old housewife for the rest of the evening.

When Granny finally got her certificate and started her practice, she had a lovely brass plaque affixed to the door at 147 Springfield Road that said; "Nurse Gordon – Midwife." Her seven children took turns using brass polish to make it sparkle. They also loved to peek in her "doctor" bag and try to figure what the odd looking things were for. We get to shine the plaque now when we visit.

Back on the bus Mari tells us about all the famous buildings in London like Westminster Abbey and Big Ben. She says she even visited The Tower of London where some queens had their heads cut off long ago. We have so much to tell Mammy and Daddy when we get home.

Mari has to go back down to Granny's where she's staying. She tells us that she really enjoyed our company and hopes someday, she might have children of her own that are as well behaved as we are. Mari is anxious to see her brother, Frank who was out of town when she came home from England. He should be there by now.

Uncle Frank is one of Mammy's younger brothers. He is really good looking, so he is, and goes with girls and everything. He says he is going to buy a car someday. We have never been in a car because hardly anyone owns one. He has promised to give us a ride when he gets his, and we can hardly wait.

***

It's a cool spring morning several weeks after Aunt Mari's visit, and I stand on tiptoes to see in the mirror and brush my hair. When I come downstairs, Mammy is standing in the open doorway with her hands on her hips, looking up the street, across from our house. I'm trying to see what she's looking at, and notice our Irene at the top of the hill. She's got her schoolbag on her back and she's leaning on McCrory's fence with one leg lying across the back of the other.

"It's those chickens again," Mammy sighs. "Irene's infatuated with them, so she is. We'll be getting another late notice from the school." She shakes her head and walks to the front gate. Taking a deep breath, she yells as loud as she can. Irene jumps and starts walking away from McCrory's garden, stealing a glance back at the chickens now and then.

"Maybe we could get a few chickens for ourselves, Mammy."

"No, Patricia, not now. It'd just be more mouths to feed."

"But we'd have fresh eggs, wouldn't we? And Irene would be on time for school every day?"

"Let's go in for breakfast now, Patricia." Mammy's just about to close the front door when she stops. "Jesus, Mary, and Joseph."

"What's the matter, Mammy?"

"It's the gypsies again. Quick! Run and lock the back door."

I do as I'm told and hurry back to Mammy. We watch as the man walks up our pathway leaving a cart standing by the kerb. It has pots and pans and other accouterments, hanging from a frame around it's sides.

"Mornin' Missus, how are ye doin' this beautiful day?"

"Just grand, thank you."

"Well, I wonder if ye have any need of a hardworking man's services. I can mend any pot or kettle that has a hole in it. Mind ye, I'll make it good as new."

"I haven't any holey pots at the moment," Mammy says. "Maybe next time."

"Right you be, Missus." He walks toward the front gate and gives a loud whistle, like he's calling a dog. Mammy closes the door, and we run to look out the parlor window just in time to see a scruffy boy of ten or eleven coming around the side of our house from the back garden. He joins the man and they push their cart towards MacCarrick's.

"See, Patricia, if you didn't lock the back door, we would no doubt have been robbed."

I wonder why someone would steal from other people, and I also wonder why Mammy didn't just keep the front door closed and ignore his knock.

"Patricia, would you ever run up and warn the neighbors that the gypsies are on the street." I'm happy to be of help and anxious to get a closer look. I've only seen them from a distance when they camp in farmer's fields. Their horse drawn caravans are always brightly painted, and hold their beds and everything else they own. Up close, the only difference is their tatty hair and colourful clothes.

Mrs. Morgan is so grateful for the warning that she gives me one of her freshly baked scones with lots of butter. By the time I get home, I have to tell Mammy I won't be needing any breakfast. She laughs as she puts the kettle on for her tea and suggests that maybe I could use a glass of milk to wash down the offering.

***

It's a warm Saturday in April, and Daddy comes in when we're eating breakfast. He looks like he's been running and Aunt Marjorie is with him. She asks us if we'd like to go for a long walk. "How about taking the Turf Loney this time?" she asks. The three of us are tickled with that. It's our

24

favourite way to get up the mountain, so we run to get dressed.

We're walking up the lane toward the Divis Mountain, past fields with white cows that look like someone spilled their school ink wells over them. Marjorie lets us climb up the metal gates that keep the animals in. But when we come to a field with a ferocious looking bull, she warns us to keep walking and act normal. We pluck wildflowers as we go, and wish the blossoms on the blackberry bushes were already fruit. But they won't be ready till summer, so we'll have to wait.

Suddenly through the bushes comes a group of runners that Marjorie says are called harriers. They seem to go on forever, and the men wink and smile at Marjorie as they pass in a single file. Jumping into the muddy ditch and out again on the other side, they spray dirty water all over themselves. Their shirts have numbers and Marjorie says they're either training or it's a long distance race.

Whatever it is, we have to move to the side to let the men pass, and I wonder why they would want to get wet, tired and muddy just for the fun of it. But it's the same thing every spring and summer. Harriers run for miles all over the countryside, and they seem to enjoy it.

We sit on some rocks halfway up the lane where fresh water gushes out of a hole in a low wall. The underground spring seems to have an endless supply and it fills a stream that gurgles and rolls over pebbles on its way downhill. Marjorie lets us have a drink first and then she enjoys the cool taste. The cold water makes us shiver after a while and she suggests that we run up the lane to warm up.

We soon reach the upper Springfield Road. At this end it's just a country road with a farm here and there. If we were to go down this road towards the city, we'd come to Granny's house where Marjorie lives, but we keep going up the hill and find a large chestnut tree. Under the shade of the tree is a sea of bluebells. The breeze makes them look like ocean waves. Buttercups and daisies grow in the sunny part of the field and the colour of all these flowers is a sight for sore eyes. Yellow primroses grow in the shade of the tree among the bluebells. We sit among them and Pauline holds a buttercup under aunt Marjorie's chin. "There's a yellow reflection on your throat, Marjorie, that means you love butter." She repeats the test on the rest of us and it looks like we all love butter.

Irene has wandered to a grove of trees and she calls us over. When we arrive at the spot where she's standing, we see a ring of toadstools.

"Look, a real fairy ring," she says. "Maybe if we are quiet and hide behind those trees the fairies and leprechauns will come out."

"They only come out in the wee hours of the morning," Marjorie informs us. "They're scared of mortals."

"That's why none of us has ever seen one," I say.

"Why don't you close your eyes and imagine them," Marjorie suggests. I close my eyes and can see the fairies, dancing in the air around the toadstool ring, their tiny wings fluttering. I can also see a wee leprechaun sitting on top of each giant mushroom, with pointed hats and shoes curled up at the toes. They have tiny hammers and are busy making shoes. I'm just hoping the real ones don't turn up, for I wouldn't know what to expect. This is a spot where I'd like to stay forever.

When Marjorie finally takes us back home, there's a strange lady in the house and Mammy is nowhere in sight. Daddy comes in just as we're wondering what's going on.

"Your mammy's at your granny's and you have a new baby brother." He smiles and tells us that we can go down and have a look at the baby tomorrow.

"The lady in the kitchen is called Mrs. McNulty, she'll take care of you while your mammy is gone," Daddy says. "I have to go to work now, see you tonight."

Marjorie leaves as well to help Mammy with our new baby. I go into the kitchen and stand next to Mrs. McNulty. "May I have a piece, please?"

"Bread love?" she asks. I nod. "What do you usually put on it, love?"

"Jam or sugar, please." She makes me a piece of bread with butter and jam and I'm so relieved that she can do it just as well as our Mammy. I only hope they forgot to tell her about the cod liver oil. We pinch our noses while swallowing to drown the awful taste. I think I *should* remind her of the syrup of figs though. That stuff is very nice and is supposed to give you lots of energy and keep you regular, but we only get it once in a while.

Irene and I ask the lady if we can borrow some knives, forks, and spoons out of the kitchen drawer.

"All right, but bring them back when you're done."

We go up to the landing at the top of the stairs. It's one of our favourite places to play house. We've set up a bunch of books for the walls of our rooms. One book for each wall. The knives are the men, forks are ladies and spoons are children. Irene walks a knife up to the space between the books that's the front door of our make-believe house.

"Knock knock," she says in a low, man's voice.

"Oh, hello," I say in a high pitched lady's voice as I hold the fork inside the house looking out at the knife.

"I'm just after getting the news that you had a new wee baby boy," the knife says to the fork.

"Oh yes, isn't it grand? He was ten pounds, a real healthy baby. Why don't you come in and have a look," the fork replies. I bounce the fork to the room in the back of our play house. Irene bounces the knife after the fork and there's the spoon lying on a washcloth on the floor. "Here he is," the fork says to the knife, "did you ever see such a lovely baby?"

The knife congratulates the fork in its low voice and says, "It's about time you had a wee boy in this house."

"I know," says the fork. "I thought we'd go on having girls forever." Just then a wailing sound comes from the spoon on the floor, and the knife and fork bend down to to take care of it.

Mrs. McNulty tramps up the stairs looking tired. She's about to use the lavatory and notices our stuff. "What's this young ladies? You've got crumbs all over the floor that I'm just after polishing. Cleanliness wouldn't be in it with you wee'uns." She's shaking her head from side to side.

Irene and I grab the cutlery family and books and scoot into our bedroom to continue our story. "Sorry, Mrs. McNulty, I'll clean up the crumbs," I say.

"Since you'll be going down to see your new wee brother in the morning don't forget to wash behind your ears tonight." She thumps back down the stairs and we start setting up house again.

The next morning Pauline, Irene, and I take a bus down to Granny's. We're very excited as we climb the stairs. Waiting outside the bedroom door we are guessing who the new baby is going to look like. Marjorie opens the door and we follow her in.

Granny's bedroom is really big and has a bay window that looks out onto the Springfield Road. The view is not that good though, just a big linen factory wall with a smoke-stack. In the curve of the bay window there's a vanity with three mirrors, and a chair to sit on. You can move the two smaller, side mirrors around in such a way that you can see rows and rows of yourself. The reflections seem to go on forever, "to infinity," as Pauline always says.

I've spent hours in this house, in this room, and trying to see through the stained glass window on the landing outside the lavatory. Sometimes late at night when I sleep over, I'm awakened by the men singing rebel songs outside the pub after it closes. I open the window a little and can see the wives coming to collect their men, who are still singing. As I've heard grownups say "They're feeling no pain." They don't seem to mind walking home linking arms with the women. They probably have a hard time waking up for Mass the next morning, though. Granny says that the money would be better spent on the wee'uns.

Mammy is lying in Granny's bed with a bunch of pillows behind her and a wee bundle lying next to her. She puts her finger to her lips and Pauline tiptoes over to the bed. Her eyes light up as she leans over and looks at the baby that Granny must have found in her nurse's bag. Irene goes next and she smiles with delight at our new wee brother. Finally, my turn comes and I'm gazing at a rosy, angel face and tiny fingers on chubby little hands. The baby starts to cry and mammy opens her nightgown. Soon the baby's mouth is working away on Mammy's chest, holding on like he's starving, or maybe he's afraid she'll disappear before he's had his fill.

"He was ten pounds," Marjorie announces. "The biggest one yet."

Mammy turns to Marjorie and says, "It was so bad, I wouldn't have cared if I was lying in the middle of Royal Avenue." This doesn't make too much sense to me, as it might be very dangerous to lie there with all those buses and lorries going by.

"What are we going to call him?" Pauline asks, and we're told that he'll be called Denis, after Daddy, whose real name is Denis even though everyone calls him Danny.

"Your mammy will have to stay in bed for awhile so that I can look after her, "Granny says. "Mrs. McNulty will look after you when you get home from school. Pauline can fix cereal in the morning. Daddy has the night shift this week, so he'll be there with you in the morning, Patricia." This all sounds very complicated to me, but I'm sure it will be worked out.

I'm wondering what it will be like to have a baby brother. He should enjoy having three big sisters to pester him, and Marjorie reminds us that he'll wake the whole house up in the middle of the night.

"Don't worry," Pauline says as she rolls her eyes, "I can still remember when Patricia was a baby."

When it's time to leave, Pauline taps Granny's barometer in the hallway. She says if it moves to a lower number it's going to rain. It almost always drops. We enjoy rapping on the glass with our knuckles to see if there'll be a change in weather.

As we walk back down the Springfield Road past the Blackstaff Weaving Mill, Pauline looks across at Hughes's Bakery where the aroma of fresh bread never fades. She begins to sing the song that we've heard children in Granny's neighbourhood chant as they skip rope:

Barney Hughes's bread
It sticks to your belly like lead
It's not a bit of wonder
You toot like thunder
When you eat Barney Hughes's bread.

"Not so loud, Pauline, what if he hears us," Irene says.

"Don't worry," Pauline says with a smile. "Mr. Hughes has all his orders. He's probably on lovely holiday somewhere spending some of the money people say he makes."

"Do you think Mammy will miss us tonight, Pauline?" I ask.

Pauline grins. "What do you think? She sees us all the time. Don't you think she could use a wee holiday from us for a change?"

"I suppose you're right, but I still think Mammy *will* miss us," I say, "being as she's so used to us and everything."

"Hurry, Patricia, there's a bus coming. Let's run for it before the sky opens up for the tenth time today."

Chapter Four

On my first day of school I'm nervous. Mammy holds my hand when we get off the bus. I'm going to be in junior infants and the teacher smiles at me. Mammy hugs me and leaves, and I'm trying not to cry, so I am.

The teacher asks us if we can say the alphabet and how far can we count and stuff like that. Mammy taught me my alphabet when I was three, so I know it by heart. Pauline and Irene have taught me how to count as well. After asking me my A B C's and all, the teacher takes my hand and leads me out of the room and I'm worried that I'm going to get hit with the bamboo cane. But she takes me to another room and says, "You're ready for senior infants," and she leaves. In senior infants we learn to add by using colourful spills like the ones we use to light the fire. The teacher has cut long ones into little pieces the size of matchsticks. We lay them out on our desk and she asks us to put five in a row. Then we have to add three. Now how many are there now? After a week in this class, the teacher walks me over to first class. *I'm only five and a half,* I think to myself, But I wouldn't dare say it out loud. So, I'm paraded into another class full of new girls and being shy makes it hard. The girls are friendly, though, and I'm soon fitting in.

The new teacher's name is Miss Bergan. She is really lovely and has short blonde hair and gorgeous blue eyes. She is very happy-go-lucky, so she is, and that makes it easier.

The girls are at one side of the school and the boys at the other. There's a wall separating the two playgrounds, and some of the older girls spend an awful lot of playtime on their tiptoes looking over the wall. I can't imagine why.

When it rains, which is at least three days a week, we have to play inside the big hall that has a stage. We throw beanbags to each other and when we do jumping jacks, I usually end up sitting down, because I'm so out of breath.

Our reading book is all about a dog. "Look at Spot. See Spot run."

The girl sitting next to me is called Sylvia Henley and she's very nice. She lives down behind our school in an area called The Bog Meadows. She says that when we have heavy rains, all the houses down there get flooded out. I think we're going to be very good friends. It's just too bad she doesn't live up our way.

Our school, St. Kevin's Primary, is next to St. John's Church and right across from the Protestant cemetery and the lower end of the Fall's Park. At the upper end of the park on the same side as our school is Milltown Catholic cemetery with its Celtic crosses and angels. I always feel sorry for the people in the graves when it's pouring down rain, but Irene says they're already in heaven.

When it's raining, it's hard to sit on a bus because so many people wear woolen coats and the whole bus stinks of wet sheep. I stay downstairs in the bus when I go to school because it's only about three stops. The conductor stands at the bottom of the stairs so that he can pull the cord for the driver to stop when people start walking toward the back to get off.

There's a wee shop on the way home from school, and I found out from the older children that if you walk fast instead of taking the bus you can spend your bus money to buy an ice lollie called a dimple. I always buy a pineapple dimple and when it's almost time for school to end, I watch the clock and imagine the cool pineapple juice seeping down my throat. Mammy never even notices when I'm a wee bit late from walking home. She probably thinks there's a garden full of chickens between the bus stop and our house. Just up from the sweet shop where I buy the ice dimple is a big house in a grove of trees that's so thick that it's always dark and cold in there. The house is an orphanage and the boys who live there are very different. They sort of stick together and don't mix with the other boys. I'm always a wee bit nervous passing there, but I don't know why.

Miss Kearns, the headmistress of our school, lives in one of the fancy houses on the upper Falls Road. The field behind our house separates our back garden from the row of houses on the main road where she lives. Sometimes when we're in our bedroom, we look across the field and try to figure out which house is hers.

At school she's really tough and keeps her bamboo cane hanging up in her office. She visits the classes from second on up with her cane. Pauline says the worst words you can hear are, "Hold our your hand." I'm not looking forward to spellings, because she gives three whacks on each hand for every word spelled wrong. Pauline says you can hear the whoosh as the cane whips through the air towards the palm of your hand. Pauline and Irene have come home many times with red burning welts on their hands even though they listened to each other the night before to make sure they'd get the words right. Irene says you have to suffer in silence, so you do, or you'd be in for more. "It's just not fair to the children who aren't as smart as the rest," she says. "You should only be punished for misbehaviour, not incorrect spellings."

Pauline hates sitting in the front row when Miss Kearns is teaching Gaelic. The language is very guttural, like Arabic, and Miss Kearns spits on the girls in the front row when she repeats the words over and over.

"Getting soaked with someone's spit is not my idea of a perfect day," Pauline says, rolling her eyes up to heaven. "Patricia, if you know what's good for you, sit far back if possible." She's lying on the bed studying her Gaelic book for tomorrow's test.

"Yes, but maybe she'll start walking up and down the aisles when she's teaching by the time I'm old enough," I say with a sigh.

"Maybe she'll have retired by the time you have to learn Gaelic."

"Oh, I hope so, Pauline. I think the spelling business would be enough to bear."

Pauline is lucky it's her last year at this school.

When we go downstairs, our Denis is crawling around and pulling himself up on the side of the sofa. He got a brightly coloured ball for Christmas, so he did, and throws it with his little hands. It's always ending up under the table, and after I crawl underneath to get it, he throws it again with a squeal and I have to crawl back under.

We now have a bucket in the back porch that's full of dirty nappies. It gets awful smelly by the time it's filled. On rainy washdays, nappies hang inside the house all over the place, including the fireplace screen. I remember once, Mammy took one of Daddy's white shirts off the line and it was frozen solid. She looked so funny carrying it in, and it reminded me of a ghost, with the arms sticking straight out the way she pegged it on the clothesline.

Last Christmas I got a beautiful leather schoolbag. It has straps for your arms to go through when you put it on your back and two buckles on the flap to keep your books from falling out. It smells divine and I just love it, so I do. Along with the schoolbag, I got the most perfect pencil case with a sliding top and a pencil sharpener, as well as six pencils. Mammy had to get upset with me once for sharpening one of the pencils down to the size of my little finger. But I told her I had to get some practice before school started again.

Daddy is still driving the buses and his route takes him up the Falls Road. It's the main road at the bottom of our street and when he has the evening schedule, Mammy usually sends one of us to our bus stop with a tin can full of tea for his break. There's a wire handle on the tin to carry the tea and you have to hold the can out so the hot tea won't burn your leg.

It's my turn tonight and Daddy and his conductor, John, give me a ride to the end of the line about a mile away. There they have a break and pour their tea.

Daddy likes to do a trick to impress me. He steps off the bus, spins the half full can around and around until it's upside down and he never spills a drop. This is one of the favourite times when I really love my Daddy. There are other times when he loses his temper and we all stay out of his way.

His bus conductor, John, is a Protestant, but he's not the least bit bigoted. He lives over near the Crumlin Road and invites Daddy over to his house a couple of times a month to play chess. After trying to learn the game, the three of us girls have decided that it's definitely a game for men.

It's a warm summer evening, and Daddy drops me off at our bus stop after I bring his can of tea. It's half nine and still daylight. On our longest day of summer, it will still be bright at eleven o'clock in the evening or even later.

Stepping off the bus, I say goodbye to John and Daddy, turn to see Irene and Mary Cunningham over at the dump and run over to join them.

"We're going to look for stuff to build a fort, Patricia. Do you want to come?" Irene asks.

She leads the way and soon we're climbing over all sorts of rubbish. We see some older girls that Irene says are from the Beechmount area and Mary look sideways at Irene.

"Everyone say they let boys touch them where they shouldn't. They're said to be real common, so they are."

We all look at the girls and they stop walking, stare at us, and give us real dirty looks. They say something nasty and now we're embarrassed, so we are.

"They're probably up here looking for boys," Irene whispers and we move on.

We find some boards and old bits of plywood and set them aside for the fort. It's getting dark now and everything begins to look scary. The others have moved on and I'm trying to keep up.

All of a sudden, I feel something soft and warm moving over my sandal. I'm almost afraid to look down because of the growing darkness. When I do, I let out a piercing scream.

"What happened, Patricia?" Irene calls out. She sounds nervous, and as she runs toward me she suddenly jumps aside as the giant rat runs in her direction.

I'm shaking and sobbing uncontrollably and shivers run all through my body.

"Let's get out of here, Patricia. C'mon Mary, this is no place to be after dark." As we hold hands and run, there's a loud scream from the Beechmount girls farther down the dump in the darkness.

"They'll wish they had stayed in Beechmount tonight," Mary says and Irene laughs.

"What's the matter with Patricia?" Mammy asks when we come in the back door.

I'm still sobbing and the tea can falls on the kitchen floor with a loud clatter.

When Irene explains what happened, Mammy tries changing the subject to distract me, but I can't stop thinking of the ugly rat that walked over my foot. I can still see his horrible whiskers and that disgusting long tail. The thought of it makes me jump again and I feel my heart pounding like a drum.

"I'll never go near that stinky dump again as long as I live," I sob.

"You're not the only one," Irene says.

"Why did God have to make such awful creatures, Mammy?" I ask.

"He must have given them some purpose or they wouldn't exist," Mammy says.

I think for awhile and then, suddenly, realize that the reason for their existence must be to feed cats like our Ginger.

A few months after the dump scare, I'm coming up our street from Higgins' grocery shop with half a stone of spuds and a packet of Woodbine cigarettes for Mammy. She only gets the ones with the picture of a ship captain, and the fancy words "Players Please" when she's had a good night of poker. Woodbines are skinny and according to the neighbours, who have regular discussions about it, they don't taste half as good as Players. But they're dead cheap.

I'm thinking how nice it would have been to spend the cigarette money on fig bars or those lovely Kemp apples from Canada that Mr. Higgins gets in every year at this time. Mammy, and just about every other smoker in the area say it's the only pleasure they have in life. She says the bit of sewing that she does for the neighbours makes her feel less guilty about spending the money on herself. I feel that she deserves her pleasure, especially when she has to endure a sewing machine needle going through her finger once in a while. I just know one thing for sure, and that's when I grow up, I'll never smoke. I'll get my pleasure out of toffee bars and Kemp apples.

I see a couple of big girls ahead as I shift the spuds from one arm to the other. They live up the Whiterock road and I think our Pauline knows them from school. The neighbours say, "The Whiterock crowd all came from those wee row houses that don't have indoor lavatories. The government gave them those brand new houses and what do they do? Keep their bleedin' coal supply in their baths." I wonder how our neighbours know this. Do they go down to the Whiterock area and inspect everyone's bathrooms?

I catch up to the girls and figure they're about eleven years old. I'm just about to ask them, "Do you keep your coal in your bath?" when I remember that I've also heard from the same source, that they're a real rough crowd down there. I decide to keep my mouth shut, remembering that this valuable information about the coal has been whispered across many a hedge by people who are experts on the ins and outs of the Falls area.

"Do you know which house Pauline Owens lives in?" The tall skinny one asks.

"She's my big sister, I'll show you the way," I say with a smile. I open the gate and knock on our front door looking out of the side of my eye at a girl who's probably from a rough crowd. I set the spuds down on the stoop and wait for someone to answer.

Pauline looks startled when she comes to the door and sees the girls standing there. I watch with interest as the tall one says, "We came to take you up on your offer of free sweets from your sweet shop down the Donegal Road."

"What shop?" I say, and Pauline's eyes open wide and she gives me a sharp look.

The tall skinny one says, "You know, the Owens Sweet Shop that Pauline said was your family business."

"Ooh," I say and I look at Pauline with a puzzled expression.

"Patricia, go and feed the cat, she's hungry." I go through the house and out the back door. *We never feed Ginger, she catches all the food she needs in the back field*, I say to myself. I sneak around the side of the house towards the front and hear the tall girl shouting. "Jist you wait 'til my ma tells the headmistress–you're gonna be in for it!" She stomps down the path and almost slams the gate on her friend's leg. She's acting that tough.

Irene is coming down the stairs and sees Pauline leaning on the bannister at the bottom looking absolutely petrified.

"What's going on?" she asks, and Pauline begins to sob as she tells us that the Whiterock girls told her they saw a sweet shop with our last name on the front. Pauline, wanting to feel important had said, "Oh, yes, that's our shop. I can get you free sweets if we go there. I never thought they'd come all the way up here. Now what am I going to do?"

"Don't worry, Pauline," Irene says, and she pats her on the shoulder. "They won't tell their mothers anything." But Pauline still looks upset and is worried about getting caught in her lie.

"Patricia," Mammy calls from the kitchen. "I'm waiting for those spuds!" I grab the bag and bring them to her, hoping that she didn't hear any of the business at the front door. She starts to wash the mud off the spuds and I plop them into the pot. I'm thinking it's strange how the water rises higher and higher with each one that's added.

"Where's my pack of cigarettes, Patricia, I hope you didn't forget them again." I reach in my pocket, hand her the cigarettes and she lights up right away. It reminds me of the day last summer, when our family came home from Sunday Mass. Mammy went into the kitchen to check on the leg of lamb that she had popped into the oven before we left. She had the oven door open, and was just about to light up a cigarette, when, too late, she smelled the odour of gas.

There was a strange flat sound as the kitchen window blew out. Mammy's hat shifted to the back of her head and there was a smell of singed hair as both the fuzz on her arms and her eybrows disappeared.

Daddy was sitting in the armchair in the living room, with the newspaper blown across his face, and plaster from the ceiling in his hair and all over the room.

When Daddy spoke, we couldn't hear him, and when we spoke he couldn't hear us. It took quite a few minutes before our ears were back to normal again.

There was a knock at the front door and while Mammy answered it, Daddy stared at the holes in the ceiling.

Mr. MacCarrick stood at the door, and outside on the street, a large group of neighbours had gathered to see if we were all right. Denis was still sound asleep in his pram in the garden where we had left him after Mass.

The neighbours said that the explosion could be heard all over the neighbourhood, but it's amazing, that to us, it was just like a b-l-a-a-t sound. Daddy said it had something to do with temporary damage to our eardrums. I think since that time, everyone in our area, and especially in our house, checks for gas odours before lighting matches.

Pauline is a nervous wreck every morning now on her way to school. She says that every time Miss Kearns comes into the room, she thinks she'll be called up about the sweet shop business. But after a week or so when nothing happens she says, "I really learned a lesson about lies, white ones or otherwise." She rolls her eyes as usual.

Whenever Pauline and Irene get into a fight now, Irene always uses the sweet shop line to enrage Pauline. It's funny how Irene, being the middle girl, gets into arguments with both Pauline and me. Pauline and I are much further apart in age and we never fight with each other. Poor Irene gets it from both sides.

The worst thing we ever say to each other is, "You cheeky cat!" and we are shocked with ourselves afterwards that it could come to such vile rantings and ravings. We never let Mammy or Daddy hear us use such language, or there'd be hell to pay for sure.

***

It's been two weeks since our Denis's first birthday. I'm minding him for twenty minutes or so while Mammy runs to the shop. We're in the back garden playing with our cat, Ginger. She loves to play with string if you keep moving it out of her reach. Pauline and Irene are up the street taking turns on the family bike. It has been handed down to us from Mammy who, used to ride it when she was younger. In fact, that bike is responsible for her falling in love with Daddy.

Mammy lived on the Springfield Road at the corner of Oranmore Street, and Daddy lived halfway up Oranmore Street. She had her eye on him and he had his eye on her, so Aunt Mari has told us. He belonged to a bicycle club for men and women, so she joined as well. The club used to go cycling to Bangor, Lough Neagh, and even as far away as Dublin. They probably spent a lot of time together on these trips and before long they were courting and later married.

Pauline rushes into the house and she's all out of breath. "Patricia, would you go down the street and see if Mammy has left the shops yet? Irene's just after having an accident on the bike. Some ruffians were going too fast and crashed into her."

Irene is hopping up the back steps and there's a slice in her shin where a kind of 'ground meat' like stuff is hanging out.

I'm almost fainting as I run down the street. Mammy follows me back, drops the groceries at the back door and rushes in.

"Good girl, Pauline, you did the right thing to wrap it up in a towel." Irene is very pale and she's being so brave. She leans on both of them as they head towards the bus stop.

When they return from the Royal Hospital, Mammy is looking tired and Irene is still pale. "They didn't even give her a pain killer," Mammy complains. "Stitched her up with a big needle without as much as a numbing compound. I told her to put her fist in her mouth and she was as good as gold through the whole ordeal."

Irene is eating a Mars bar and her leg is all bandaged up.

"Just wait 'til I get my hands on those Murphys," Pauline shouts, "tearing down the road like hell's blazes."

"Watch your language, Miss," Mammy warns.

"But Mammy, it could have been much worse, she could have hit her head on the road."

"Indeed aye, it could've," Mammy says, and she ruffles Pauline's hair.

Irene gets to stay home on her last day of school before the six week holiday, but I'd rather go to school than be stitched up without painkillers.

The next week they go back to the hospital and have the stitches removed. While they're gone, I'm playing in the back garden. Mrs. Farrell from next door, who just got the baby boy she'd always wished for, shouts from her upstairs window. She wants to see Irene when they get back. I wonder what the problem is. Irene's usually very good and doesn't cause any trouble.

When Mammy and Irene return they show me the white marks where the stitches used to be, and Irene looks concerned when I tell her Mrs. Farrell wants to see her.

I'm waiting on pins and needles for her to come back from Farrell's, and when she does, she plops herself on the bed next to me.

"How do you figure this, Patricia? Irene says. "Mrs. Farrell wanted to thank me for praying that she'd have a new baby. She even gave me a shilling. I just couldn't tell her that I completely forgot to pray when she asked me to last year. Do you think I should give her back the shilling?"

"I don't think so, Irene. Maybe Mr. Farrell was praying and God answered *his* prayers and all that counts is she got her baby. What does he look like?"

"He's red and wrinkly, but they said he'll look like Josie when he grows up."

"Oh, heavens, will he have her red curly hair and freckles, too?"

"That wouldn't be so bad, Patricia. Look at Peter Cummings, he's very nice looking and he's got those features."

"Are you in love with him, Irene?"

She blushes and says she's going to get a jam sandwich and rushes out of the room.

Daddy calls me downstairs. "Patricia, would you like to take a ride downtown? I need to pick up my pay packet."

I always jump at the chance to to go downtown for any reason. When we reach the city centre and hop off the bus, there seem to be an awful lot of people milling around, and Royal Avenue is blocked.

"Oh, dear, looks like they're getting an early start on the twelfth," Daddy says.

"The twelfth, Daddy?"

"Twelfth of July, the day for Orange parades. Actually it's also the day your mammy and I were married. We were one of five couples who just walked up to the altar together and took our vows. No pomp and circumstance like you see these days."

We have to stand and watch the parade before we can cross the road. It's a lot of men dressed in regular suits but they have shiny orange sashes draped over their shoulders and down to their waists. On their heads are wee bowler hats that remind me of Charlie Chaplin. A few of them are carrying big banners of King William on his horse. Some are beating on heavy looking drums, and many of them are playing tin whistles. The rest are singing songs. We have to listen for there's nowhere to go.

Kick the Pope in Boyne water... "What's Boyne water, Daddy?" I ask.

"It's a river in the Boyne valley," he says. "Where King William of Orange defeated the Catholic King, James. It was back in the sixteen hundreds before any of us were born.

The parade has finally passed by and we cross the road and walk toward the docks, one of my favourite places to be. It's like a different world down here, so it is. The small ships sit, rolling gently on tiny laps of waves. They creak and groan and almost seem to be alive. I always wonder where they're going next, and where they've been.

"There'll be lots more parades between now and the twelfth of July," Daddy goes on. "They're just straining at the bit to rub the Catholic noses in it." I look puzzled and Daddy smiles and pats the top of my head. "Don't you worry yourself about it, Patricia. You'll understand soon enough."

On the bus going home Daddy tells me about one of the things he did as a boy. "We used to tie a long string around the knockers of about five or six houses in a row, kind of looping them all together, then knock on the end door and run."

"What happened then, Daddy?"

"The first person to answer the knock would cause all the other knockers to rattle and you'd have five frustrated people who couldn't get their doors open."

"Oh, Daddy, how wicked! Did you ever get caught?"

"Never, they couldn't get their doors open fast enough to catch us."

"Do you think the children on your old street still play that trick?" I ask.

"Aye, maybe," Daddy says when I ask. "But don't you think the folks should be on to it by now?

Chapter Five

Pauline looks upset when I come downstairs this morning.

"What's the matter?" I ask her.

"It's just not fair Patricia, Granny goes on these great holidays and she always takes you with her, never me. I'm the eldest."

"I wish you and Irene could go too. Why don't we see if Mammy can ask Granny."

"I know how you feel, Pauline," Mammy says, "but your granny can only afford to rent one room in the boarding house and Patricia never has accidents in the middle of the night."

I'm feeling sorry for my sisters and a wee bit guilty, but I say a silent prayer to God for helping me be the one.

This year Granny has chosen Portstewart on the North coast of County Antrim. I really love the sea.

We're on the train starting on the long journey of sixty miles or so and Granny is busy chatting with another old lady across the aisle from us.

Once we get out of the city, we pass fields dotted with sheep, then cows, and then sheep again. I try counting the roundy haystacks in the field and soon I'm fast asleep.

When I awaken, the train has stopped and I ask, "Are we there?"

"No, love, this is Ballymena. We've a long way to go yet."

I watch the telephone poles fly past the train. The wires between them are rising and falling, rising and falling and soon I'm dozing off again. The *c l i k e t y-c l a k* of the wheels on the rails makes me sleepy.

I wake up with a start when the train groans and hisses to a stop. We're at another station with people rushing back and forth with heavy bags, mothers holding onto the hands of little children and hurrying them along.

"This is Ballymoney, Patricia. It shouldn't be too long now." I listen to Granny telling the woman about raising seven wee'uns on her own and the old lady is saying, "I may as well have been alone for all the support I got from my auld man. He always took the long way home on paydays, past the bookie and the pub. I thank my lucky stars I had sons first, for they helped me stay out of the poorhouse when they turned fourteen and got jobs. I don't think either one of them has ever touched a drop. The auld man taught them their lesson in life about the drink leading to poverty."

When we reach Coleraine, it's pouring down rain and I ask Granny, "Is it always raining here? Is that why they call it Coleraine?"

She laughs and says, "Ach, it doesn't matter where you are in this country, it's always coming down in buckets somewhere and if it isn't pouring where you are, it's getting ready to."

The train windows are fogged up and impossible to see through, so I daydream about what Portstewart will be like and before long the train hisses and blows into the station.

We wave goodbye to the old lady as she leans on her cane and slowly disappears into the crowd.

Granny puffs and pants as she carries the bags and we find a taxi stand outside. In the rear view mirror of the taxi you can see the train station disappear as we go towards the ocean. The sun has come out and the water is sparkling and shining beyond the sea wall.

When we finally arrive at the boarding house, I'm impressed with the plush furniture in the lounge. The china cabinet has sets of delicate English china and Irish crystal.

The lady in charge gives us a big smile and shows us to our room.

"Dinner will be served shortly," she says and she starts down the stairs.

There's a big bowl in our room with a jug sitting inside it and I ask Granny for a glass of milk, but she tells me it's only water for washing up. The lavatory down the hall has to be shared by four rooms so you have to knock before trying to open the door. Later when I'm sitting on the toilet, I hear a loud bong like someone beating on a drum. I can't get out of there fast enough to see what's going on. Granny says it's the dinner gong and we're sure to hear it many more times before the week is over.

It's strange sitting around a big table eating dinner with a bunch of strangers. Granny is speaking politely with the other guests and I'm enjoying the lamb chops and mashed potatoes. When we go to Granny's house for dinner she always says, "Eat up you're at your granny's." This is one time she doesn't have to tell me to eat up. The food is great and I think Granny is right about hunger being the best sauce.

The next morning we go for a stroll along the ocean front. There's a man standing on a wooden box who keeps throwing his hands up in the air and shouting about salvation. "Unless ye be saved, you cannot enter the kingdom of Heaven. You must repent of your sins and wicked ways before it's too late! The devil is waiting for you to fall so that you can join him in eternal damnation."

I'm a wee bit nervous and ask Granny, "What's eternal damnation?"

"Don't worry, Patricia, you've been christened and you'll go to heaven when you die as long as you live a good life and don't do anything really bad." This makes me feel a lot better and I hope I can stay on the right path.

We're passing a row of small shops and I stop and gaze in the window of one that has a lovely display of seaside buckets and spades for children. There are crabs and starfish on some and others have pretty scenes.

Granny looks at me with a smile, takes my hand and we go inside. I choose the bucket with crabs and starfish and it comes with a long handled spade. I'm so thrilled I can hardly contain myself. The tin spade rattles against the bucket when I walk. I'm skipping along and Granny says, "You should get lots of use out of those in the next week."

Eternal damnation has flown from my mind and I don't have a care in the world.

The following morning, on the strand in front of the boarding house, Granny is stretched out on a deck chair and I'm paddling in the water. My dress is tucked inside my knickers and I'm staring down at my feet as the waves are sucked back to the ocean. It makes me feel like I'm moving backwards at high speed. Some of the other children from the boardinghouse are playing with a wee plastic boat. They throw it into the waves and watch it float back to them.

"What's your name?" I ask them and I learn that the boy is Nigel and his sister is Margaret. We spend the day making a big square car out of sand. It has front and back seats and a gearshift made out of a piece of driftwood. This is the most fun I've had in ages and I hope we can do this every day. Margaret and Nigel hope so too.

"What are those red things?" I ask Granny a few days later at breakfast.

"They're fried tomatoes," she whispers in my ear and I stare at the soft, soggy slices next to the fried eggs, bacon and sausage. "Just give them a try, it won't hurt you."
I'm used to cold, hard tomatoes and I screw up my face until one of the women across the table laughs at me.

I take a bite and am pleasantly surprised that it isn't as bad as it looks. Margaret and Nigel are down at the other end of the table and they have already finished their soggy tomatoes. It must be something they're accustomed to. Granny looks shocked when I take a round yellow blob from a dainty dish and pop it in my mouth.

"That's butter, Patricia." But it's already too late, and I have to swallow it before anyone notices.

The women at the table are discussing the ages of their children and Granny tells them that I'm in the first class at school and I'm six years old. "She goes into second class in August," she says with a smile.

"What school do you go to, Patricia?" Margaret's mother asks.

I smile and say, "St. Kevin's, on the Falls Road."

There's a holding of breath and a widening of eyes all around and the conversation comes to an abrupt end. The women finish their breakfast in silence and scoot the children off to get ready for the seaside just across the road.

Granny grabs her deck chair when we're done eating and we set out to do the same. I'm looking forward to playing in the sand car again with my new friends and I'm relieved when I see that it's still there. I see Margaret and Nigel at the edge of the water and run over to join them. Just as I get close to them I hear, "Margaret...Nigel... we must go now." They run off to join their mother and I go and sit in the sand car, but it's not as much fun alone.

After a while I notice the yellow bathing suit about a hundred yards down the strand and I know it's Margaret. I ask Granny if I can go down that way and she says, "Aye, it's all right with me."

I'm skipping down with my bucket and spade and I see their mother dozing in her deck chair with a newspaper hat covering her face. When the children see me, they look at each other nervously and Nigel keeps looking over at his mother.

"I'm sorry, Patricia. We aren't allowed to play with you any more. Mummy says we're to stay away from you."

I'm mortally wounded and try to think of what I could have done to hurt them and wonder why their mother is mad at me. I've been really good, especially since the man on the box made it quite clear that eternal damnation lay ahead for those who were bad. For the rest of the day I play alone and try to figure out what I've done that would make me such a bad person.

When I tell Granny, she explains it in a sorrowful voice. "It's just the way things are, Patricia. They thought we were Protestant because my name is Hyacinth Gordon. You see your grandfather became a Catholic to marry me. But the name is Scots and those who don't know me assume I'm a Protestant." She gently strokes my back and continues. "When you said you went to St. Kevin's, that gave us away. You must be prepared to be looked down on, for the rest of your life, as a Catholic in Northern Ireland."

I'm still puzzled about how the children were playing with me, and having a good time, and now just because we go to a different church, I'm to be feared. I like Margaret and Nigel just the same, because I remember it was their mother who seemed to be having the problem with our difference and it makes me sad. I feel like they would like to play with me but have to do as their mother says.

The following morning, there's very little conversation at the breakfast table and the children keep their eyes on their plates and avoid mine.

After lunch, my great Aunt Rynes (short for Mary Agnes) comes by on her way to Moville, in Donegal where she and Granny were born. She has one of her twelve children with her, and Kathleen, who is really only my second cousin, wants to go swimming. While the sisters catch up on the latest news, Kathleen and I go paddling in the water. We're splashing around and Kathleen, who is about twelve, dares me to go in up to my waist. I'm being very cautious, since I haven't learned to swim yet. But she wades out to the deeper water to show how safe it is. The water is very calm in this area because of a sea wall runs through the water making it more like a bay.

Just when I'm feeling secure, Kathleen, who is much taller than me, plants her hand on my head and pushes me under. My ears and nose are being filled with burning, salty water. I've lost my balance and my eyes are stinging terribly. As I flail my arms, I'm thinking at least I won't go to eternal damnation because I've been good so far. Kathleen finally pulls me up to a standing position and she's having a great laugh about the whole thing. I don't think she realized that I'd never had my head underwater before and she is beginning to look a bit worried.

"Don't tell my ma, Patricia, she'd have my life."

I assure her that it will be our secret and quickly leave the water. She is apologizing over and over and I say, "Well, if you're so worried about me telling your ma, you can just play with me for the rest of the afternoon in that sand car back there." I don't have to worry about being alone any more and soon we're laughing and having a grand time until Kathleen and her mother leave to continue their journey.

Granny and I leave a few days later for Belfast and although there were a few unpleasant happenings toward the end of the week, I really loved the holiday.

***

It's strange to be back in our streets again with the women going to the shops every day for groceries because the meat would go bad if they didn't. The milkman leaves bottles on the front step every morning and the inch of cream on top is kept for the tea. Edwin's daddy drives an electric bread van and there's a man with a horse and cart who brings potatoes and other vegetables. A lot of the neighbours compete to see who can be first into the street to pick up the horse droppings. Daddy is very proud of his rose bushes and tall lupins. He's also very quick on his feet, much to the dismay of the other men, who want the droppings for their vegetable plots.

Behind our row of houses on Andersonstown Crescent, is a big field. The owner rents out portions of it to anyone who would like to grow a vegetable garden. There's always a discussion about who grows the best carrots or cabbage and who keeps the tidiest plot. Daddy grows wonderful beets that look great sliced with lettuce and tomatoes at tea time. Mr. O'Neill is growing some very strange vegetables. They have long stalks and pom pom type balls on top covered with tiny white flowers. He laughs when we ask him about them.

50

"Haven't you ever seen onions growing before? The balls on top contain the seeds and the onions are hiding under the ground."

Every plot is a little different, and a lot of vegetable trading goes on. We enjoy helping to pull weeds until we realize that the weeds grow much faster and taller than the vegetables.

***

It's Saturday evening again and we're down at Granny's. Our parents are playing poker with Tom, Lucy, Marjorie, Eileen and Granny. Denis and our cousin Anne Marie are with us under the table between all the sets of legs and shoes. Our cousin Vincent is on the sofa drinking milk out of his baby bottle. The noise gets deafening when money is slapped down on the table and they're saying things like, "I'll see you," and "I'll raise you."

Everyone is smoking, except Granny and Daddy and there's a haze hanging over the room that makes us cough. The adults are laughing now and talking about bluffing, and I have no idea what that means.

The front door opens and Freddy, our youngest uncle, comes in along with a huge draught of cold air. He has a long overcoat and a cloth cap, and he's swaying slightly and wearing a crooked grin. We follow him into the front parlour where he removes his overcoat. Leaning over, he throws me up on his shoulders saying, "Up you go, Patricia. We'll shock them all, won't we?" Freddy puts the overcoat back on except my arms go in the sleeves and his cap ends up on my head, covering my ears. I've never been this tall before and I feel like a giant. Anne Marie is tugging at the coat wanting a turn. "Hold your horses now, we'll be back."

We waltz into the kitchen and everyone looks up at me and laughs. I flap my arms and Freddy starts to lose his balance.

Granny is getting upset at his shenanigans. "Freddy, I think you need to be looking for a normal job, so you do.

You're after having too many pints while serving the drink today."

"Ach, Mama, I'm happy at the pub and I'm sure they couldn't survive without me." He puts me down and staggers into the scullery to see if there's any leftover food from tea time. We're watching him make a ham sandwich and I ask him why his hair is so red and fuzzy.

"I think the milkman had hair like mine, Patricia. Aye, that's it, the milkman."

"Jesus, Mary, and Joseph, Freddy will you get yourself upstairs and stop demoralising the wee'uns," Granny shouts, and he does just that.

I have to go to the lavatory, and someone's in the upstairs one. Its dark outside so I ask for the torch. Granny doesn't have a garden like us. She has a cement yard, walled in on all sides. There's a two-seater lavatory inside a shed in her back yard. It's like a long window seat with two holes cut out. High above are matching water tanks, and chains to pull when you're done. It's very handy when you're playing outside, but tonight it's pitch black in there, and the torch doesn't make me feel any better. Granny has mice in her scullery, and I think there may be some in the shed as well. I go so fast and sing so loudly, that it's sure to scare the mice away.

When the poker games are finally over Granny shuffles her newest pack of cards. She always takes great care of them and doesn't want any to get bent or marked up. Placing them carefully on the mantle, she turns to ask Uncle Tom something about his teaching job. Her eyes widen suddenly when she sees one of her new cards float through the air and land in the glowing fire.

Irene is hanging her head. She looks upset. She was touching the cards on the mantle and now the flames are turning blue and then green as they eat up the six of diamonds.

"I'll buy you a new pack. After all, I won the biggest pot tonight," Mammy says. Granny nods and looks down at Irene.

"Ach, don't worry love, I know you didn't do it deliberately," she says, and she pats Irene's head. Aside from the mishap, Mammy and Daddy are pleased with their win tonight, and we'll be able to buy lots of groceries next week.

***

We're having a spelling test this morning and everyone is nervous. In fact, Sylvia Henley is sobbing quietly in the seat next to mine.

"I'm so worried, Patricia, my granny was taken to the hospital last night and I had to go along. I didn't have a chance to go over my spellings."

"Don't worry, Sylvia, you're very smart, and it shouldn't be too hard."

"I hope not, my hands are still stinging from the slaps I got for yesterday's mistakes."

I studied really hard last night myself, in order to escape the head mistress's bamboo cane.

Just as we have our pencils poised, there's a knock on the classroom door and a stern looking nurse with her hair in a bun, enters and drops a large box on Miss McCann's desk. She takes out a plastic cape, a lamp with a long cord and a jar of liquid with fine tooth combs soaking in it.

"I'm with the Department of Health to inspect for lice," she says and her eyes squint as they sweep over the room. My head has started to itch just thinking about it and I pray that it's clean. We're called up to the front of the room, one at a time, and she asks each girl sit in the chair.

She throws a cape over the girl's shoulders, and shining a bright light on the subject, she divides the hair, wets it and starts combing through each section with the fine tooth comb. Her eyes are locked on the scalp so she won't miss anything. When she finds any of the little buggers, she sends that girl to the next room for treatment. The girls who are clean go back to their desks, and I can see the relief on Sylvia's face as she walks back to her desk and starts to study the spellings that she didn't have time for last evening.

The nurse leaves for a while and returns with about seven of the girls who were sent next door. They look embarrassed and I feel bad for them. Their hair smells like the chemical used to clean toilets and they're shivering because it's a cool morning and their heads are wet. Miss McCann passes out papers to be given to all the parents, regarding the outbreak of lice and everyone moans.

Just our luck, we end up with the dreaded spelling test, but Sylvia gets all but one right and I do the same. Now we watch the door in fear, waiting for Miss Kearns to make her rounds.

It's evening now, and Pauline and Irene are sitting by the fire reading books. Denis is asleep in his cot. When I finish my homework, Mammy says, "Patricia, bring some newspapers and spread them out on the table." She gets the fine tooth comb and starts looking through my hair. "We have to check every night, so you might as well get used to it."

I groan and bend my head down so that Mammy can comb out every section of hair. After a while my scalp is burning and I beg her to stop.

I'm not sure which problem is the worst, dealing with lice or boils. Just a few months ago I had a big boil on my leg. Daddy told me we had to get the poison out so he put some porridge on the stove to cook. He wrapped the cooked oatmeal in a tea towel, and pressed the hot poultice on my boil, then told me to bite down on a rolled up sock and try and bear it as hot as I could. My eyes began to water and the pain was terrible, but the core of the boil came away when he removed the oatmeal. The poisonous core began to squirt slowly out of the boil. It looked like a tube of light green ointment. I had a hole in my leg where the boil had been, but it felt so good to be rid of the pain of that ugly red bump. We all have this problem from time to time.

Now this lice business has made everyone upset, and in class we are always waiting to see the nurse come back through the door with her nasty smelling solution.

I'm sitting listening to Miss McCann explain about subtraction, when I see a little white louse crawling up the sweater of the girl in front of me. It's heading towards her hair and I'm tempted to tell her. Instead I edge my desk back a few inches. I'm hoping the louse doesn't decide to jump on me.

"Miss Owens, go and stand in the corner. We can't have people scooting their desks around. There must be order in the classroom."

I'm embarrassed, but at least in the corner there's less chance of lice jumping on me. I certainly don't want that toilet cleaner stuff in my hair.

Finally, Miss McCann tells me to sit back down, as we are ready to practice the prayers for our First Holy Communion.

The Apostles were given the power from Christ at the Last Supper when he broke the bread and gave wine and said "Do this is memory of me." Now the priest, who has received this same power from Christ, holds up the Host and says, "This is my body," and holding up the wine says, "This is my blood." We have faith and believe that the change is really happening and the Host is really the body and blood of Christ. We are all going to have a chance for the first time to receive Jesus into our bodies and souls.

We also go over the words that we need to say in confession: "Bless me, Father, for I have sinned. This is my first confession."

Miss McCann explains the difference between mortal sins: killing someone, and venial sin: telling lies, gossiping, etc.

Sylvia leans across and whispers, "I'm going to wear our Nora's white dress and veil."

Miss McCann is still writing sins on the board, so I say quietly, "Is it long or short?"

"Long, with satin ribbons flowing down the front and back," she whispers.

"Mine is simple and short and the veil has a rose above each ear," I say.

"Miss Owens, back to the corner. You just don't seem to understand that when I say order, I mean order." Miss McCann speaks sternly. I stare at the wall and think of the beautiful patent leather shoes I'll be wearing tomorrow and say a wee prayer that it won't rain.

The class is now saying, "Oh, my God, I am heartily sorry for having offended thee." The prayer that we have to say after God, through the priest, forgives our sins. We repeat it over and over so that we'll know it by heart. After lunch, we'll go over to the church and confess our sins. I hope I can think up enough of them to make it worthwhile for Fr. Grady.

I've survived confession and was relieved that the screen inside made it impossible for the priest to tell who I was. He was nice and only gave me three "Hail Marys," and I said them very quickly.

Mammy told me to have a bath a whole day early. My most favourite thing in the whole world is when my hair is washed and Mammy wraps a towel around my head. She then pulls my head to her stomach and I lean in to her while we stand by the kitchen sink. She gently rubs the towel on my hair to soak up the moisture. I look forward to closeness and warmth of this weekly event and I don't ever want to grow up and have it taken away.

She's wrapping my hair up in rags tonight so that I'll have ringlets tomorrow. As she winds my hair around the long strips of cloth, I tell her about going to confession.

"I don't think you'll ever have to worry about committing a mortal sin, Patricia. Going to confession isn't all that bad and it leaves you feeling so good, when you come out."

It's finally Saturday and our family rides the bus down to St. John's. There's quite a crowd when we get off the bus and I wave at Sylvia who looks beautiful in her long dress. Mammy made mine and I love it even though it's not elaborate. Everyone says I look great, and I feel special.

The boys are wearing sparkling white shirts with their best Sunday clothes and they all seem to have brand new knee socks as well. Even their ears are clean and shining. All the girls look beautiful in their dresses and veils, almost like angels on this special day.

After the priest changes the bread and wine, we sing a hymn and the teacher motions to the front row and that group stands up. The rows move toward the altar one by one and when it's my turn I can hardly believe that I'm finally going to receive Jesus. We kneel at the altar rail and hold our folded hands under the white cloth that's connected to it. The priest moves along the line, and the altar boy holds a shiny gold plate under each chin to take care of the problem of anyone accidentally dropping the host. When the priest says, "Body of Christ," we answer, "Amen."

When I receive the wafer it feels very dry and sticks on my tongue. When I close my lips it immediately sticks to the roof of my mouth. I'm trying to get it down with my tongue while we're filing back to our seats. I notice that the girls who are already kneeling in the pews are also moving their mouths around, trying to dislodge the host in order to swallow it quickly. We have been warned not to chew and I can understand that. When it hits me, that Jesus is inside me, I kneel quickly, cover my face with both hands and bow my head. I say the prayer we have been taught with a feeling of wonder:

Jesus, you have given yourself to me
Now let me give myself to you.
I give you my body, that it may be chaste and pure.
I give you my soul, that it may be free from sin.
I give you my heart that it may always love you.
I give you every breath that I shall breath,
and especially my last.
I give you myself in life and in death,
That I may be yours forever and ever.

When the Mass ends, the First Communion children file out and each girl ends up walking next to a boy. The rest of the people in the church are all smiles and there's a lot of talking and laughing outside. *Thank God it's a nice day, with only a few clouds in the sky*, I think to myself.

"Granny wants to see you, Patricia," Mammy says. "We're having early dinner there." Our family hops on the next bus heading down to the Springfield Road.

Granny says I look great and suggests that I go up to see my Granny Owens as well.

"Irene should go with her," Pauline says. "I need to help you with the dinner, Granny." Irene grimaces and grabs my hand. We go out the back door into the entry and start walking up Oranmore Street.

Granny Owens, lives halfway up and usually, when we go up this street, we get down on our hunkers while passing her house so she won't see us.

We're hoping she isn't home, but on knocking, she opens the door and we smile, shyly. She's a great big woman, who wears silky dresses with little flowers all over. Her hair is always rolled up on top of her head and her glasses and pursed lips make her look scary to us. We don't know her that well.

She invites us in and we're hoping that she's out of fruitcake. No such luck. Out comes the tin, and she's cutting pieces that are awful big. She pours cups of tea and tells me I look very nice.

"Did your mum make your dress, dearie?" I nod. "Cat got your tongue, dearie? You're a big girl now, you can speak up for yourself." She talks funny, like the people in the English movies at the cinema. Daddy, who is pro IRA, can't stand the fact that his mother was born in England. He calls her Min when he talks about her, although her name is Lavinia. It's like he doesn't even like her. Maybe someday I'll find out what the real problem is.

Granddad Owens comes down the stairs and shakes our hands. He's a short man with a small moustache, and has a heart of gold, so he does. Taking two shillings out of his pocket he slips them to me and I thank him profusely. While we sit at the table he tells us about how he worked as an electrician on the Titanic. He describes how hard it was for Catholics to get a job in the shipyards. "My name saved me, you know. I think it's Welsh. Though I was born in Dublin, someone in my past must have been a Welshman."

"Joe, wrap up, and put more money in the gas meter," Granny says sternly. Granddad jumps, and takes a coin out of his pocket. We're fascinated with how this system works and ask why we don't have a meter where we live.

"Because you live in a modern house, Love." He smiles and lets me drop the coin in the slot. A little hand on the meter box goes up to the top and points to full.

Granny Owens doesn't have a parlour; the house is very small and joined to other houses on both sides. They have to go the toilet in a shed outside, and when they need a bath, they have to drag a big metal container into the scullery. Daddy says that he used to freeze while taking his sponge baths in winter. I'm sure he really likes living in our house now with a real lavatory an' all.

We nibble on the cake that might be good, if it didn't have so much peel in it. Mammy makes hers with raisins and currants only, and we like that a lot better.

Granny is about a foot taller than Granddad and I've heard that he spends a lot of time in the pub to keep out of her way. It also explains why Daddy has taken the pledge and doesn't touch a drop. He told us that the drink is the ruin of Ireland.

After our tea and cake we thank Granny and Granddad Owens and go back down the street. Granny Gordon is at the top of the stairs when we get to her house, and she calls me up.

She leads me into Uncle Frank's room where he's lying in bed holding a towel to his jaw and looking miserable.

"Frank has an abscessed tooth, Patricia, but he wanted to see you in your finery just the same."

"Does it hurt really bad, Frank?" I ask. He opens his mouth and shows me the swollen gum around one of his lower back teeth.

"We're waiting for the doctor to come and lance it," Granny says, and I cringe at the thought of it.

"Ach, he's in such pain right now, Patricia, that it should be a relief to have the poison taken out," she says. Frank points to his chest of drawers. There's a shiny half crown lying on top.

"He wants you to have this for your First Communion, Patricia." She hands me the money. I thank poor Frank, and as we're going down the stairs I ask Granny why so many people have false teeth.

"Oh, it's just the way things are done," She says. "Every time you have a bad one they yank it out and before you know it there aren't enough left to eat with. They replace them with false ones. Your mammy and Marjorie are perfect examples."

I remember earlier this year, I had two bad teeth and the dentist put me to sleep and pulled them out. When I was asleep I could see pink elephants floating in the air all around me.

"Looks like I'm well on my way to losing all my teeth too," I say.

"God forbid that you'll ever have that problem," Granny says with a laugh.

When we get down to the parlour, Uncle Tom, Aunt Lucy and our cousins, Anne Marie and Vincent are there. Tom wants to take a picture of me out in front of the house and Anne Marie stands next to me.

"Anne Marie, take your thumb out of your mouth," her Daddy tells her and she puts it back in just as he pushes the button.

I have several pounds and some change by the end of the day, and Mammy says I can open a savings account at the post office. It'll be exciting to have a wee book that shows how much money I have. I can take out thrupence or sixpence once in a while if I need it. The post office man will just mark it in my book.

Going home on the bus several people give me smiles and nods even though I'm not wearing my veil anymore. They can tell by the white dress and shoes that this was a very special day for me.

Chapter Six

It's been a week since my First Communion and Mammy is checking my hair again. She finds some nits and starts combing like mad, shaking the nits onto the newspaper and smashing them with her thumbnail.

"Sorry, Patricia, but if we don't get them this evening they'll be lice tomorrow, so grin and bear it. You have to be cruel to be kind." She's trying all the little sayings to make me feel better, but it doesn't make any difference. My neck is killing me and my scalp is burning.

"Patricia better sleep somewhere else tonight," Pauline says, "I'd be mortified if anyone at school saw lice in my hair."

Pauline goes to a fancy secondary school called Fortwilliam, and a lot of the girls in her class are well off. She could have gone to St. Dominic's, down the Falls Road, but the O'Hare girls went to Fortwilliam all the way over by the Antrim Road. They're always singing its praises, and Mammy thinks the long bus ride is worth it for a better education.

Anyhow, Mammy keeps working on my head and I don't think a single nit could have escaped her thumbnail. At least I shouldn't have to get that smelly treatment.

It's hard to sleep though because my head is still burning. Please God, this infestation will soon be over.

***

Edwin MacCarrick and I are walking down the cement path toward our back garden. We're taller than usual today because we're walking on tin cans. I have to hold my string tightly, so that the cans will stick to the bottom of my feet. Edwin is better at this than I am and he isn't nervous at all.

Mammy opens the kitchen window and whispers, "You two had better take those cans off or go out on the street. I just spoke to Mrs. Farrell, and she's just after getting Tony down. You're liable to wake him up with all that racket."

We jump down and swing the cans over our shoulders by the string. Then we notice Daddy at the bottom of the garden. He's on his hands and knees by the tree, and reminds me of the men in Pauline's geography book who pray with their heads to the ground. Suddenly, he gets up, runs past us to the kitchen window and yells, "Bessie, could you come out here a minute?" He's running back to the tree and is down on his knees again, twisting his head this way and that, looking at something. If we didn't wake Tony up, Daddy surely did.

"Ach Danny what are you doing,?" Mammy asks. She bends down to see what he's so excited about.

"I've found the source of those filthy rats," he's saying. "Aye, indeed I have. See that big nest in there?" He points to a hole in the bottom of the tree.

Just yesterday, we were sitting eating dinner at the kitchen table, when our cat, Ginger, jumped up on the windowsill right outside. She plopped down a rat almost as big as herself.

Pauline and I were sitting right next to the window and we jumped. I covered my eyes and tried to get away from the table so fast that I spilled my milk. While I was cleaning up the mess, Mammy said, "Ginger's just showing off her accomplishment and letting us know how much we need her. It certainly would be better though, if she would pile the rats up next to the dust-bin instead of right under our noses."

When I think of the ugly rat on our windowsill, I can understand why Daddy is so determined to get rid of them.

He's stuffing things inside the hole now. "I'll smoke them out, so I will," he says.

"What will Ginger do then, Daddy?" I ask.

"You don't have to worry about her," he says. "The ones we smoke out will just be a drop in the bucket, and she still won't have to wander far to have her dinner."

It's late now, and although I've been in bed for hours, I can't get to sleep. The vision of those rats living in the tree keeps coming into my mind.

Just as I'm starting to doze off, I hear a crackling sound and it startles me. Pauline and Irene moan when I pull back the covers and get out of bed.

"What are you doing, Patricia? You're freezing us out, so you are."

"Get up, get up," I wail. "Look out the window!" We're all shivering now as we gaze at the bright orange flames shooting out of the tree at the bottom of the garden.

Pauline runs to the front bedroom yelling, and soon Daddy is outside in his pajamas dousing the flames with the garden hose. Denis has been awakened by all the commotion and he's jumping up and down on our bed. Every once in a while he pulls the curtains back and watches Daddy with delight. We have opened the window slightly and can hear Daddy say, "Don't worry, folks, I've got it under control."

Mammy runs a hot bath to warm Daddy up now that he's got himself all wet and is probably freezing. She's mumbling about smoking out more than the rats. The next morning, we all sleep late and barely make it to twelve o'clock Mass. Daddy gets a ragging from some of the neighbours.

"Do you need any new members for your rat patrol, Danny?" Mr. Murphy says with a smirk.

"Started smoking I see, Danny," Mr. Farrell says. Daddy is a very private man and he's embarrassed and mumbles to himself under his breath. Later when Mrs. MacCarrick and Mammy are talking over the back hedge, I hear Mrs. MacCarrick say, "He's never going to live it down as long as he's on this street," and they both roar with laughter.

It's well Daddy has already gone to work when this conversation takes place or Mammy would be getting the silent treatment again.

Usually, when we're lying in bed, we can hear the drone of our parents voices coming from downstairs, but when Daddy is mad about something, there's a complete silence that can go on for days. He has become so suspicious of Pauline, now that she's thirteen, and when Mammy sticks up for her, he gets angry. If he only knew! Pauline is completely innocent. She can't figure out what the problem is and says, "Our Daddy is pure paranoid if you ask me." I don't know what that word means so I can't agree or disagree.

Shortly after the tree burning incident, Daddy sends me down to the petrol station on the Falls Road to buy some paraffin oil for our wee Primus stove. Instead of taking the long way down, I decide to take a shortcut through the field in back. I'm making my way past the stream that runs along the edge of the field when I hear a loud splash. I look into the water and am appalled to see a big ugly rat swimming away from me. I'm reliving the whole experience of the rat running over my foot in the dump, and take off as fast as I can, jumping over rocks and not looking back.

The man in the petrol station looks at me strangely as he fills the can. I'm shivering and trying to hold back the sobbing sounds that keep sneaking up from my throat. I heard someone say once, that for every rat you see, there are two hundred that you can't see. Just thinking about it makes me shiver. I wish I could be brave, but I can't get rid of the rat thoughts. I run up the Falls Road and around to our street the long way. No more shortcuts for me.

When I get home, I go to the back garden to give Daddy the oil and see him drowning newborn kittens in a bucket. I don't think he wanted me to see this, but it's too late.

"Why can't we keep just one, Daddy?"

65

"One cat is enough, Patricia. It'd be one more mouth to feed."

"But, we never feed Ginger and I just saw a big rat in the stream. There's plenty of cat food out there."

"Whist, Patricia, cats multiply too fast and one is enough for this family."

If there were enough cats in the neighbourhood the rats would be under control, I think to myself as I leave.

Just as I reach the street, I meet Maggie McArdle.

"Want to play, Patricia? I've got a new skipping rope."

I grab mine and we go up the street to her house. We're skipping for quite a while when it starts to rain. We run into the shed in Maggie's garden and play a game with the potato pile until we're tired of that.

I'll show you my cushion, if you show me yours," I say. We have an inspection and both agree that they're pretty ugly, "But not as ugly as little boys," I pitch in, for I remember being shocked when I saw my baby brother for the first time without his nappie.

We agree not to tell anyone what we did, but I feel guilty for a long time.

***

Summer is here at last and I'm on another holiday with Granny Gordon, this time in Moville, County Donegal, where she was born. We're out walking along a cliff path when we hear someone calling. It's Mammy and Pauline who have come up for the weekend. Pauline catches up to me and she's out of breath. As soon as Mammy and Granny are out of earshot, she leans over and says, "You're in big trouble, Miss Patricia, so you are." I'm wondering what I did and she says, "Maggie's big sister Noreen said that Maggie spilled the beans and told what you two did in their back shed." I'm mortified and realize that it was pretty stupid of me to think that it would be kept a secret. You'd better go to confession as soon as we get back, Patricia, and confess your sin," Pauline says.

I don't really enjoy the last two days of the holiday, with this looming over my head.

The first Saturday after we come back I'm shaking as I kneel in the dark confessional in St. Theresa's Church.

"Bless me, Father, for I have sinned, it's two weeks since my last confession. I told four lies, I stole a penny out of my Mammy's handbag, I called our Irene a 'cheeky cat.' I made fun of Desi O'Connell and I uh...uh...uh..."

"What is it, child?"

"I uh...uh...looked at my friend's cushion and she looked at mine!"

"What is your name, child?" *How can he be asking me this? I thought it was all kept secret.*

"Uh...it's Patricia Owens, Father."

"How old are you, child?"

"I'm just turned eight, Father."

"Well, Patricia, you know that you must always avoid the occasion of sin. For your penance you must say three decades of the rosary. What you have done is a very serious matter. Now say your act of contrition."

"Oh, my God, I am sorry, and beg pardon for all my sins..."

He is making the sign of the cross giving me absolution, and I stumble out of the confessional box. There's a long line outside and I pray they didn't hear my terrible sin.

I kneel down and prepare to say my penance. Three decades of the rosary is three "Our Fathers" *thirty* "Hail Marys" and three "Glory Be to the Fathers."

I should be here for quite some time. At least Father Glynn didn't yell out loud like some priests do. I'm happy to be relieved of my sin and say my penance with reverence. By the time I finish, everyone is gone, even the priest.

Chapter Seven

The Farrells next door are crazy about their wee Tony, who is around eighteen months of age already. They talk about him all the time and spoil him to pieces.

It's a warm Sunday morning and our family is sitting enjoying the wonderful eggs that we can afford to eat only on weekends. Pauline holds two fingers against her lips and we stop talking to see what she's trying to tell us. When there's silence, we hear a strange wailing sound coming from next door, and when we go to investigate we see Mr. Farrell running over to Dr. Harton's across the street. He looks frantic and everyone is trying to figure what could have happened. When the doctor emerges from the Farrell's house later, he looks despondent.

We later find out that Tony is dead. He woke up early, stood up in his cot, reached through the bars and opened the drawer of his mammy's dressing table. There he found a box of Fersolate tablets that have a candy coating and ate most of them.

Mammy is sobbing "Jesus, Mary, and Joseph, how could this happen? They wanted that wee boy so badly and he made them so happy. It could have happened to us. He ate the same pills that I'm taking for the headaches I get from the sewing." Irene and I are looking sideways at each other. If Mammy only knew that every time she gets a new box of pills, we climb up to the top cupboard when she's at the shops and suck off the green candy coating. We put them back in the box, but now they're white in colour. Thank God, we never swallowed any by accident.

Mammy and Mrs. MacCarrick are talking across the back hedge. "It could have been the fersolate tablets that caused my stillbirth last year," Mammy is saying. I've never heard this word before and go to find Pauline.

"Last year Mammy did stay at Granny's for a few days," she says, "and when she came home she had lost a lot of weight. I found her crying a few times. Maybe she had a baby and it died, I don't know."

A few days later there's a long black hearse covered in flowers, out in front of the Farrell's house. A large crowd has gathered on the street, and the little white coffin is being carried out of the house on the shoulders of four men. The Farrell family follows and they are weeping. It's hard to watch them, and soon most of the women and children are also crying.

The hearse begins to move forward slowly, followed by the men carrying the coffin that moves up and down with every step they take. I'm trying to imagine what Tony looks like now that he's no longer alive. We have seen older people laid out in their homes. The coffins are usually placed across four kitchen chairs facing each other, but Mammy didn't want us to see Tony. She thought it would be too much for us and I think she was right.

Mammy, Daddy, and the MacCarricks join in the procession. Pauline will be in charge of us until they return. I can imagine how we'd feel if it was our wee Denis in there and I say a prayer and ask God to help the Farrell family.

Tony is with the angels for sure, because he was so young and innocent. It just doesn't seem fair for the Farrells to have finally gotten a son and then have him taken away so soon.

***

Granny Gordon's friend is a midwife also. She lives at the bottom of the Springfield Road and her name is Nurse

Peale. She has a wee cottage by the sea in a village called Ballyhornan, and our family has rented it for a whole week. We go by bus with Granny, and Daddy will come down for the weekend. The cottage is in County Down, and when we're on the bus we travel through the small town of Downpatrick, where St. Patrick is buried.

Arriving in Ballyhornan the bus stops about one hundred yards from the cottage and we are delighted to see that it has a thatched roof. The entrance has a half door or Dutch door. You can keep the bottom half shut and open the top half then just lean over the lower part to look out. Maybe it was designed to prevent little children from crawling out or animals from wandering in. Whatever the reason, it's a novelty for us. Inside there's a large central room that includes the living area, kitchen and eating space. Off to the side, are three bedrooms with lots of beds with sheets, blankets, and everything.

The fireplace was built using big rocks, and attached to the side of it is a thick movable metal ring that can be pushed over the fire when there's a pot of food or a kettle of water on it. Seems to me we'll be eating lots of stew while we're here, because you can only heat one pot at a time.

There's no electricity and the oil lamps are fascinating. I can hardly wait until evening to see how they work. There's also an old privy in back that stinks, and I hope I don't have to use it too often.

The village shop sells everything under the sun, and has a small post office inside. Down at the end of the road on the other side of the cottage is a village green that sweeps down to the sea.

Pauline, Irene and I can't wait to check out the strand. Mammy warns us to watch the tide. There are low flat rocks at the edge of the small waves and they have tidepools tucked within them. We run all over this area and find crabs and sea anemones. Pauline calls us over to show us a rock that she has found that's shaped like a sofa.

"This is my house," she declares, sitting on her rock sofa. Irene and I scramble to find our own houses. We decide that we can visit each others homes, but any crabs or little see-through fish that Pauline calls "spricks" are the property of the house they end up in. We spend ages playing in our imaginary houses until we see Granny pushing Denis in the tansad. She calls us in for lunch.

After lunch, Mammy sends Irene and me up to the dairy across from the village shop with a big milk jug to be filled. Irene lets me carry it up and she'll carry it back when it's full.

The barnyard has a strong smell of cows, and as this is a completely new experience, we're a wee bit nervous. The farmer's wife waves us into the milk room and fills our jug from a big, shiny can. The milk is still kind of warm and foamy on top as the jug fills up.

I notice Irene looking over at the other side of the room and turn to see what has caught her attention. There's a young lad with dark curly hair churning milk to make butter.

"Tell your ma that we have the freshest butter she ever tasted." He smiles, and Irene blushes. He's about twelve. I think she has a notion of this handsome boy already.

"We'll tell her about the butter," Irene says, and flutters her eyelashes.

Back at the cottage we hand the jug to Mammy.

"Do you think you could run to the shop now and get a loaf of that good homemade wheaten bread?" Mammy asks. "We'll have to let the milk cool before we drink it. Mind those geese as you go, though. You heard what Granny said."

As we're walking along, Irene is studying the cottages. "See those rain barrels at the end of the rain spouts?" I nod, and she says, "Pauline says they collect soft water from the rain and it's great for washing your hair. It's supposed to give you a great lather from the soap compared to the hard water we have in our city pipes."

"Maybe we could put a bucket outside the cottage and try it on our hair if it rains this week," I say, and Irene agrees.

On the way back from the shop we see a farmer walking a herd of cattle down toward the sea.

"Quick, Patricia, give the bread to Mammy and let's follow." I run into the cottage and set the bread on the table, hurry out and run to catch up with Irene who is just behind the herd.

"What on earth is he thinking?" she says gasping. "He's walking the cattle into the sea."

When we reach the shore we realize that the wee island, a short distance out in the sea, can be reached when the tide is all the way out. The cattle walk across and don't drown. We run back to the Cottage and ask Granny about what we've seen.

"That's Guns Island, and the tide comes and goes twice a day, so the farmers take advantage of the situation to find fresh grazing for their cattle," she says.

It's noisy during the evening meal with everyone talking at once about their discoveries so far.

"Geeze, Geeze!" Denis is shouting at the top of his lungs and we look at him in puzzlement.

"Ach aye, that's right," Granny says. "There's not only a flock of chickens in front of the village shop. There were two geese today that were more than a wee bit aggressive. I had to run the tansad at them to keep them from attacking us. Denis thought it was great fun. I don't think he realised how bad it could hurt to be pecked in the leg. The lady in the shop said the geese think the grass is greener outside the fence and she has a hard time keeping them in."

When it starts getting dark, Granny shows us how to light the oil lamps. Pauline wants to read her book by lamplight just for the novelty of it, and decides it's almost as good as electricity. I like the warm glow it gives the room, and it's great for making shadows on the wall. Denis wants us to play the shadow game before he goes to bed, and Mammy shows him how to make an ostrich.

The day after we arrive is Sunday and as the church is in another town, the villagers show us where to wait for a pony and trap. It takes a whole trap for our family and it's very exciting being pulled by a horse. Granny sings a song to Denis as we go:

Horsey, horsey, don't you stop
Just let your feet go clippety clop
Let your tail go swish and the wheels go round.
Giddy up, we're homeward bound.

Denis really loves it, and when the driver flicks the whip to make the horse go faster, he squeals with approval. The horse must have a musical ear, because he trots in perfect time to Granny's song.

We don't know a soul in church, but the Mass is the same as it is at home, with people constantly coughing and drowning out the priest's words.

After the Mass is over the locals stand around outside talking and some of the men wander down the road toward the pub.

On the fourth day of our holiday, Granny suggests a nice long walk so she can show us something unusual.

We leave the village and take a road that gradually rises until it's on top of a cliff above the ocean. We have to cut through a barnyard, and Granny tells us not to worry, the farmer is friendly and doesn't mind people passing through. Several goats with long beards and horns come over to greet us and Denis just loves it. I think he'd rather stay here than continue our walk. Beyond the farm, the cliff path continues and purple heather sways in the breeze all around us.

"Hold your whist, everyone," Granny says, "and listen to the heather." We stop babbling and can hear the rustling sound that it makes when it blows in the breeze. As we round the corner of the cliff at its highest point, Granny points to what she wanted to show everyone, and we stand quietly looking out at a rusting hulk of a ship that had gone aground many years ago. It looks so forlorn lying at an angle with one side under the rolling, foaming sea.

"Do you think anyone lost their lives, Granny?" Pauline asks.

"I'm not sure. You can see it's not very far out, but the rocks here can be very treacherous."

We sit on the grass, and I try to imagine the people being rescued by the villagers of long ago, and hope that the story had a happy ending.

Denis is so excited with the fresh air and beauty of it all, that he's running through the heather chasing imaginary butterflies. We have to keep our eyes on him because of the cliff edge.

When we walk all the way back to Ballyhornan, we're tired and hungry. Pauline is first in and she comes back out with a shocked look on her face.

"What's the matter?" Mammy asks, and Pauline points inside the cottage with her mouth agape. There in the middle of the central room is a big, brown cow, contentedly chewing her cud and ignoring us completely.

"Shoo, shoo, outside where you belong!" Granny shouts, flapping her arms up and down. She reminds me a lot of the geese up the road when they flap their wings. The cow leaves reluctantly by the open back door, most likely the way she came in, giving a sorrowful moo as she goes.

"Who used the privy last?" Mammy scolds.

I raise my hand halfway and say "It's not every day we have a cow in the kitchen," and everyone laughs. "Be sure and close the back door from now on," Mammy says, with a grin, and we get down to the business of cleaning up the animal's calling cards from the flagstone floor.

When everyone has settled down, Mammy gives Pauline the potatoes to peel, while she fills the big pot with water. Irene peels the carrots that will be thrown in with the potatoes, and I set the table.

This morning Granny stopped a fisherman who was pushing his cart past the cottage. She bought a plateful of fresh herring caught off the fishing village of Ardglass. On our way to Ballyhornan, we passed this village, and could see the people standing at long tables cleaning fish and throwing them in big containers.

While setting the table for dinner, I can hear Granny singing a song she sang in the last century when she was young. She says it might put Denis to sleep:

Mary Ellen at the church turned up
Her father turned up and
Her mother turned up.
Her little sister Jane and
Her rich old uncle Ned
And the parson with his
Long white robes turned up
But no bridegroom
With the ring turned up
But a telegram boy with
His nose turned up
With a telegram that read
That he didn't want to wed
And they'd find him in the
River with his toes turned up.

Instead of sleeping, Denis is laughing, so Granny changes her tune and starts to sing. "Toora Loora Loora."

When he finally nods off Granny comes out and sits in the big rocking chair by the fire and rocks herself to sleep.

The potatoes seem to be taking too long to cook, and we can't wait to taste the fresh herring. In the city you don't see them often in the shops. We usually have sole one Friday and monkfish the next Friday. One is white the other brown. I prefer the brown fish, but nothing can compare to fresh herring.

After a very tasty dinner, we go outside, and Pauline introduces us to a few of the village children that she met yesterday.

Eilish is about eleven, like Irene, and Maeve is more like thirteen, or Pauline's age. There don't seem to be any eight year olds around, so I'll have to make do.

Maeve asks if we've ever seen an eel, and we say we haven't. "Well you're in for a treat," she says, grinning. She leads the way down the road towards the ocean. When we come to the end of the road, we make a right turn past a row of holiday houses and a few wee cottages that face the sea. When we see an old two story house with a ramp for boats that is almost in the ocean, Maeve tells us that it's called the boathouse.

"The owner rents it out occasionally to holiday makers like yourself."

The view from the windows must be just marvelous. You can see Gun's Island and fields of heather along the cliffs, and upstairs you can probably see for miles around. Near the boathouse is a wide wall that goes a long way into the water.

"Follow me," Maeve says. She runs along the wall towards the deep water and we trail carefully behind. Eilish is also careful, maybe she doesn't know how to swim.

Peering down into the deep water, we can see the long, slimy looking eels swimming around among the fish.

"Some people eat them, but they're said to be dangerous to swim around. They have a kind of electric charge that can hurt you." We aren't too anxious to be spending lots of time here and suggest that they show us some other sights.

"Do you want to see the old barracks left over from the Second World War?" We nod, and soon we're going back the way we came. We pass Nurse Peale's cottage and see Granny through the window. She's adjusting the oil lamp. We walk up to an open area next to the cottage.

"The British army used this place to guard the coastline," Eilish informs us, "and since the end of the war it's been abandoned. We play in here once in a while."

The gate is missing from a space wide enough for a lorry to pass through, and a few stray cows have wandered into the compound.

"There's the cow that was in our kitchen today," Pauline says.

"How can you be sure? They all look the same to me," Irene replies, and we laugh.

We run in and out of the metal army huts shouting commands, like we're soldiers, until it's completely dark.

There's no choice now but to go in for the evening. At night it's pitch black here. they don't have lights like we do in Belfast. Maeve and Eilish say they will call again tomorrow and see if we can play.

On Saturday morning Daddy arrives on the first bus, and we're anxious to show him the tidepools, the old boathouse, and the slimy looking eels. He's impressed with Guns Island and says he and Mammy will walk over to the shipwreck after Mass tomorrow.

After lunch, we go with Daddy for a long walk along the strand. The waves are small and gentle, unlike the wild breakers in Bundoran, and the sea seems to be shallow beneath them.

"I'd have to walk a long way for a good swim in that water," Daddy says. "I think I could even walk across to that Island."

"The cows did the other day when the tide went out," Pauline says.

When we get back to the cottage, Maeve and Eilish are looking for us to see if we can play.

"Let's go and play in the barracks," Maeve suggests. I run ahead and try to beat them through the space where the gate is missing. The sun has come out from behind a cloud and it catches my eyes and makes me squint. Just as I reach the space, I see a string of barbed wire.

I'm going too fast to stop and turn my head sharply to the left. I feel the wire cutting into my right ear and pull myself away from it. The rest of the girls are looking at me with their mouths hanging open.

"Oh dear, Patricia, let's go back and have Mammy look at your ear," Pauline says. She looks worried. I glance down at my dress and see a trickle of blood running down the front. I try not to cry but my insides are trembling.

"Your ear is split down the back, you'll need stitches," Mammy says.

"But it doesn't even hurt," I say.

"There's no way around it, Patricia. I'll take you back on the bus to the Royal Hospital. Your daddy can come back tomorrow evening with the rest of them." She tears up a pillowcase and wraps it around my head and ear doing her best to stop the bleeding.

I'm a wee bit embarrassed on the bus with the bandage on my head. People seem to be staring. The trip seems to take forever. I sleep for a short while and when we reach the hospital it's already dark.

When I'm finally called in, they put a mask over my face and it knocks me out. By the time I awaken, I'm horrified to realise that I've wet the table I'm lying on.

"Don't worry, Patricia, it's not your fault. You were out like a light," Mammy assures me. It doesn't make me feel any better though, and I'm glad to get out of there at last.

On the way back to our house Mammy says, "They installed the barbed wire today while you were down at the strand. It was unfortunate, but you paid the price of warning everyone else to the danger. You have seven stitches, according to the doctor."

"I'm lucky Mammy, it almost got me in the eyes, but I turned my head just in time."

"Indeed, aye, it's a blessing you weren't blinded."

On Sunday we spend a quiet day together, and Mammy lets me sleep in and miss Mass since I qualify with seven stitches.

I never got to see the cows come back off the island, but Daddy assured me that they watched them come over safe and sound. Irene shows me a matchbox filled with sand. "I brought a wee bit of Ballyhornan home with me," she says with a smile. She always thinks of such nice ways to remember a place.

I'm lying in bed dreaming of beautiful Ballyhornan, the most perfect place in the world. I'm on the strand, playing in the tidepools, looking at the island so close, the heather growing on top of the cliff, and the boathouse. I'll never forget the oil lamps, fresh milk, tasty herring, and even the scary eels. I wonder do the people who live there realise they're in Paradise? I hope and pray we can go back again someday.

Chapter Eight

"Will you both hush for heaven's sake." Our Pauline is upset at Irene and me since we've been arguing about who should hold the toasting fork. We're sitting by the fire on a Saturday night, and the embers are perfect for toast, red with no flames.

Pauline's in charge for the evening, and we're staying up later than usual. She's turning the knobs on the wireless, trying to find the station that has the Saturday night mysteries.

"And we continue with our story from last week," the broadcaster says in a low, mysterious voice.

"George is plodding through the station after stepping off the train."

We can hear whistle sounds, "All aboard" sounds, and people walking and talking. There are occasional shouts in the background as passengers are greeted by their friends or families.

We listen with rapt attention, imagining the train station full of people, and then we hear George speak.

"Where can I find the baggage cart?" He thanks the station master and picks up his suitcase. You can hear him call for a taxi. The driver complains that the suitcase is extremely heavy as he puts it in the boot of the vehicle.

Pauline pours tea for the three of us, and we eat our toast with lots of butter,

We listen to eerie music now from the wireless, as George takes his suitcase, pays the driver, and walks up the

steps of his building. The narrator is explaining that George has put the suitcase under his bed, and you can hear him yawn.

He is now lying on the bed reading a book, and you can hear him starting to snore as he drifts into a deep sleep.

Pauline gets up to turn off the light. We're really enjoying the warmth from the fire and with the lights out it seems so cozy. As we're usually in bed by now, we relish this extra bit of freedom.

From the wireless now are sounds of twittering birds and traffic noises. We imagine George waking up. You can hear shuffling sounds as he walks across the floor in his slippers. He fills his kettle and you can hear him strike a match to light the gas. He's making a clatter now as he gets a cup and saucer down from his cupboard. We hear him shuffling back to the bedroom where he yawns and says to himself, "I should unpack."

There's a scraping sound as he pulls the suitcase from under his bed. "What's that sticky stuff on my floor?" George mutters to himself as the music gets loud and dramatic.

There's a creaking sound as George opens the suitcase and then a loud gasp.

Irene has put her hands over her ears now, and her big green eyes have grown even bigger. Looking at her has made me even more jittery than I already was.

On the wireless George has let out a high-pitched wail. "My God, I've taken the wrong suitcase! And whose bloody body does this head belong to?"

We let out a scream, and Irene spills her tea while trying to turn off the wireless.

"For heaven's sake, you're going to wake our Denis with your antics," Pauline says. "It took me ages to get him settled." She sinks down onto the sofa. "We'd better go up to bed as soon as we get this mess cleaned up."

Irene and I look at each other. "I'm not getting into bed unless someone looks underneath first," Irene says. "What if there's a suitcase with a head in it."

"Me neither," I whine.

"All right," Pauline says. "We go up together, and all look under the bed at the same time."

Thank God, there's nothing there, but when we get into bed we cuddle up together and leave the light on.

I'm still awake when Mammy returns, looks in, and turns off the light. I pretend to be asleep. It's going to be very hard to go to bed from now on without checking for suitcases, and I hope that when I do get to sleep I won't be having nightmares.

***

Pauline, Irene, and I are taking Irish dance lessons at Madden's School of Dance, down the Falls Road. Irene is really good at the slip jig, so she is, but I'm still trying to get the reel without any mistakes.

We're all lined up and Mr. Madden is urging Anne Murphy to keep up with the line.

"You'll get stepped on if you can't keep up. You'll be holding up everybody else." He moves his arm up and down to show her how to keep time. Then turns on the music, and has us start all over again.

"We move to the right across the floor with the left foot following the right, counting to seven. Then to the left seven times with a toe-up one-two-three at the end of each seven steps.

Pauline and some other big girls are in another room practising the *Seige of Ennis* and the *Walls of Limerick*. They are group dances, or set dances, and are usually done with boys and girls together. In this class some of the girls have to pretend they're boys just so that they can learn the dances. Boys don't often volunteer to learn dancing because they'll be tormented by their friends.

Next year Pauline will be going to ceili dances at the Ard Scoil where she'll be dancing with real boys. I don't think I'd have the nerve, and I'm not really looking forward to it. But our Pauline is thirteen and the boys are already starting to look at her. She doesn't seem to mind at all.

It's dark as we walk back up the Falls road, and Irene and Pauline are engrossed in an argument about certain steps of the hornpipe. We're tired as we reach our house and I wonder why that the downstairs is in darkness. We go in and notice Mammy standing in the dark parlour. We can see her profile from the street lamp. She's looking out the window at the front garden and is dabbing at her eyes.

"What's wrong, Mammy?" Pauline asks, putting her hand on Mammy's arm.

"It's our Denis; he's in a bad way, the laryngitis has gotten much worse. I heard the gate and was just looking to see if your daddy was back with the doctor."

We follow her upstairs, and see a look of alarm on her face when she checks Denis. His face has started changing colour to a sort of blue, and he's hardly breathing at all.

Mammy runs into the bathroom and fills a big enamel basin with hot water. "Get me a couple of towels, Pauline," she says, as she rushes back to the bedroom. She props Denis up in the bed and stuffs pillows behind him. Folding a blanket, she places it on the bed between his legs. Now she sets the basin on the blanket and leans his head over the steam. She covers his head with a towel to keep the steam in a kind of little tent.

"This should do some good, please God... Irene go down and open the front door wide so the doctor can come up the minute he gets here." Mammy is praying now, asking God to make our wee brother breathe easier.

Suddenly Denis, who is only three and is confused by the steam tent, starts to cough and the towel over his head falls in the water. He coughs again, then throws up all over the towel. The vomit is mostly yellow phlegm. His face has turned pink now and Mammy is crying and thanking God for his great mercy. It's such a relief. Denis could so easily have died if he hadn't thrown up.

When the doctor arrives, he examines Denis and says. "I'd better give him an antibiotic and something to loosen the phlegm. Be sure and give him plenty of water and the steam treatment should work if he has any more breathing problems."

When I look at Denis, I feel ashamed. I'll push him on his tricycle from now on without complaining. He could easily have been with the angels in heaven, just like the Farrell's wee Tony.

***

As Lent has arrived again Daddy takes us to St. Theresa's for the Friday evening Stations of the Cross. On the way up I'm singing the song that I've decided to sing at our Irish dance party next week. Mr. Madden wants everyone to recite a poem or sing a song as a change of pace from the dancing.

"You're going to do real well," Irene says. "I need to practise my poem a bit more."

We have gone ahead into the church, as Daddy is having a word outside with Mr. Morgan. We move to the centre of the pew, pull down the kneeler in front of us and start to say some prayers, as the stations haven't yet begun.

When Daddy comes in he genuflects in the aisle while looking up at the altar. As he enters the pew he is still looking up, and drops quickly to his knees thinking his kneeler is down like ours. It's still up and Daddy expecting to stop long before he actually does, completely loses his balance. His head disappears under the pew, somewhere near the floor, and his legs are left sticking up in the air. He's trying with all his might to get right side up, but his legs are still sticking up making him look like a ballerina who is being held up in the air by a ballerino or whatever those men are called.

I look over at Irene, and she has both hands clamped over her mouth trying to stifle the laugh that is sure to come. Her eyes are jerking back and forth as well. Just looking at her makes me giggle too, and Daddy, who has now righted himself, is too embarrassed to turn around and scold us. He's kneeling upright finally and his head is down on his hands like he's deep in prayer. I think he may be just feeling awful, and wondering how many people have noticed.

Through the whole Stations of the Cross, we answer the prayers in all the right places, but Irene and I are in agony trying to stifle our giggles. They just keep coming back every time the vision of Daddy's legs in the air returns. When the Stations of the Cross are finally over we run ahead down St. Meryl Park laughing our heads off all the way.

A few weeks later Irene and I are playing in the street with Sandra and Edwin. The sky has grown darker and suddenly rain is coming down in buckets. We rush into their house squealing and soon hear loud claps of thunder. Huge bolts of fork lightning fill the air, and when we count between the thunder and lightning we realise it's extremely close. We're scared to death, and end up hiding under Sandra's bed upstairs. The storm lasts about half an hour, and when it's over we come downstairs and play the board game *Ludo*. Edwin wins, and Irene vows to get him next time.

As we open the MacCarrick's gate to go home, we see the postman walking past.

"You girls are in for it, he says. "Your father's looking all over the neighbourhood for you, and he's got his belt in his hand." Pauline and Irene have had the belt once, but I've been lucky so far.

"Oh, sweet Jesus, what are we going to do?" Irene says. "Hurry, Patricia."

As we're going in our front gate we see Daddy coming round the corner near Florence's house, and he's raging, so he is. We run inside, rush upstairs, and lock ourselves in the lavatory. We're shaking with fright and and can't imagine what's going to happen to us. Daddy's pounding on the door, but we're too afraid to come out.

"Daddy, we were right next door, so we were. We went in out of the storm and forgot the time," Irene calls through the door. We can hear him muttering and then Mammy's voice pleading with him.

"Come on out, girls; it'll be all right," Mammy is saying now. She must have talked Daddy into putting his belt back on. Irene and I look at each other and try to decide what to do. After opening the door a crack, we see Mammy standing there and run out and hide behind her, holding on to her dress for we know he'd never strike her. He's yelling about us not being in sight when our meal was ready.

"Sorry, Daddy," we say together, while hanging our heads.

"Well, just don't let it happen again."

"Right, Daddy."

We stay behind Mammy all the way down the stairs, and when we reach the living room Pauline is clearing the table and whispers, "You should have said where you were going!"

It was just a spur-of-the-moment thing, going into MacCarricks instead of our own house, but we've learned our lesson and been saved from the belt for the time being.

Daddy can be very funny one time and raging the next, but thank God Mammy is more easygoing.

The next week we stay near our house, especially at mealtimes, and resort to the old street games usually played on long summer evenings.

There's about a dozen of us lined up against the hedge in front of our house.

"I want to be the angel," Mairead Cafferty says.

"I'm the devil," Desi O'Connell says, and Pauline is chosen as the gatekeeper.

The angel and the devil stand in the road by the kerb facing Pauline, with the rest of us lined up against our hedge.

Pauline steps in front of Mairead, the angel, who knocks on an imaginary door and says

"Knock, knock."

"Who's there?" asks Pauline.

"The angel with the golden hair."

"Whaddiye want?"

"A box of colours."

"What colour?" Pauline asks.

"Yellow," the angel answers.

Sandra was secretly assigned that colour at the beginning of the game and she goes and stands behind Mairead, the angel.

Pauline steps in front of Desi now, and it's his turn to knock on the imaginary door.

"Knock, knock."

"Who's there."

"The devil with the long black horns," Desi answers.

"Whaddiye want?"

"A box of colours."

"What colour?" Pauline asks again.

"Purple," Desi answers.

Edwin has been assigned that colour and runs to stand behind Desi. Slowly but surely the lines grow behind the angel and the devil, until the children against the hedge have all been chosen.

Pauline gets the rope and the teams face each other for a tug of war. Sometimes it's lopsided if the older ones end up on the same team, or maybe there are more boys on one side. But anyhow, it's one of the long, involved street games that make our lives interesting.

Most of the parents don't mind their youngsters staying out late. The sky is still bright, and I think it's music to their ears to hear us calling out the game commands. It gives them a little time to themselves that they certainly don't get on wet evenings when most houses are filled to capacity.

Our living room is about twelve feet by twelve feet. With the dining table and chairs, the sofa and easy chair, it's a bit crowded, so it is. Most of the families are bigger than ours. As of now we only have four children. We take every opportunity to stay out and play, because when it rains we're stuck in the house. I often ask Mammy how she can bear to stay inside all day cooking and cleaning. On a Sunday afternoon, Daddy will take us for a long walk up to

McKenses' Glen while Mammy stays behind and bakes apple tarts and wee buns for our tea.

My very favourite game is throwing balls against the side of Granny's house. Her gable wall is right next to the footpath because she has the last house at the corner of Oranmore Street.

We get two tennis balls, take turns throwing them up against the wall, one after the other, and catch them, one at a time, as they come back. It's almost like juggling.

Then we throw them at the wall. Let them bounce once on the footpath and catch them as they come back. When we're catching the last ball, we have already dashed the first ball to the ground let it hit the wall and caught it in the air on its way back to us. You have to keep the balls going in order, repeating the three different things. You start with three ups, bounces, and dashes, then six of each, then nine and twelve. It's very fast and exciting, and if you fail to keep it up and drop a ball, it's another girl's turn. Excitement builds as the balls fly. Up, bounce, dash, up, bounce, dash, faster and faster until someone drops a ball. The most any of us has been able to do at once is twelve of each.

A crowd usually gathers when the best players are up, and everyone cheers them on.

Some of the boys have hurley sticks and hit hard balls back and forth. You have to stay out of their way or you could end up with a split shin. You'll often see one of them limping home after being hit by the ball or a hurley stick, trying to be strong by not shedding a single tear.

Other times you have to move aside when you're walking to avoid stepping on boys who are down on their knees playing marbles. They are so possessive about their stuff and have their mothers make wee bags with string on top to cinch the bag shut. You can hear the marbles clicking together when they walk down the street. The game is taken very seriously.

On Hallowe'en we dress in our parents' old clothes and go door to door singing:

Christmas is coming and the geese are getting fat,
Could you please put a penny in an auld man's hat.
If you haven't got a penny a ha'penny will do,
If you haven't got a ha'penny,
God Bless you and Yir auld man too.

Many times we're lucky and the door will be opened, and a penny or halfpenny dropped in our hats. It's also the time of year when the boys get to take it out on the girls by throwing fire crackers their way and scaring them half to death. Bangers are the only fireworks we seem to have around here, and they are deafening .

It was right after Hallowe'en that Irene told me how she came home for lunch one day, and found the gas on but not lit. She was terrified, especially after our previous explosion and ran out in the street crying. A man who lives up at the end of our row saw her and stopped to help.

"What's the matter, child?" he asked.

"Our stove is on but it's not lit and the house is full of gas," she answered, sobbing. The man was very nice and came into the house and turned off the knob on the gas stove.

"You'd better open all the windows to clear the air," he said.

Irene smiled and said shyly, "Thanks mister, I don't know what would have happened if you hadn't come by." Irene was so grateful to the man that she always talks about him like he's a hero.

The most exciting time of the year is Bonfire Night; For the Protestants it's on the eve of their 12th of July celebrations, and for us it's on August 15th the Feast of the Assumption. Young men in the area go around collecting items to burn in the fire. Since our house is at the intersection of another street, like an upside down letter T, the fire is usually right in line with the front of our house. We always have a great view of the growing pile of rubbish and for about a month we watch from our front windows as it gets higher and higher.

We Catholics put an effigy of King Billy (William of Orange) sitting on a chair on top of our bonfire and the Protestants have an effigy of the Pope or Catholic King James on top of theirs.

As the weeks pass, the pile grows with old bits of lumber, sofas, chairs with legs missing, tree branches, old window frames, cupboard doors, picture frames and countless other items that help to make the bonfire a roaring success. It's a neighbourhood project that is enjoyed by all, except maybe the few people whose windows crack from the intense heat.

When the big night arrives and the pile is almost as high as a house, everyone gathers and sings songs as the flames leap in the air. Then they hold hands in a circle around the fire, dancing and yelling with excitement as it grows. The heat soon makes it impossible to stand too close, and parents have to keep an eye on their wee'uns.

This can go on for hours until the flames finally die down to red embers. Then the women fetch unpeeled potatoes, and set them among the hot embers. It isn't too much later that the potatoes are being devoured by the people who helped to make the fire the best ever. It's too bad that we only get to have this type of potato once a year. The women only seem to know how to cook mashed or boiled potatoes, so the kind baked on the coals are a nice change.

The next morning and all week following the celebration, the ashes are shoveled into wheelbarrows to be used in the winter gardens. The bonfire will be forgotten until next year when the collection of wood will start all over again.

Irene and I are still trying to stay in Daddy's good graces since the incident with the belt and are sticking close to home. We're playing skip rope with Sandra in the middle of the road in front of our house. Old Mr. McGonigle hobbles up the street and stops to watch.

"Ach, I remember a time when I had that kind of energy, girls. Keep moving while you can." He rubs his stubble of a beard. "Before you know it Father Time will take a hold of your life and drain the energy out of it. It creeps up on you, and before you even notice the time passing, you're old and weak in the knees like myself."

We've stopped skipping and are standing with rapt attention, listening to his every word. We're not sure how to answer him, he's sounding so sad, so we just smile and wave as he shuffles on up the street. It's hard to imagine him as a young lad. He has a slight hump on his back, wrinkles all over his face and needs a cane to get about.

Our skipping is suddenly interrupted again. This time by the sound of loud music and someone speaking through a megaphone. We step quickly off the road and on to the footpath as we see a lorry coming around the corner toward us. It's seldom we ever see a motor vehicle up our way, except for an occasional taxi.

In the back of the lorry, some men are holding placards, and around the sides are signs requesting votes on election day. "Vote for Michael Brennan if you want more rights for Catholics," one young man is shouting. "We need jobs, better housing, and an end to this unfair gerrymandering. Let's stand up for our rights. Why settle for second best? We're just as good as the rest of them."

We lean on the hedge and watch. Some of the neighbours come out to see what all the commotion is about. They wave and follow the lorry up the street until they're out of sight.

Daddy is standing shaking his head sadly, and I'm wondering what he's thinking.

"What's gerrymandering, Daddy?" I ask.

"It's a very unjust system, Patricia, that hangs over this city like a plague."

"What does it mean, Daddy?"

"Let me see if I can explain it properly," he says as he leans on the hedge beside me. "When you have a large Catholic area, they split portions of it up and join them with larger Protestant areas. So that no matter if every Catholic got out and voted for the candidate of their choice that candidate wouldn't have a chance in hell of ever getting elected. You see, the Protestant votes will always outnumber us."

"So what's the use of voting at all then, Daddy?"

"My point, exactly. We have no chance, so therefore we have no rights!" He plucks some leaves off the hedge and throws them in the air. "The only way to get fairness in this province is to fight with methods that will affect the pocketbooks of those who hold the power. Our voices have been drowned out, but the IRA will be heard and justice will be served some day. They'll all get their fair measure, be it in this life or the next."

I feel very bad, and hope that when I grow up the powerful people in England will realise some of the injustice that has been dished out to the Catholics in Northern Ireland because we are in the minority. The Orangemen angrily call us Papists during their parades, as if we *adore* the Pope or something. They even seem to hate us. They should be happy that we believe in the same God as they do, and don't go around saying God doesn't exist like people do in Russia.

Later when the election is over, it's no surprise to anyone that our man didn't get in. The people discuss it on street corners, in the shops and outside the church on Sundays, and it's depressing to listen to them. There are secret meetings where young men in our neighbourhood are being recruited into the IRA, and Daddy seems to think it will only be a matter of time before the Irish people start to protest again and fight back like they did in the South before 1921.

Chapter Nine

Aunt Mari has gone to live in America. She came back from England to say goodbye to everyone and we went down to see her off on the boat to Liverpool. From there she took a big ocean liner to New York and flew to San Francisco. It all sounds so exciting. Maybe someday when I'm older I can sail away on a ship or fly in an aeroplane.

Mari now lives on Channing Way, in the city of Berkeley, close to San Francisco. She has a job as a nurse, and we are dreaming about how wonderful her life must be now that she lives in California, where it's always warm and sunny. Mammy says she can probably go to look at the Golden Gate Bridge any time she wants.

She sends a picture of herself walking along in downtown San Francisco. She has a book under her arm, and we can just make out the name on the cover, *The Quiet Man.* Mammy says she must be homesick already and reading books about Ireland.

After she's been there a few months, she sends all three girls notepads with envelopes. Our names are embossed in blue in the top right hand side, and on the left side, each girl has a different flower. Mine is a yellow rose and I love it. I keep taking the writing paper out of the box to have another look, and Mammy suggests that we write to Mari on the new stationery.

I write the following:

30 June 1950

Dear Aunt Mari,
    Thank you very much for the note papers,
    they were lovely.
    I have started the library.
    Mammy got the bangle that you sent to
    Granny's house.
    Pauline is going to Donegal on Tuesday.
    We have plenty of fun up our way.
    We have plenty of roses on our rose bushes.
    I am eight years of age now.
    My name is embossed on the front.

Love from Patricia xxxx

When Mammy checks the letter for me she says, "Sure Mari knows your name is on the front, isn't *she* the one who had them made especially for you?"

"Does that mean I have to write the letter all over again?" I moan. "It took donkey's ages to write it, so it did."

"Don't worry, Patricia. She just might see some humour in it."

Aunt Mari has asked her sister, Eileen, to start saving and come to America. She is willing to sponsor her and all. Eileen, who always complains about the constant rain and bitter cold, is thinking it might be great to live in California. She could easily find a job in a doctor's office as a receptionist and typist.

Uncle Freddy has moved out of Granny's and is married to a girl from Cavan. They have two wee boys now, and are moving to Birmingham, England. We'll miss him, so we will. As an uncle, he was a ton of fun.

Uncle Frank had a girlfriend not long ago, and he was going to marry her. The only problem was that she made fun of the way Granny answers her part of the rosary saying; "Hoooly Mary Mother of God pray for us sinners," and Frank got upset and took back the ring.

Mammy says there was probably more to it than that.

Some Saturdays when we're over at Granny's house, Denis and Anne Marie play together, as they're the same age, while Pauline, Irene and I get to wander all over the strange neighbourhood. Once we have gotten down on our hunkers and made our way slowly past our granny Owens's house, we stand up again and sometimes walk for miles. We usually have to step around women who are down on their hands and knees scrubbing their front stoops. It gets to be a real competition with the women as to who can have the cleanest place. Sometimes it gets out of hand and they end up scrubbing the footpath as well, almost all the way out to the kerb.

We can always tell what neighbourhood we're in by glancing into the little porches between the outside door and the inside door of each house. The Catholics have a picture of the Sacred Heart or the Pope, and the Protestants have a picture of the King of England. Sometimes we'll be walking through the neighbourhood for quite a long time before we realise that we're in a Protestant area. Maybe we've been too busy talking, or skipping to avoid cracks in the pavement. But when we start to notice the King's pictures, we walk swiftly while trying to act natural, so that we won't seem out of place.

This afternoon we've ended up in the middle of the Shankill district.

"Jesus, Mary and holy Saint Joseph," Pauline says with a startled look. "This place is world famous for its hatred of Catholics!" Irene and I look at her in alarm and she grabs our arms to stop us. "I know how we can get out of this situation safe and sound," she says in a loud whisper. "Let's sing 'God Save the King,' like we're forced to at the end of the films. That way everyone will think we're Protestant." She has a satisfied look on her face now, like she solved a major problem. We start to sing, and our Pauline has the most beautiful voice you ever heard.

There's a couple of old women wearing the shawls that people wore back in the olden days. They're standing talking, and you can tell by the way their eyes are squinting that they're probably gossiping about one of their neighbours. The wee skinny one is standing on her front porch and the other one is on the footpath with a shopping bag in her hand. She sets her bag on the ground when she sees us, and looks like she's going to say something.

"Here, lassie, hold on a second. We're looking for a child with a voice just like yours.

Would you like to come over to the Orange Lodge next week and sing the very song you're singing, love?" Pauline's big brown eyes are nearly popping out of her head now and she stutters, "Em... em... I'll have to ask my mammy first, Missus, if that's all right with you."

"Well love, y'ill know where to find me. Right there, in the one with the beautiful window box." She points to one of the houses that all look the same, but she does have some nice chrysanthemums under her front window.

"I'll let you know, Missus," Pauline says with a shaky voice, and the three of us skip away, trying to act as much like Protestants as we can. When we finally reach the end of the street and turn the corner, Pauline and Irene double over laughing and I don't feel nervous any more. "Did you ever notice that there are a lot more pubs in the Catholic areas?" I ask.

"Yes, Patricia, and a lot more children too," Pauline says, and she and Irene laugh again.

Being in a district where we are hated reminds us of what Daddy told us about the dreaded Black and Tans. We walk swiftly back to the safety of our own area while Pauline explains more about it.

"They were convicts released from English prisons and sent to Ireland to keep the Catholics, or Papists, under control and dampen their spirits," she says seriously.

"The headmaster of Daddy's school escaped death by not being home when the Black and Tans broke into his parents' house," she goes on. "His father and brothers were murdered, but not before being brutally tortured. The same thing happened all over the South before it became a free state. The Black and Tans were feared because they were so savage and vicious."

"Why were they called Black and Tans, Pauline," Irene asks as we try and keep up with Pauline's quick pace.

"I think it must have been from the striped prison uniforms they wore, in those colours," Pauline replies. "Daddy said the campaign to terrify the Irish only angered them and made them want to stand up and fight back. The IRA led this fight, and when the South finally gained its freedom in 1921, it was the first country to break away from this nation that did nothing but hurt us and look down on us," she explains.

Pauline tells us how she's been studying the subject in school this year.

"Before the uprising, the Black and Tans killed farm animals, destroyed farm tools and burned down villages," she goes on. "The people were forbidden to speak their language or practice their religion. That's why there are Mass rocks all over the countryside in Ireland."

"Oh, yes," Irene says, "I saw a few the last time we were in Donegal."

"People would meet behind bushes and hedgerows and celebrate Mass in secret, using the large flat rocks as altars," Pauline continues. "The children were taught their school lessons in the same secret manner. Daddy said the English couldn't keep the people ignorant like they wanted to, because nothing could dampen their spirits. The more that was taken away from them, the more they fought back."

"Is that why they call us the Fighting Irish?" I ask. Pauline and Irene laugh and thump their chests with their fists.

As we keep up the pace toward Granny's street, we discuss what Daddy told us and breathe a sigh of relief when we see Clonard Monastery at the top of Oranmore Street.

"I'm going in to offer up a prayer of thanks," Irene says. We follow her into the church that is every bit as beautiful as a European cathedral. The ceiling looks like it's a mile high, and there are round columns and arches all the way from the back of the church to the three beautiful altars in front. We see a plaque telling how the monastery was built in 1896 and the church was built from 1908 to 1911.

"Daddy was born in 1911," Pauline whispers, "His daddy worked as an electrician on the Titanic. I wonder if he worked on this church as well. It's only about a hundred yards from their house."

"Why don't we ask Daddy about it later," Irene whispers, as she kneels down and buries her face in her hands to pray.

When we get back home in the evening and tell Daddy all about our day. Irene and I begin to ask him about the way the Irish were treated at the hands of the British.

"Pauline, go into the parlour and get me the book, *The Story of the Irish Race,* by Seumas MacManus," he says. "I'd like you to get it straight right from the start." When she brings the book he opens it, and asks her to read a footnote.

After reading, our Pauline leans back in her chair and thinks for a moment.

"They were a bunch of holy terrors, weren't they?" She says. "It says here that the ex-prime minister said that he discovered things being done to the Irish that were a bigger disgrace than the worst happenings in Europe. The labor party sent investigators, and were horrified at what they found. They said Britain's name should be stinking in the the rest of the world's nostrils. Can you imagine, they actually admitted to their wrongdoing?"

She plops the book on the table and starts pacing the floor. "Now I can understand why the IRA came to be, Daddy," Pauline goes on. "They were just like the American Revolutionary movement we read about in school last year."

"Maybe someday before we die, our six counties in the North will be able to break away from the ties of England, and be free like the rest of Ireland," she says.

Daddy shakes his head. "Michael Collins was wrong when he gave in to the British, you know. We had the upper hand and could have had a free Ireland in 1921 but he made a deal with them and let them have the six richest counties, the ones with all the industry. The Irish were left with the poorer agricultural areas."

"Yes," Pauline says, "but I can understand their desire to get what they could after the long fight."

Daddy puts the book away and asks if anyone wants to take a walk.

"We already walked our feet off today," Pauline says. Irene and I laugh and agree with her. None of us are willing to go for a walk even to the street corner.

When I sleep that evening my dreams are full of people being tortured by the Black and Tans and I wake up shouting. Pauline calms me down and I thank God it was only a nightmare.

***

It's been almost a fortnight since Christmas and it's freezing cold. Mammy is holding on to the fences coming up the hill from the shops. The footpath is icy in spots and she's not taking any chances. I'm behind her holding on to Denis's hand and carrying the potatoes. Mammy is only a wee bit of a thing but her stomach is swollen and she looks tired, so she does.

In front of Campbell's house she stops and talks to Mrs. Campbell, and I can hear her saying, "Any day now."

Denis, who is almost four, is dragging behind. He's peeking through the McMullans' hedge watching their cat jump in the air in sudden bursts. Denis protests when I start to pull him on, and I end up dragging him the rest of the way up the street.

Daddy is on the night shift this week, and I'll be bringing his tea down to the bus stop. He said if it's raining not to worry, but I know the tea will perk him up, rain or no rain.

The next morning is cold and damp, and when I wake up I realise that it's the feast of the Epiphany when the three kings found the manger in Bethlehem. That means there's no school and suddenly it's a wonderful day.

I climb out of bed trying not to wake Pauline and Irene. Pauline is almost fourteen now, Irene will be twelve in June, and I'm going on nine.

When I get to the kitchen, I find a note from Daddy saying that himself and Mammy are down at Granny's house. It says that we are to take care of Denis until Daddy returns. I make myself some tea and toast and glance through the *Irish News*.

Before long Denis is hopping down the stairs. He must have smelled the toast, but he wants corn flakes as well, so I go out to the front step for a fresh bottle of milk. It's almost frozen from being there for hours. Denis is eating and colouring with his Christmas crayons at the same time, and I have to warn him that the corn flakes are getting soggy. He eats half of them and I have to finish off the rest of the mushy mess. He drinks some tea to warm him up, and goes over to the sofa by the fire to finish his colouring.

By the time Daddy comes back, Pauline and Irene are up. Daddy smiles and winks at us.

"You've got another baby brother, so you do, and he's at your granny's. You can see him tomorrow. Today your mammy needs her rest." I feel like I've heard those exact words before.

We're wondering if the new baby will be rosy and plump like Denis was, and will he have the same gold coloured hair.

"Looks like we'll be having some more sleepless nights," Pauline says. "But it'll be worth it to have a new baby in the house again."

"It's well we didn't give away the pram," Irene says with a smile.

"I've been up all night with your mammy, girls, so please keep it quiet down here," Daddy says. "I need a few hours sleep before my shift this afternoon." He looks like he's ready to drop right there, and we promise to be as quiet as possible.

The next afternoon, we march up Granny's stairs and tiptoe into her bedroom to see our new wee brother.

Denis runs in and I pick him up and let him sit on the side of the bed. Mammy gives him a big hug and tells him he'll have someone to play with now. He peeks into the little basket next to the bed and I lean over him to get a glimpse of our new baby with the pale skin and platinum blonde hair. His fingers are tiny and he's just like a wee doll, so he is.

Marjorie smiles and says "Go ahead and touch him if you like," and when Denis holds the baby's hand the little fingers cling to his bigger one and he beams with pride.

"This makes me a big brother, doesn't it?" He puffs out his chest, then asks, "How long will it be before he can walk?"

"Oh, soon enough Denis, let's enjoy him this way first," Mammy says, and she looks happier than I've seen her for a long time.

"What's his name?" Denis asks and Mammy smiles.

"He'll be Michael Francis, now isn't that a nice name?" Denis nods, and strokes wee Michael's head.

When we go downstairs, Uncle Frank has come home. He works out near Nutts Corner at Aldergrove as a aircraft mechanic, and has finally bought a car to take him to work and back.

"Who wants a ride, before I change my mind?" The four of us are more than happy to get in the car. He has to crank a metal thing in front to make it start. It's pouring down rain when he drives us home. To go right he turns a knob and a plastic flag comes out of the right door frame and sticks straight out. The same thing happens at the left side when he wants to go that way. I wonder how the people behind could possibly see the flag in all this rain. The window washers slosh back and forth with a rhythm that could almost put you to sleep. Slop slop, slop slop, it's fascinating to watch, and it's great to be dropped right at your own front door.

Later in the week when Mammy brings Michael home she goes up to her bedroom and sets the little basket next to the bed. She's holding the baby and calls Pauline into the bedroom and asks her to shut the door.

Irene pulls me into the boxroom which gets the name from its small size. It's so small you can only squeeze in a single bed and maybe a small chest of drawers. Irene presses her ear to the wall and signals for me to do the same. When I listen I can't believe what I'm hearing. Mammy is telling Pauline about where babies come from. I've heard girls at school whispering a lot of crazy stuff that I thought was made up, and here Mammy is telling our Pauline that it's true. Irene and I are wondering how the baby could possibly get out, and when Pauline reappears we ask her.

"Mammy didn't mention that part," she says, "but I'm sure the belly button must open up or something like that." We're all lying across the bed in the boxroom, trying to figure out how our wee Michael came into this world, and ourselves too, for that matter, and we decide it has to be through the belly button.

Michael is very sweet and we don't mind helping to change his dirty nappies or pushing him in the pram. The neighbours always stop us when we have him to admire his looks and great disposition. He's as good as gold, just like our Denis, and we're grateful for that.

Edwin next door says that he wishes they could get a new baby in their house as they only have two children. We're now up to five, a small family for this neighbourhood, but large for a Protestant family like the MacCarricks.

***

Pauline, Irene and I are jealous of our McDonough cousins who live in Dublin. They have such lovely Irish brogues and the Tri-Colour flies over their city in all it's glory. Granny's brother, who is their father, very rarely comes up to Belfast. And who could blame him?

When Mammy and Marjorie took us to Bray, just south of Dublin for a holiday last year, the one thing that everyone wanted to do on Sunday was to go to the cinema. In Belfast it's forbidden. We can't even go to the playground on Sundays where they have the swings and merry-go-rounds because everything is locked up. Sunday is supposed to be a day of rest and relaxation. What better way for children to enjoy the day than to swing or go to the cinema like everyone in the South can do. The Protestant government in the North seem to look at things differently.

The department stores downtown are also closed, and Belfast is like a ghost town every Sunday. Oh, how we wish we'd been born in the Republic of Ireland like our cousins, and have the freedom to do what we want on Sunday. I suppose they don't even realise how good they've got it down there.

I've asked Daddy why his father, who was born in Dublin, moved to the North, and he said, "To find work in the shipyards." His daddy told him that out of ten thousand workers at Harland Wolff only about five hundred were Catholic, and they had to watch their backs because "accidents" were always happening to them.

Aunt Mari has written, and said that Americans don't care what church you go to, or even if you go at all. If you work hard and save, you can have whatever you want. And anyone can be a policeman if he can pass the test. It really sounds like Paradise, so it does.

Michael is a few months old now, and I've just had my ninth birthday. The weather is still cold and we even saw an inch of snow yesterday. It didn't last though and soon turned to slush. They say March comes in like a lion and that it did this year. Let's hope it goes out like a lamb the way it's supposed to.

I've been coughing for days now and no matter how hard I try, I can't breathe when I lie down. I try to avoid telling Mammy about my problem breathing but eventually it has to be done. She runs downstairs saying, "Be right back, Patricia, just sit up 'til I get there."

She returns with a big fluffy pillow from the parlor sofa under her arm, and the inevitable glass of warm milk mixed with a shot of brandy. Her cure is very difficult to swallow.

"This should help you get a good night's sleep, and tomorrow we'll visit the doctor," she says as she puts the pillow behind me and adds my own so that I can sleep sitting up.

All night I sleep fitfully in the sitting position, between coughs and wheezes. The doctor says I have chronic bronchitis. "It's very common in the cold and damp," he says. I suppose he knows all about the ice we can scrape off the inside of our bedroom windows. The one fireplace downstairs is not enough to warm up the whole house in winter. I'm given some cough syrup and told to drink lots of liquids and spend the rest of the day in bed.

It's the middle of the night and I wake up to see the blankets from the bed hanging from the light fixture in the middle of the ceiling. I'm standing on the bed trying to pull them off and Pauline and Irene are shouting for our parents. When I see Daddy coming through the door, I notice that the walls of the room are starting to move in and out like an accordion. I scream at Daddy to watch or he'll be squished.

"There aren't any blankets on the light, Patricia, see they're here on the bed, you're just delirious."

"But I can see them Daddy, look there, can't you get them off?"

Mammy runs the bath and tells me to get in. It's warm and she is gradually adding cooler water until I'm feeling much better. I'm hoping this doesn't call for more warm milk and brandy, but tonight I'm lucky and get a drink of water instead.

It's morning already, and I'm looking around the room while holding the blankets up to my chin to keep in the warmth. The window has a thin layer of ice and I imagine I can see a tiny donkey and cart moving through it. The little man on the cart is hitting the donkey and it moves faster until it reaches the other side of the window.

Pauline and Irene must have gone to school and I can hear Denis and Michael downstairs. I have the day off because of the bronchitis, but I'd rather be in school instead of feeling like this. The ice has melted on the window now

103

and there's a pool of water on the windowsill. Mammy comes up with a cup of tea and some toast.

"I heard you talking to yourself, Patricia, so I brought a cup of tea to warm you up."

"I wasn't talking to myself, Mammy, I was yelling at the man who was beating his donkey."

"Oh, that was just in your imagination."

"But he was right there moving through the ice on the window, I swear I saw him."

"Don't worry about it, the sickness is making you imagine things. You were half asleep too, so it isn't any wonder that you were seeing men on donkeys."

I realise that it seems far-fetched, and I was probably imagining the whole thing. I really can't complain about a little bout with bronchitis though, for only last week we had an ambulance on our street for the first time in my memory.

The O'Kane's wee girl, Helen, came down with scarlet fever. A lot of the neighbours were standing around talking about how many children around the Beechmount area had contracted the disease. When Helen was carried out she was a bright red colour. Mrs. O'Connell who lives a few doors down from the O'Kane family said she was worried that her wee'uns might catch it too. "It can cause rheumatic fever, you know, and that means permanent heart damage." The other women crossed themselves in unison hoping to protect their children from such a fate.

There has also been a rash of polio incidents in the city in the past few years. A very beautiful young girl called Christine Donovan up on the next street was in an iron lung for a long time. Although she survived, she is in a wheelchair and only eighteen. It's very sad. She should be thinking of getting married and having a family, but now she can't. Polio is a dreadful disease that everyone fears. Being so closed off, lying in an iron lung must be frightening. We've seen pictures of these machines in newsreels at the cinema, and also in the Irish News, and many rosaries have been said in hopes of protection from this horror.

Christine and her family even made a pilgrimage to Lourdes, in France last year in hopes of a miracle cure, but were unsuccessful. Mammy agrees with me that we should count our blessings, and not complain about an occasional bout of bronchitis.

The following week I'm on the mend and meet the postman at the front door. He's holding a big parcel that has come all the way from America. Aunt Mari hasn't forgotten us, and we are shaking with excitement as Mammy opens the box.

Inside are bars of chocolate called Hershey's, different from anything we have here. Also packages of confectioners sugar that Mammy says should be great on her sponge cakes. There's a jar of stuff called popcorn that we've never seen before, and last, but not least, are the most wonderful paper dolls made out of thick cardboard with stands so that they can be dressed standing up. The clothes look so "American." Some of the skirts are all pouffy with petticoats underneath and one has a poodle dog on it. There's a lovely dress that's a new colour to our eyes. It's sort of a mixture of blue and green. We'll have to ask Mari if there's a name for it.

Later while Irene and I are playing with the paper dolls, Mammy is following the directions for the popcorn. Everything looks good until a popping sound erupts and there's white puffy things shooting all over the kitchen. We're doing our best to catch them but they're so fast that a lot of them have gone down behind the stove.

"It must be magic," I say, and Mammy is beginning to think it's funny now.

"I think I've done something wrong," she says and laughs.

They're hitting the ceiling, and it's raining the funny looking stuff. Denis is jumping up and down screaming with delight and Irene and I grab two bowls so that we can catch some. By the time the popping stops we have caught quite a lot in the bowls.

"Mari's going to get a laugh out of our ignorance when we write to thank her for the parcel," Mammy says. We sit down to enjoy our very first bowl of American popcorn and are pleasantly surprised at the flavor.

"I don't think I can eat any more," Mammy says. "They're getting stuck in my false teeth. Thank God I didn't pour the whole jar in. Next time I'll cover it up."

It's amazing how much stuff could come from that thin layer of hard yellow seeds. We're so fascinated with it, that the very next day Pauline writes a letter of thanks for all the great things Mari sent us. She has a list of questions concerning the popcorn. Where do those little hard things come from? How do they grow so big? And how do you keep them from snowing in your kitchen? etc. I think she asked the last question just for the fun of it. We probably won't get a reply for a month or so because it takes almost two weeks to get letters from that far away.

Chapter Ten

Aunt Eileen is going to America. Her best friend, Rosaleen McNee, will be traveling with her. Aunt Mari, who has moved down to the Los Angeles area from San Francisco, will sponsor them. She even has a job lined up for Eileen. A dermatologist friend of Mari, whose receptionist is retiring in a month, said that Eileen should be perfect for the position.

Taking the trip down to the dockside, we wave goodbye as the ship pulls away from the quay. Wailing sounds are bouncing back and forth between the ship and the dock and I realise that most of the people leaving may never see their families again.

Eileen is dabbing her eyes with her hanky as she waves to us. I imagine this is much harder for her than any of us staying behind. She is leaving the country where she grew up, as well as her friends and family. The ship is headed for Liverpool, where most of them will board a huge ocean liner bound for America. I hear some people saying that many are going to South Africa as well. Granny's sister-in-law, Great Aunt Birdie, left for South Africa shortly before I was born, so I don't think there's any chance I'll ever get to see her. Mammy said her daddy's family were very tolerant of the fact that he became a Catholic to marry Granny, leaving them with Catholic nieces and nephews. It's a pity it can't be that way all over the North. Things would be so much easier for everyone. She also says that the neighbours always commented about her daddy being a much better Catholic than those who were born into the faith. He even attended daily Mass.

Granny is weeping as the ship gets farther away, and Eileen is only a wee speck now standing there on the deck. All you can see is her bright blue head-scarf next to Rosaleen's yellow one. Eileen has told Granny that someday she hopes to see her in America too, and she will certainly have a place to live if she does come. The ship is just a dot in the ocean now as it moves up Belfast Lough toward the Irish Sea. They will sleep on the ship and when they wake in the morning they will be in Liverpool, England. It sounds like such an adventure, so it does.

Granny is taking it very hard though. It's her third child to go overseas, but at least she still has Uncle Frank and Aunt Marjorie in the house with her.

Marjorie got herself a dog. He's a beautiful black and white border collie, with a smiling face and a tongue that always seems to be hanging out. She calls him Laddie and just loves him.

When Marjorie takes him for walks she sings as she goes, and people always stop to say "hello" to Laddie and rub his head. Marjorie says that dogs are truly man's best friend, and cats are only in it for what they can get from you. Our cat never comes inside, but takes care of herself very well, with her endless array of rats on display. I'm not so sure Marjorie is all-knowing on the subject, since she hasn't any experience to speak of. But she's right about dogs, they are fun and give you a lot of love.

***

Our wee Michael is walking around the furniture now and saying Da-da. His hair is almost white and blinds you when the sun hits it. His eyes are a beautiful shade of blue, and his favourite thing to do is crawl all over Denis. He keeps us laughing with his antics.

Mammy and Daddy have been looking at new houses just being built at the top of Gransha Park off the Glen Road.

They say we need more room and it's true. The living room in our house has only enough space for a small sofa and the table where we eat. Now that there are seven of us, it's a bit of a squeeze, and the other rooms are always too cold to play in except in the middle of our short summer.

We're thrilled about the prospects of a larger house with a bigger garden. Mammy says the reason they were able to save to buy a new house is because Daddy neither smokes nor drinks. He hands over his whole pay packet every week and doesn't spend a penny on himself. "You should be grateful that your daddy is like this," she says. "It's not every man who takes care of his family so well."

I think Mammy has made a great contribution as well, by sewing every piece of clothing that we've ever worn except our knickers. She's worked hard as a seamstress for others as well in order to bring in a little extra.

We'll miss our friends, although they won't be that far away. It's just a little over a mile from Andersonstown Crescent to Gransha Park. The new house is in the last row of houses below the Divis mountain, and all around are open fields with cows grazing right behind the thin wire fences of the back gardens.

When I lie in bed at night and think of moving, my mind wanders to Jim Armstrong. Although I'm only ten I know for sure I'm in love. Now I promise myself, when I have children in the future, I will know for sure that it's possible for them to be in love at the youthful age of ten. I've been having dreams for the past few weeks and they're always the same. Jim comes over to me when we're playing street games and kisses me right on the mouth. It feels wonderful and I'm upset when I wake up. I just want to get back to the dream, so I do!

Why do we have to move right now? Jim doesn't even know I'm in love with him. He probably likes someone who is twelve years of age like himself. I love his quiet ways and his lovely red hair. I will really miss looking at him. That much I know for sure.

When moving day finally comes, Sandra's upset that Irene is leaving, and her brother, Edwin has promised to come and visit me in our new house. He has been such a good friend for the whole of my life and I'll miss him. They look almost as sad as we feel to be saying goodbye.

Pauline, Irene and I are wandering through the rooms of 21 Andersonstown Crescent as they are emptied by the moving men.

We stand in our bedroom and touch the walls that Daddy and Mammy put so much work into with paint brushes and wee sponges, making the walls look like expensive wallpaper. They painted a coat of dark pink and followed it when dry with little dabs of a lighter pink over the darker colour. The process is called distemper. It took a long time but saved them loads of money, and has lasted much longer than wallpaper.

Their bedroom is done in two different shades of blue and has a very cool, calm feeling. It will be difficult to imagine someone else enjoying the results of our parents' toil, and imagination.

We stand looking out our bedroom window into the back garden for the last time. The wild roses growing over the hedge, the tree at the end of the garden that Daddy almost burned down in his determination to destroy those horrible rats, the bush with the little yellow flowers the colour of sharp cheddar cheese. We enjoyed eating the flowers and called it our bread and cheese bush when we played house.

We crane our necks to look one last time at the gooseberry bush in the MacCarricks' back garden that we watched with anticipation in summer as the berries grew plumper, gradually changing from green to pink. They were finally devoured by the neighbourhood children who had the good fortune to lie on blankets in Sandra and Edwin's garden on the few hot, humid days of summer. We'd watch the dark storm clouds play hide the button with the sun on days when the temperature could rise to a sweltering 75 or 80 degrees Fahrenheit.

It was so hot then that all we could do was to lie around in the heat talking, dreaming, and wondering how the people in the Eastern or Southern United States and those people in countries close to the Equator could possibly survive.

Next we wander into the boxroom, the wee room where Denis and Michael slept. Through the window the Divis mountain can be seen in all its quiet splendor. We try to see if our house on Gransha Park is visible, but there are too many homes in the way.

For the last time, we stand on the landing at the top of the stairs where we did involuntary jigs at one time or another while waiting for the lavatory door to open so that we could rush in and relieve ourselves. The same landing where various relatives slept fitfully during the blitz, when they fled the city to escape the German bombs, according to Pauline who can remember that terrible time.

Then we walk into Mammy and Daddy's room where we all, at one time or another, crept in the dead of night after a bad dream, and squeezed in between their warm bodies for comfort and slumber.

We walk slowly downstairs and stand in the parlour where Mammy banged on the piano playing by ear the latest tunes heard on the wireless. Her favorite, *The Third Man* with all it's sharps and flats, a difficult piece to play, but no problem for her. This room is also where she fitted countless neighbours and strangers for new dresses, coats, and school blazers.

By the time we are looking around the kitchen we are having to blow our noses to stem the emotion. Here we have memories like the time the gas stove explosion blew out the window but somehow didn't hurt any of us.

Lastly, we stand in the small living room where we sat on straight-back chairs in the evening by the fire reading books, studying for tests, or just watching the flames from the coal fire change from blue to gold to red, as they leapt and danced. Sometimes they were encouraged by a sprinkling of sugar when they began to die. We touch the little shelf in the corner above the empty spot where the sofa sat. The shelf where the wireless sat and entertained us for many years even as far back as when we, each in our own time, believed there were tiny people inside doing the talking.

We glance at the windowsill where Ginger, our cat displayed her dead rat trophies for our approval, and we're already weeping when Mammy says it's time to leave. Just before hopping into the van, Irene runs into the garden and fills a matchbox with grass, so that she'll be taking part of the old place with her.

It's a different feeling to be getting ready for bed in our new house. Gazing out the window I watch as our new, glorious view of the mountains is gradually obscured by the fading twilight.

After checking under the beds for suitcases, we lie and talk about the possibilities of finding new friends in the neighbourhood. Irene is happy because Mairead Cafferty, who used to live on our old street, moved to the lower part of Gransha Park several years ago. She has a sister Agnes, who is around my age, so I'll have someone as well. Pauline knows some girls from school who live very close to this street, and Mammy has assured us that we shouldn't have any trouble finding new friends.

We can hear Denis whimpering in the other room. "I want to go home, Mammy!"

"But you are home, Denis. This is our new home."

"I like our other house better, Mammy."

"Don't worry, you'll get used to this one too. Michael's asleep already and we don't want to wake him now, do we?"

As we lie whispering in the dark we can hear Mammy downstairs. She's putting things away in the kitchen cupboards. They have glass doors that let you see where everything is and she's really tickled with them. She also loves the gleaming new stove with the rack on top to warm up the plates while you cook dinner. The linoleum floor is dazzling and should be so easy to keep clean, and now she can look out the window when she's washing dishes. There's another window in the kitchen next to the stove, and a covered porch by the front door that's big enough to keep your bicycles out of the weather. Everything in the house is situated exactly the same way as the old house except on a larger scale.

The first thing I do when I wake up in the morning is look out the window at the mountain. I wonder if the people who bought our old house are doing the same. The difference is that on the old street you could only get a glimpse of the top half, and here we can see the whole mountain without a thing in the way. The new house faces the opposite direction, so our bedroom in back faces the mountain, and in the old house Mammy and Daddy had the view.

The bottom half of Gransha Park has big, detached houses that were built years ago. I wonder if their owners are upset that a whole new row of houses has sprung up at the top of their street, semi-detached and all exactly the same.

After we're settled in I walk back to our old street and ask Edwin if he can come up and play at our house.

He's wearing his Protestant school blazer with its little insignia on the pocket. We're walking up the Gransha Park hill when suddenly a group of the well-to-do boys at the lower end of the street start shouting rude things at him.

It upsets me. "Mind your own business and leave him alone," I shout. "He's not doing *you* any harm, and he's *my* lifelong friend.

Edwin is embarrassed as we hurry past the bullies to our house, and I'm ashamed and distressed that Edwin has been humiliated by Catholic boys for no reason. They don't even know him. How can they judge him?

We play some games of snakes and ladders, and ludo, and end up out in the back field. Trying to avoid cow dung, we sneak up to catch a glimpse of a wee cottage that sits right in the middle of the field, surrounded by trees and bushes. The residents of the lower part of the street think that the old woman living there is a witch. She doesn't have electricity and gets her water from a well, and hardly anyone ever sees her.

Wandering back up the field we've decided to build a fort with some boards that are lying around. When it's time for Edwin to leave, I'm hoping he will come up often to play, and help finish the fort. He must feel bad about the taunting he received on his arrival. As I say goodbye he doesn't seem too enthusiastic about the prospect of repeating the experience.

***

Right next to McErlean's shop where we now buy our groceries, is a field that is usually full of weeds. Daddy has come in from work with a contented look on his face.

"Imagine this, girls," he says while rubbing his hands together, "I've found a dandy crop of nettles."

Irene and I groan and drop our heads, trying to avoid the inevitable, but it's no use.

"Why did Daddy have to get bursitis in his knees?" I whine as we walk down to the Glen Road carrying a bundle of newspapers.

"It's the draught that comes into the bus while he's driving," Irene says, as she pulls the gloves out of her pocket.

"I can understand him cooking them and drinking the juice," I say, "but how can he sting his knees with them? I think he must have gone bonkers, so he must."

"Well," Irene says, "he's not the only person on this island whose bonkers."

We cross the Glen Road and walk casually into the field, hoping not to be seen by the many women entering and leaving the shop.

Getting down on our hunkers we start gathering the long stinging nettles with our gloved hands. We have spread the newspapers on the ground and place the weeds carefully on the paper. It reminds me of an ancient Irish song and I start to sing with feeling:

Down by the glenside I met an old woman.
A pluckin young nettles nor e're saw me comin'
I listened a while to the song she was hummin'.
Glory oh...Glory oh...to the bold Fenian men.

We laugh and I imagine the old woman wearing her shawl and maybe gloves like ours. "Why do you think *she* needed the nettles?" Irene asks. "She couldn't have been a bus driver too." We laugh again, and when we see a double-decker bus full of people passing, we drop to our stomachs so that no one will see us.

"Hello there, girls, nice day for picking nettles." We're mortified that we have been discovered and watch Mr. Devlin wave at us before crossing the road and walking up our street.

"Hurry, Patricia, get as many as you can before someone else sees us."

We pull like mad 'til we each have a big armload of the dreadful weeds wrapped in newspaper to prevent us from being stung. The embarrassment continues as we rush up the street followed by whistles from the bully boys. It's absolutely humiliating and we sigh with relief when we reach our gate at last.

Daddy has a big pot of water boiling on the stove when we return, and he throws some of the nettles in the sink to wash them before cooking. He sets the rest aside. As he throws the washed nettles into the pot he smiles with contentment. "I don't know what I'd do without you girls," he says, as he sits on a cane chair. Rolling up his trouser legs, he starts stinging his knees with the dry nettles until there are red welts all over his skin. He then pours a glass of the dark green juice he has created from the weeds and drinks it as soon as it cools down.

"How can you bear to do that, Daddy?" I ask.

"Well, Patricia, it's a case of necessity. If I didn't do this the pain in my knees would be a lot worse."

"Hope the next crop doesn't grow too fast," Irene says raising her eyes up to heaven as we go out the back door to play.

The Cafferty girls have become good friends with Irene and me. They have given us all the ins and outs of the different families on the street, and introduced us to the children who are part of the established crowd. The lady next door to us has a new baby, and if we ask, she'll let us push him in his pram. Sometimes Agnes pushes him and I push our Michael. We can walk for miles that way and meet other friends along the way.

The neighbours here are generous as well as nice. Several of them have glasshouses in their back gardens, and we have been supplied with wonderful tomatoes, delicious enough to be eaten like apples. We usually have them at tea time with lettuce, ham, and heavy wheaten bread.

In the field behind the houses, a local cricket club has taken shape. Young men and older boys participate. They enjoy the game on long summer evenings when it's daylight until ten or eleven o'clock. Daddy says he's not interested in playing. He's too old, and since it's an English game he wouldn't be caught dead playing it anyway.

It would be great if they could play hurley instead, but there isn't enough ground cleared in the field, and with cricket they can all use the same bat.

It's a beautiful warm evening as I'm walking down the street to see if Agnes can come out. There's some kind of commotion in front of Crilly's house. People are saying that Mr. Crilly was hit on the temple with the cricket ball and seems to be unconscious.

As the ambulance screams up the hill and turns right toward our row of houses, the women cross themselves and murmur to each other. Mrs. Crilly is crying as her husband is carried out, still unconscious. She has to be helped into the ambulance to be with him. The siren starts again as the vehicle disappears around the corner and down the hill. People are speaking in hushed voices as they wander slowly back to their homes. Mrs. Braden has offered to mind the

Crilly children until their mammy returns. She's trying to comfort them saying. "Don't you worry yourselves now, it'll be all right."

It's been over a week, and Mr. Crilly finally regains consciousness. There's a feeling of relief and many prayers of thanks from the people who were concerned about him. Cricket is over for the time being and may never start up again.

Since Daddy doesn't play cricket he gets his exercise from walking, but his real love is cycling. He's got loads of experience since belonging to the cycling club where he met and fell in love with Mammy.

We've started taking long bicycle trips on summer mornings when he has the evening shift. We have gone as far away as Holywood and Lough Neagh. The road to the lough is like a giant washboard; mile after mile of smooth ripples. Once you get a start up the first hill the momentum of going down takes you up the next hill and so on. The feeling of freedom and well-being is hard to explain. The road seems to go on forever and it takes so little effort to sail up one hill and down the next. It's almost like we're in some sort of pleasant dream.

Out there the air is so still, the quietness broken only by the soft whirring of our wheels and an occasional bird call. In all the trips we've taken to Lough Neagh, I've never seen a vehicle of any sort on that particular stretch of road. Daddy's bicycle has fixed wheels, and his feet are enclosed in little wire stirrups. He can't stop pedaling like me, but must keep his feet going round even downhill. He likes it that way because he's used to it. But it would scare me not to have my feet free to put down quickly if I had to stop in a hurry.

When we cycle to Holywood we usually doze or daydream on the sand after the long ride, while listening to the waves gently lapping on the shore. Daddy always enjoys a swim after this to refresh himself.

The last time we went, Daddy taught me how to swim. He said all ten-year olds should know how. I was very nervous at first but he put his hand under my back and taught me how to float with my legs straight out, and after that I had more courage. The breast stroke is the only one I've learned. I couldn't bear the thought of putting my face underwater and having water up my nose.

It's great to be able to swim, but there's only a short time in summer when it's warm enough. I ride the bus to the indoor pool near the library. What I see is a crowd of big boys horsing around and causing an earsplitting din. I think I'd better swim in the ocean from now on, even though the opportunities will be few and far between in this climate.

Chapter Eleven

Uncle Tom and Aunt Lucy have moved to an older three storey house at the corner of the Limestone and Antrim Roads.

They used to have a nice new house on the Ballysillan Road, but after Anne Marie and Vincent grew old enough to go out and play, they were ostracised. The grownups gave Tom and Lucy the cold shoulder too, so they decided to sell and buy a house in a more Catholic area. Just down the street from them now is a Catholic church and school, so they are quite happy with their decision.

Mammy's first cousins, the O'Hare clan, live just down the road in a row of big houses called *The Glen*. Their back garden is really long and backs up to a park. I suppose the boys cut the grass and the girls help with the housework. I think there must be at least four boys and three girls still at home, and the twins, Anna and Joan, have told Mammy about their piano teacher, so now I'm soon to be taking lessons.

"Why don't you come over and see our place on Saturday after your lesson, Patricia," Lucy suggests when she finds out. "Anne Marie and Vincent would just love it." She has given me directions and all, and it sounds simple enough.

Early Saturday morning I get on the bus with my brand new music bag. It has a handle on each side of the opening and is kind of flat since it's empty. I love the smell of the new leather, and as the bus is crowded with people headed

119

downtown to do their shopping, I soon have to move it onto my lap.

An old man with most of his teeth missing has spied the empty spot next to me, and before I know it he's plopped himself down beside me and my music bag.

He must have lost his razor for his whiskers are sprouting in all directions, and the aroma drifting toward me is like a combination of sour milk and whiskey. Before long the movement of the bus has him closing his eyes and nodding off to sleep. The next thing I know, his head has stopped nodding and landed right on my shoulder. His leg is touching mine!

"Jesus, Mary, and Joseph," I pray, "please don't let me get pregnant."

I've heard that pregnant girls get kicked out of their homes as a rule, and at ten years of age, I don't know how I'd even take care of a baby. My heart is racing and I'm starting to perspire as I try to edge my way over in the seat. But there's nowhere to go and my other leg is already jammed up against the side of the bus. I'm also hoping that this man doesn't have lice, for that business is no fun either.

Thank God I have to change buses on Royal Avenue. The wee man is starting to mumble like he's sparring with someone in his sleep. His arms move around and I have to shift my bag for fear of him grabbing it. Now I'm almost certain I must be pregnant. I'll have to ask Lucy after my music lesson if she can tell one way or the other.

Finally I pull my body out from the increasing weight that is crushing me. I pull the cord for the driver to stop and when I stand up straight the old man drops down onto the nice warm place I've left for him. There's no chance of anyone else sharing the seat because he's taking up the whole thing, sprawled out like Sleeping Beauty.

As I get off the bus I begin to wonder if I should have wakened him so that he wouldn't miss his stop. Then again he can get a good sleep if he goes to the end of the line, and the driver will most likely give him a free ride back to where he needs to be.

I sigh with relief on the next bus, as there is space beside a young woman who's wide awake, and reading a book. Before long I hop off at Clifton Street and start walking up toward the Antrim Road.

At Carlisle Circus I notice the Mater Hospital where Mammy spent some time after an operation on a duodenal ulcer. She was in a ward with at least twenty other people, and I think she was happy for the bed rest, even though she suffered a lot of pain.

I pass a newsagent's shop and am shocked to see, right out on the footpath, a rack of magazines with naked women showing everything, for all the world to see.

I cover my eyes to avoid embarrassment and walk right into a dog leash that has a dog on one end and a swanky lady on the other end. She accepts my apology and looks at me strangely as if I'm not all there. I untangle myself from the dog and thank God he was just a springer spaniel and not some large ferocious type. I know for sure that Daddy would be just as shocked as I was about those terrible pictures, and there's no way they would be found in a Catholic district like ours.

After walking up the Antrim Road for some time, I find Miss McSherry's house, and knock on her door with the shiny brass knocker.

"Hello there," she says, "you must be Patricia. The O'Hare girls have told me all about you. Come in, come in, why don't you?"

Miss McSherry is only about two inches taller than me. She has her long brown hair wrapped up on top of her head, and she has a bounce in her walk. Asking me to wait a few minutes on a bench in the hallway, she disappears into the sitting room. I can hear someone playing a Strauss waltz in a very halting manner and I look around at the nice furnishings. There's a hall stand that has a pretty oval mirror with fancy carvings across the top. Attached to it is an umbrella stand like Granny's, but more elaborate. The stairs are carpeted, not linoleum like ours.

After some time, the sitting room door opens and a handsome boy of about fourteen or so comes out. I drop my eyes as he passes and hear him open the front door.

"See you next Saturday, Miss McSherry."

"Cheerio, Peter. See if you can get that piece a bit smoother by next week." I follow her into the room and sit next to her at the piano. She shows me where middle C is and how to position my hands for the scales. I'm supposed to hold my wrists up from the keyboard and go up the notes starting with my thumb on middle C. She shows me how to do the left hand too and then both hands together. We go over this for a long time, and she says next week we'll work on learning treble from bass and whole notes from half notes.

"Now I want you to practise every day until you can play the scales like this."

She positions her fingers and runs through the scales really fast. I hope I can do it that well by next week. "I'll try," I say, and she smiles.

I hand over the shilling and thank her. When I go through the hallway there's a wee girl of about six years of age waiting on the bench.

Miss McSherry introduces me to her elderly mother who is standing by the front door. I notice that she's even shorter and daintier than her daughter. I say goodbye and I'm on my way. That was enjoyable enough, I hope the practise is as well.

Walking further up the Antrim Road I finally come to the Limestone Road. On the corner sits a three storey house, on a triangular piece of property like Lucy described to me. It reminds me a lot of Granny's, with no back garden, just a cement yard.

Lucy answers when I knock. "You're just in time for sandwiches, Patricia." She shows me their wonderful walk-in pantry just off the kitchen and Anne Marie comes running downstairs and hugs me round the legs. She's only five like our Denis and her brother Vincent is around three or four.

We sit down to eat, and the sandwiches of lettuce, tomato and meat are really delicious. I didn't realise how hungry I was. "That meat's very tasty, Lucy, what kind is it?" I ask.

"It's tongue, Patricia, I'm glad you enjoyed it. There's plenty more."

"Oh no, I've had enough, thank you. I never thought I'd like tongue though," I say. "I'll have to tell Mammy about it. Maybe she'll get some for us." I never would have believed I would enjoy eating a cow's tongue. This has been a very eventful day altogether.

I keep asking Lucy questions just to hear her beautiful Irish brogue. She's from County Carlow and met Uncle Tom when he was in a teacher's training college in the South. I don't know how he could have talked her into moving to the North of Ireland with their Royal this, and Royal that, but anyhow they make a great couple and seem to be very happy.

After a quick tour of the house with too many stairs, Lucy asks if I would like to take the children over to the Water Works Park across the Antrim Road. Anne Marie and Vincent are rearing to go, and after kissing Lucy goodbye they show me the way.

We sit on the grass watching courting couples in little boats on the lake, and Vincent has a great time chasing the ducks. After a few hours of exploring the place we return to the house and Lucy suggests that I come again next week after my lesson. I have a feeling that she enjoyed the peace and quiet this afternoon.

Uncle Tom comes in before I leave, and he shows me a beautiful book he got from the library. It's all about California. He's been following the progress of his sister Mari from San Francisco down to Los Angeles, and being a school teacher he wants to learn all he can about the place. He's fascinated with the whole state and points out the desert, the beautiful coastline, and the National Park called Yosemite. We're not sure whether to pronounce it Yose-mitty or Yose-might. Now we have another question for Mari and Eileen who live there. Tom also shows me pictures of tall palm trees that grow all over the Los Angeles area, and we discuss how it must feel be to be warm all the time.

Lucy tells me where to catch a bus to the city centre, and how to get the other one to the Andersonstown area. I won't have to walk at all, thank God, for I wasn't looking forward to passing the newsagent's shop on the way home. This time I go upstairs on the bus, for you never see too many old people up there, especially ones that reek of whiskey. I never had a chance to talk to Lucy about the possibility of my being pregnant because Tom was there. Maybe next time.

The following Saturday, I learn how to read notes and find them on the piano keyboard.
Miss McSherry gives me a music sheet with a simple piece and asks me to practice every day.

When I get to Lucy's she suggests Alexandra Park across the Limestone Road this time. At the entrance is a huge bed of red, white and blue flowers. In the center is a crown made of blue pansies and it's surrounded by red and white flowers. The letters H R M are below the crown in the three Union Jack colours. It's really beautiful, but I wish it signified something Irish instead of British.

Anne Marie wants to know what the large letters stand for and I say, "Her Royal Majesty, that's what."

The former Princess Elizabeth just became Queen of England this year, and there was a big celebration in England. She was driven through the streets in a beautiful carriage drawn by horses. It was pictured in all the newspapers, and talked about all over the radio as well.

I feel that the new Queen is a bit too hoity toity with her sophisticated accent and stiff way of moving. She looks like she might break if she turns her head too fast. I like the Queen Mother. She looks like any regular wee lady you'd meet on the street and doesn't act so uppity.

We find a lake in the park with three beautiful swans floating along gracefully. You'd swear they had hidden motors making them glide. They move not a feather, and get from one side to the other like magic. I have to warn Vincent not to chase or scare them because they're in a class all their own, far above ducks.

Anne Marie points out the O'Hare cousins' back garden. It reaches all the way back to the park. Great Aunt Rynes has a cat named Musha and a budgie that sits in his cage and talks up a storm. He has a very large vocabulary and even knows how to say the cat's name. It's a treat to listen to him chatter. The cat doesn't seem to mind either. She just rolls herself up lazily on the hearth rug and ignores him completely.

I'm wondering if great Aunt Rynes would mind if we stopped in some Saturday. I'll have to ask Lucy what she thinks. Now I have two things to ask Lucy about.

After sitting under a tree in Alexander Park watching the swans, we mosey on back to Tom and Lucy's and I get up the courage to ask Lucy about my predicament.

"You say the man's leg was leaning on yours, that's all?" she asks.

"Yes, but he actually fell all over me when he went to sleep, Lucy."

"You're in luck, Patricia, it doesn't happen that way."

I'm so relieved that I can't help smiling. "I was very worried and didn't sleep well last week thinking of it," I say. "You've taken a real load off my mind."

"*I'm* pregnant myself, Patricia. Haven't you noticed I'm not as tall and lanky as usual? Just tall and portly."

"Oh, that's nice," I say.

"Anne Marie and Vincent are going to be surprised when the time comes. You shouldn't say anything to them though, they don't know where babies come from yet." She doesn't offer any more information about how the babies get started, so I'll have to wait for that secret. Hopefully by the time I'm eighteen someone will tell me how it all happens.

I wave goodbye and get on the bus with a spring in my step, for I've been saved this time from the worry of being with child. Irene's going to be very relieved at the news that sitting beside a man on the bus is not enough.

Chapter Twelve

A big open field lies between the top end of Gransha Park and the Glen Road. Everyone in the neighbourhood gathers shamrock there for St. Patrick's day. The leaves of the plant are so small that it would take about four of them to make one clover leaf. Since Ireland is the only place in the world where it grows, we feel that at least, even though this is Northern Ireland, it proves that we're really in Ireland, and not England where shamrock refuses to grow. Even though England lays claim to this part of Ireland, it's *still* Ireland.

Irene and I love to wander through this field and explore the little stream that trickles down from the Divis mountain. There's a swampy area that's fed by the stream, and we're excited when we see a big blob of a jelly like substance containing hundreds of black dots, almost like eyes.

"It's the beginning of frogs," Irene whispers as if they might hear us and disappear any minute. "Let's keep an eye on them every day and see how long it takes for frogs to develop."

"All right, Irene, but in the meantime let's get a jam jar and take some home to watch their progress."

Denis is trailing behind us and we don't stay long for fear of him falling into the swamp and being sucked under like the film we saw at the Broadway last week. He's just too adventurous for a five year old, and it takes ages for us to get home even though you can see our house clearly from the swamp.

Back at home, Irene is climbing up the cupboards trying to reach the empty jars on the top shelf.

"What are you doing, Irene?" Mammy asks. "Can't you see I'm trying to bake here?" She has flour all over her apron and looks a bit flustered.

Pauline comes in the front gate pushing Michael in the pram. She has the baking powder that Mammy is waiting for and hands it to me. Ann Murphy is behind her and they're giggling and talking about some boy.

"What's this about Danny Cosgrove?" Mammy asks, and Pauline blushes, takes Michael out of the pram, and carries him into the living room. I can hear Ann talking a mile a minute. That's the way she is, everyone calls her a real chatterbox, so they do.

Irene has finally retrieved the jar from the top shelf and we're about to leave again when Mammy stops us.

"First I want you both to take the clothes off the line and hang them on the fireplace screen to dry out." There never seems to be enough sun to dry them completely, and the women in this neighbourhood play a constant game of hang them up, take them in, whenever the sun shines or a cloud let's loose.

We end up hanging clothes across the backs of the chairs as well, and the ones on the screen are letting off clouds of steam as they dry. *I bet they don't have this problem in sunny California,* I think to myself.

Pauline's looking anxious now and lifts Michael up off the sofa. "Mammy, can I take Michael out again. I'm afraid if we leave him here he might pull the clothes off the screen?"

Mammy says she can, so Pauline and Ann go back down the street pushing the pram and talking so fast you can't even understand a word they're saying.

Most of the older girls like Pauline push babies in prams as an excuse to pass the homes of boys they have a notion of. I know she has her eye on Seamus McAvoy who lives down St. Meryl Park. She and Ann have probably passed that house a hundred times hoping to catch a glimpse of him. I'm sure she gets on the same bus as he does going to school in the morning. She's always in a hurry to get to the bus stop but sometimes lets several buses go by before finally boarding one.

The St. Malachy's boys are very popular with the girls. I don't know if it's the uniform or what, but Pauline and her friends are always in love from a distance with one boy or another from that school.

Irene asks me to go with her for the frog eggs, and she doesn't have to ask twice. We wave at Daddy who's coming up from work, then run all the way to the swamp. This time Denis is staying behind to play with Peter Fitzgerald.

When we're lying on our stomachs, I hand Irene a stick to pull part of the blob over to the edge of the jar.

"You scoot them in, Patricia, they give me the willies."

"All right Irene, though I don't think it could hurt you." I'm a bit of a tomboy and always get the messy stuff to deal with.

Just as we get back on our feet with the jar full and ready to go home, a strange dog approaches. He stares at us and starts to growl in the most horrible fashion, showing all his teeth. We stand frozen with fear when suddenly, the dog lunges at Irene. He grabs her cardigan in his teeth, and pulls with all his strength. Irene is screaming now and tries to get away from him but he keeps clinging to her clothing, making a low horrifying snarl. Irene drops the jar.

I'm sobbing now, trying to think of what we can do. The field has no stones and just as I'm running over to get a stick to beat the dog with, there's a loud whistle from the direction of the Glen Road. The dog's ears perk up, and he lets go of Irene and takes off toward the sound of the whistle.

We run like mad all the way back toward our house before he can change his mind and return to finish the damage he started. Irene is still crying and her cardigan has been ruined. It's dirty, stretched out, and has a big hole from the dog's teeth.

When we explain what happened, instead of comforting Irene, and hugging her, Daddy gets very angry and blames her for her own misfortune. She has been terrified by the dog and his reaction seems really unfair.

I'm beginning to wonder if Daddy has two personalities; the one who sings lovely songs in the bathtub, and the one who seems to be getting more angry every day.

He's suspicious of Pauline when she is three minutes late coming home in the evening. She might have been stopped by one of the neighbours who wanted to say hello. She's always rushing up the street at night trying to beat the clock and avoid confrontation with Daddy. Pauline is now fifteen and I don't think he wants her to grow up at all. She has lovely dark hair to go with her brown eyes and is very attractive. This brings a lot of welcome and unwelcome attention from boys. Most Irish girls have blue eyes, and brown are unusual, so boys are always making remarks like, "Hello there, darkey," and embarrassing her.

A few months ago Daddy got angry at Pauline for being five minutes late. She told him that Mrs. Braden was asking about the new neighbours who have moved in two doors up. Daddy was standing at the front gate watching her, and he knew she would have been on time if she hadn't stopped to answer Mrs. Braden's question. Being polite and not wanting to appear rude, she had to talk to her for a few minutes. She was terrified when she started toward the house and saw Daddy standing there by the gate. As soon as she reached him he started yelling and when they got into the house he slapped her across the face.

Mammy tried to stand up for her, and paid the price. For weeks we would lie in bed at night and listen to the silence downstairs. Normally we would hear mumbled voices with the wireless in the background. But not any more. We cried, thinking how sad it was for Mammy getting the silent treatment for so long.

One night in the second week, Mammy came into our bedroom in the middle of the night. She lifted Denis out of bed and brought him to her room. Then she came back and climbed into the bed beside Irene.

This went on for ages and finally one night I heard Irene get up and go into the front room. I could hear her talking to someone in a loud voice.

"What were you doing, last night, Irene?" I asked her the next morning.

"I went in and woke up Daddy. 'What's the matter with you?' I asked him. 'Why won't you speak to Mammy?' all the while crying my eyes out. He just said, 'No one cares about my opinion around here, so they don't. You go back to sleep.'"

"I'm surprised you were so brave, Irene," I whispered. "I wouldn't have the nerve."

"I couldn't stand it any longer, Patricia, it's just not fair to Mammy."

The next day Irene came home from school and found Mammy slouched over the kitchen sink sobbing her heart out. She seemed to be near to collapsing. Irene got some money out of Mammy's handbag and ran down to the call box in front of McErlean's shop. She rang Granny.

Granny told her to go back home and stay with Mammy, while she called the doctor.

The doctor came and gave Mammy something to relax her, and as he was going back down the street we saw him stop and talk to Daddy, who was walking up from work.

Things changed for the better, after that, and Mammy would sing to herself again while doing her housework.

Now, because of that dreadful dog, Irene gets the brunt of Daddy's anger. I feel like yelling at him for being so insensitive, but I wouldn't dare. Irene has to make the best of a nasty situation, and at least Mammy gives her some sympathy.

"I've got some leftover wool under the stairs, Irene, we'll have that cardigan as good as new in no time."

I don't think Irene will ever care for dogs after this, even if they're not crazy like that one. She'll probably be waking up for years with nightmares about vicious dogs, just like I do about rats. Sometimes I dream that I'm in a dark moist cave, with water dripping from the ceiling. Rats start to jump up and cling to my clothing just like the dog did to Irene, only there are about ten or more. I try to get them off, but it's impossible and I wake up screaming.

Weeks pass before Irene and I can get up the courage to visit the swamp again. When we finally do we're surprised to see tadpoles sporting legs and looking like half-fish half-frog creatures. We find the jar lying in the weeds, but the eggs are gone.

"The birds probably ate them, Patricia, maybe next year we can try again."

***

It's several months later, and a group of us have decided to walk up the mountain loney. Denis is with us too as we pass the tall structures holding electric wires, and cross the field.

Mairead and Agnes are picking dandelions that have gone to seed. They're blowing them all over the place and making me sneeze. When we reach the loney and start to wind our way up the mountain we have to step around large round cakes of cow dung. We've learned that although it might look like it's hard, if you step on it there's usually a soft gooey part in the centre that can stink and ruin your shoes.

Farmers use the lane to move their cows from one field to the other. It wouldn't be any fun to arrive when the cows are present, but apparently they were here a short time ago.

The gorse bushes are a blaze of bright yellow and when the sun shines it's hard to keep from squinting. The thorns on the plants make it impossible to touch them. I still have a scar on my thigh from falling into one of the bushes when we first moved up here. Mairead has noticed the blackberry bushes that are also covered in thorns.

"They're blooming at last, I can't wait to start picking those juicy berries," she says, inspecting the blossoms.

"I'm going to bring my wee bucket and get the biggest ones," Denis announces.

"Only if you can reach them, Denis," Mairead replies. "You know the biggest ones always grow out of reach for some reason."

We've passed the farm and are now a long way from our street. In the distance, farther up the mountain we can hear Mary Jordan's voice and she's laughing. She's only seven and we wonder if she's up here on her own.

Rounding the bend we see Mary, Claire and Annie who hang around together. They're talking to a very handsome man who looks to be in his thirties. Mary is going over to sit on his knee. He's sitting on a big flat rock, telling amusing stories, and we sit on the grass a short distance away and listen. The man is very friendly and with his sparkling blue eyes and dark wavy hair he could pass for a film star.

He's bouncing Mary on his knee and asks, "How about you lass, want to bounce next?" Claire Walsh goes over and takes a turn. She has beautiful blonde hair that hangs all the way down to her waist.

Now he's singing a funny song and making us howl with laughter. We're thoroughly enjoying this unexpected entertainment when the smile suddenly leaves Claire's face and a look of alarm takes its place. The man's hand has moved from around her waist and made its way up under her dress.

Irene stands up, takes my hand, and grabs Denis. She pulls us over to the edge of the field next to the lane.

"Oh, look, Claire," she shouts. "Here comes Father Malachy up the loney! Hello Father, how are you?"

The gorse hedges along the sides of the lane hide anyone who may be approaching and I peek around it but can't see a soul.

The man has jumped up and dropped Claire and he's dashing across the field in the opposite direction. He didn't even say goodbye. When he's out of sight, Irene gathers everyone together.

"That man was dangerous," she says. "He was doing something bad, so I had to pretend about Father Malachy coming to scare him off. I feel stupid, so I do, that I fell for

132

his good looks and charm." She gazes off into the distance after the beautiful, terrible man.

"Thank you, Irene," Claire sobs. "I don't know what would have happened if you weren't here."

"Not at all, Claire, it was nothing. I just had to think of something fast, so I did."

The eight of us file back down toward our street in a quiet mood. Irene is a hero to us, and we'll always appreciate her for that. We've decided to keep it our secret. Denis doesn't even have a clue, thank God. He was picking daisies for a daisy chain, and missed the whole thing.

Chapter Thirteen

Miss McCrory, our fifth class teacher, is pleasingly plump. Every day, while we read our geography books, she takes her tea break sitting at her desk.

She wears bright red lipstick and her lips glisten when she sips her tea. She lifts her china cup daintily, with her little finger held out, just so, like the aristocrats in the English films. Along with the tea she usually has at least four chocolate-covered wheat meal biscuits and takes wee bites as if to savour the taste and make them last longer. Glancing around the class, it's easy to see that my mouth is not the only one watering at the sight.

She is definitely one of the nicest teachers our class has ever had, and she's helping us prepare for the Eleven Plus Qualifying Exams needed for entrance to secondary school. Most of the girls are nervous, but she assures us that we will do well if we relax and don't fret about it.

My friend Sylvia has heard about an old woman near our school who sells honeycomb made in her own kitchen. She makes slabs of it and breaks it up in small pieces. When we have money, we knock on the old woman's door. For thrupence you can buy a big bagful, so we share the melt-in-your-mouth treat. I'm going to miss doing this next year when we leave St. Kevins, but Sylvia lives nearby so she can still buy honeycomb whenever she can afford it.

Sylvia will go to St. Dominics down the road next year, but I have to go to Fortwilliam with Pauline and Irene.

Our Pauline is on the netball team at Fortwilliam. She can easily throw the ball into the net, so she's a real asset to the team. Sometimes practise keeps her late after school, but she still seems to have enough time for her homework. The best part about her school, I have been told, is the lack of corporal punishment. Thank God for that, for I'll be going there before long myself. I'm almost eleven and will start next autumn. I'm tired of coming home with red welts on my hands whenever I get a spelling word wrong at St. Kevins.

Pauline likes to play camogie as well, although it's a more dangerous game with hard sticks swinging this way and that, and even up in the air. The girls try to hit the ball up the field toward the goal with the wide flat stick. If you were to get in their way you could end up with a nasty injury. The game is very much like men's hurling and the girls are every bit as aggressive.

I don't really play any organised sport because of my breathing problems, but during gym class I'm sometimes compelled to participate in an occasional game of rounders. Mari says rounders is very similar to the American baseball. She said that her friends, and countless other Americans, flock to see baseball games in summer.

I think sometimes I take advantage of my health problems to be lazy. I'd rather be reading a book. When I was eight I discovered the Falls Road Library. Mammy is always reading and she told me about it. The grown-up section is downstairs and I am amazed that so many books even exist. Tall racks, almost as high as the ceiling, fill the room from one end to the other.

On my first visit I wandered around this floor for quite a while, searching for the children's section. I enjoyed peeking through the spaces to the next aisle, until a nice looking young man's eye caught mine. I could feel my face get hot and decided to ask the librarian for help.

She sent me upstairs where a children's section did exist, on a much smaller scale, with the books stacked only about as high as my head.

The check-out counter had a glass front and you could see all sorts of wonderful books with bright colourful jackets. When I asked the lady if I could see one of them she said they were being saved for someone else. I wonder who you have to be to have one of those beautiful books reserved for you, but as usual, I was afraid to ask. The lady accepted the note from Mammy and gave me my own card.

I spent ages roaming the shelves and finally made my selection. I chose *Black Beauty*, and a collection of *Grimm's Fairy Tales,* and couldn't wait to get home and start reading.

Now, almost three years later, on my way down the library stairs, I notice a shelf full of magazines including *National Geographics*. I snigger to myself when I remember the first time we looked at our only copy of this magazine a few months ago.

Pauline, Irene, and I love to look at pictures of faraway places and unusual animals. When we first acquired our copy, we were ecstatic. But when we came to the section about the Amazon Jungle in South America we were puzzled by the fact that three or four of the pages had school composition paper pasted over them so they couldn't be seen.

"You know how Daddy is," Pauline said. "He had to be the one to cover the pages up."

"Try lifting that little space there," Irene said, "where there's no paste."

When she did, Pauline's eyes widened.

"I want a peek, so I do," I said, straining over both of them trying to see what was so interesting.

"My turn," Irene said, and when she saw what was behind the paper she started to giggle uncontrollably and almost fell off the chair.

"Hush, Irene, Mammy might come upstairs to see what's going on," Pauline warned. She started to look at the next picture by loosening up the paste.

"That's not fair," I protested. "I haven't even had one look."

When Pauline saw enough she let me peek, and I was really embarrassed. The pictures were of women in the jungle, not wearing a single stitch of clothing.

Irene had regained her composure by this time and said to Pauline, "The big roundy ones are what you're going to look like."

"Well, Miss Irene, the long pointy ones are what you're going to have."

Pauline is on the plump side and Irene is on the skinny side.

"I hope I never get those awful things," I wailed.

"Don't worry, Patricia, you don't have any choice in the matter," Pauline said. She already has some small ones that are kind of roundy. Irene is just starting to show and she hates it, so she does. She keeps her cardigan on all the time and her shoulders hunched over so no one will notice. When Mairead Cafferty comes over she does the same thing although it looks like she won't be able to hide hers much longer.

At school Sylvia Henley and I discuss the problem of growing up.

"I notice Patricia, you wear your blue and gray checkered skirt a lot," Sylvia says, looking at the broad straps down the front. "I was just going to tell you that you have two wee bumps starting yourself, but you can't tell with that skirt on. The straps cover them up."

I'm relieved to hear it. I was hoping the awful things wouldn't show through my clothing. Now, I find myself wearing the skirt more often. Mammy made it. The straps do cover the two wee bumps that are forcing themselves on me, and they're a Godsend for now, but for how long? Just like Irene, I find myself hunching over as much as possible.

"Girls, why don't you sit up straight, and hold your shoulders back," Daddy is always saying. "Do you want to end up with a hump on your back like old Mr. McGonigle?"

He has no idea what we're going through, and I wish he'd stop paying so much attention to our posture.

Today Pauline has gone into the boxroom to have another look at National Geographic. "Irene, Patricia quick! Would you look at that." We follow her gaze out the window and see our new neighbours from France kissing passionately right in front of our gate.

"They must be French kissing," Pauline says, watching with interest until they finally release each other. He goes toward their house and she goes toward the shops with her grocery bag.

"What's French kissing?" Irene and I chime in together.

"It's kissing between two French people, or one French person and a person of another nationality," Pauline responds. "Since Mrs. O'Reilly is French they qualify."

"You're not serious, Pauline," Irene says with an exasperated look. Pauline goes back to her reading and Irene and I sit looking out the window at other people passing.

It's nice to have neighbours who are different from the usual Irish type. Mr. O'Reilly is a tall, blonde Irish college professor. He met short, dark, French Mrs. O'Reilly when he was teaching English in France.

They have lived on our street for about six months now, and Pauline says their nephew from France is coming to stay with them for part of the summer.

When Jacque arrives he doesn't waste any time getting to know the children in the neighbourhood. He's about eleven and full of energy. When we walk, he runs. When we hop, he jumps in the air. When we talk, he shouts and gesticulates, waving his arms around like he's Maurice Chevalier. He almost never stops moving and we are happily exhausted after a few hours in his company.

Jacque speaks only French, and we don't speak any, so we have a great time pointing to objects and learning the name for each. He has taught us a French song that we know by heart now, but don't have the slightest idea what it means. He dances along balancing on the low walls in front of the gardens as he sings:

Sur le pont d'avignon
l'on y danse, l'on y danse
Sur le pont d'avignon
l'on y danse, tous en rond.

Mr. O'Reilly tells us later that it's a song about the bridge of Avignon where people meet to dance. Kind of like the crossroads dances in Ireland.

This morning Mammy is pushing Michael in his pram up the street. We're following Jacque like the children in the Pied Piper, and every one of us is singing in French. Mammy stops and just stands with her jaw hanging open and then she laughs until tears roll down her cheeks.

When we go in later she says, "Jacque's parents are probably enjoying a well deserved rest while he's over here, I would think. Can you imagine having a wee'un like that, Danny?"

Daddy looks up from his newspaper and laughs. "No, I can't, Bessie. I certainly wouldn't be able to read in peace if he was ours." He goes back to his reading and Mammy looks at me and says, "Patricia, while you girls are all here, your daddy and I have something we need to tell you." She calls Pauline and Irene from upstairs. "This house is ending up costing more than we thought it would. A lot of people in the area are taking in students from Trench House as boarders, and we've decided to do the same."

"But where are they going to sleep?" Pauline asks. "There's not a spare bed in the whole house."

"Your daddy and I will move into the box room and Denis and Michael will move into your room."

"You mean the five of us will have to share one room?" Pauline says with dismay. Irene just looks shocked. I'm the only one who doesn't seem too worried about it. I think it would be nice to have Denis and Michael in our room, but I kept my mouth shut.

"The boxroom will be a tight squeeze for us too, you know," Mammy says. "but we need to do this for a few years if we want to stay here."

"How many boarders will we be getting, Mammy?" Pauline asks.

"We'll have two, starting at the beginning of the school year. There'll be someone from the college coming over to inspect the place to make sure the accommodations are adequate." Mammy speaks with an optimistic tone. "It really won't be all that bad. They'll be at school most of the time. Just here for meals and to sleep."

This very day we begin to appreciate the privacy that we're soon to lose. Irene is so shy that she can't imagine collegiate men sitting around our fire in the evening. She's fourteen, and goes to the commercial side of Fortwilliam. She's learning typing, shorthand, and accounting skills, and can work as a secretary when she leaves the school. It sounds more sensible to me, but Mammy says I have to go to the regular secondary school, where Pauline goes. So that's that. As for college students in our house, I don't think Irene likes the idea at all.

Later in the week Mammy answers a knock on the front door, and I hear her say, "Hello Norah, come in, come in. Patricia, you're wanted!"

I go to the door and see Norah and Angela who live in the older, fancier houses on our street.

"Hello, Patricia. About the qualifying exams next Saturday, instead of us having to go by bus, my daddy has offered to drive us over."

"That'd be great," I say. "I wasn't sure about catching the right buses, since we're not familiar with the area."

"I know," she says, "and Lord knows how long it would take. We'd probably end up being late. Will you come down to our house at half eight then?"

"I will, and thank your daddy for me. See you then."

The exam is being given at a school over in East Belfast, and we live in West Belfast.

"I'm sure you're glad to be getting a ride, Patricia," Mammy says. "It should relieve your anxiety, and you'll be more relaxed at the exam."

When Saturday finally comes, we meet at Norah's. Her father, is a doctor, and owns a shiny black vehicle, one of the few cars in the neighbourhood. He asks if we have our pencils, then helps us in, and we're off.

"You girls need to pass the exams, you know, or your parents will have to pay for your secondary school education, so they will," he says.

"I know," Angela says sadly. "This is the only chance I have, so it is."

"Mine too," Norah says. "Have some faith in us, Daddy, we can pass. We've been drilled at school every day for weeks now."

"I'm young enough to have another chance next year, if I fail," I say. "Although I want to pass this time. I'd hate to have to take fifth class over again."

"Lucky you!" Norah whines. "That should take the pressure off, so it should." I smile and look out the window. Little does she know how nervous I feel. My stomach is tied in one big knot and my heart is thumping like a drummer in an Orange parade.

"Don't worry, you'll all do well," Mr. Hudson says "You'll pass with flying colours."

Mammy has told me that both of girls could well afford to pay for school if need be. *But my situation is different,* I think to myself, *and since we don't have that kind of money, I'm the one who should be concerned.*

"Do you know exactly where this school is, Daddy?" Norah asks.

"Ach aye, it's over in the Stranmillis area. Don't worry, girls," he says cheerfully.

After about fifteen minutes or so, we are in a completely strange area of the city that we know is Protestant. We already passed one Orange Lodge and on the sides of many buildings are pictures painted of King William of Orange on his white horse, waving the Union Jack. Large signs that say "No Pope Here" are everywhere and I'm wondering why the Pope, who stays in Rome most of the time, could be such a threat to people in this part of Ireland.

On the sides of buildings in the poorer Catholic neighbourhoods you can find the words, "Up the IRA," and stuff like that. Just as I'm thinking about the problems of this city, we reach the school.

"Here we are, girls. Good luck now," Norah's father says. "I have to make my hospital rounds, so you can take the bus back like we agreed." We thank him and just as his car is disappearing round a corner we look at the school and I get a sinking feeling. It almost looks abandoned. By the time we reach the front door, I've got butterflies playing catch in my stomach.

One office door is open and there's a lady sitting at a desk. We walk up shaking.

"We've come for the Eleven Plus Qualifying Exams," Angela says. The woman looks confused. "Eleven Plus? I'm afraid you've come to the wrong school, dear. The exams are being taken..."

I've got bells ringing in my ears, and I can't hear what's being said. It's such a shock. What are we going to do now?

"Just down the road in that direction..." the woman is saying, "about two miles or so...you'd better hurry!"

"Thank you," Angela says. I feel like I'm about to faint, and Norah and Angela look dismayed.

As soon as we reach the street we start running in the direction she told us, and we're all crying. "Oh, why did my daddy have to leave so quickly?" Norah is saying. We don't see any buses so we keep running until we can hardly breathe. Finally we're just walking at a fast pace.

"Do you think they've started yet?" I ask. No one answers. "Maybe the teachers were late getting there and we'll still make it on time," I say.

"Don't kid yourself, Patricia," Angela snaps, then she bursts out sobbing again. As we're running, I'm wondering what will happen if we can't take the test. People are staring at us but we don't care. *If only a bus would come...But maybe this is not a main road.* I get this awful feeling of desperation and try to will a bus to drive by, to no avail.

Finally, after what seems like an eternity, we reach the school where we should have been in the first place. Running to the front office looking red-faced, bedraggled and desperate, we stand before a lady who is startled when she sees us.

"You've got the right school, but I'm afraid I can't disrupt the proceedings for you," she says, throwing a disapproving look at us. "The exams started over thirty minutes ago."

"But we were dropped off at the wrong school, so we were!" Norah says.

"I'm sorry, but that doesn't change anything."

Leaving the school, we keep walking in the direction we started out in, and before long we realise we're all the way down near the Botanical Gardens and Queen's University.

"We're almost downtown," I say, "if we just go in that direction we should reach Divis Street where we can catch a bus back to Andersonstown."

"I'm parched from all that running, so I am," Angela moans. "Why don't we look for somewhere to get a drink."

"There's a wee tea shop across the street," Norah says. "We can use our lunch money."

Sitting in the small cafe, we order lemonade and buttered scones. We are a bit more relaxed now, but still worried sick about what will happen to us.

"I'm so sorry, girls, I wish my Daddy hadn't gotten us into this predicament." Norah sounds forlorn.

"I'm sure he didn't do it on purpose, Norah," I say. "I wonder what *my* daddy is going to say about this whole mess? Just thinking about it makes me nervous."

After drinking the last drop of lemonade we parade out and walk slowly to Divis Street. On the bus we sit quietly looking out the window, each lost in her own thoughts.

Daddy and Mammy are upset about what has happened and say it looks like I'll have to repeat my last year at St. Kevins next year. I can't sleep. I'm thinking, *if only we could have caught buses ourselves, like originally planned, we could have taken the exam.*

All week I'm depressed and start to notice white spots on my knees. Mammy takes me to the doctor. He inspects the spots with a puzzled look, leaves for a few minutes and I can see him in his office across the hall looking through a large manual on his desk. When he comes back to the examination room he asks, "Have you been kneeling in lime?"

I can't remember ever doing *that*, doctor," I say.

"Well, it looks like that's what you did," he says, with an air of authority. "I'll give you some cream to apply for the itch, and I dare say it should be cleared up in a week."

After about ten days the spots are multiplying and now cover my shins, elbows, and heels as well as both knees. The itch is unbearable, especially while sitting at the fire in the evening. The skin has large patches of white, flaky looking scales, and I feel like a fish or reptile.

"If you knelt in lime, Patricia, how did it get on your elbows and ankles, I wonder?" Mammy asks. "I think we should be trying another doctor, so we should."

The second doctor takes one look at my knees and says, "Psoriasis, that's what you've got, young lady. It's caused mostly by nerves, but can be connected to asthma and dry skin."

"Every winter her heels and knuckles crack and bleed," Mammy says, "so I suppose you could say she has dry skin."

"Well, Mrs. Owens, the only known treatment we're aware of is sunshine."

"You don't get much of that around here, doctor," Mammy says with a pinched smile.

"I'll give you some ointment for the itch, and because it has a tar base, it doesn't have a very pleasant odour. It will soften the flaky skin, however, and you'll notice the scales falling off." *You mean I won't be a fish for the rest of my life,* I think to myself while he hunts for the cream. He hands me a jar of ointment and a bottle of bath oil.

"Thank you, doctor," Mammy says as we stand up to leave. "I'm glad we finally know what the problem is."

"Oh, one more thing," he says as we're going out the door. "She should have a citrus fruit to eat every day. It just might help."

Out on the street Mammy looks at me sideways and says with a smirk, "Well, so much for kneeling in lime, Patricia. We'll have to stop at McErlean's on the way home and get you some oranges."

That's the only good thing I've heard for weeks. I even feel quite guilty, for they're one of the most expensive fruits. The doctor said one a day, so we count out seven gorgeous juicy oranges. Mammy must be cringing having to pay so much for them. Lovely, Canadian, Kemp apples in summer are the only fruit that most people can afford, and you have to go to hospital in order to get a bunch of grapes. Mammy got some once when she was in the Mater Hospital.

"He said it was caused by nerves, Patricia. Do you think it was brought on by that exam business?" I nod, and now have another *If Only* to think about.

I'm absolutely wallowing in self pity now. The psoriasis is driving me crazy and the tar baths stink as well as the ointment. Pauline and Irene are sorry for me but they're also a wee bit jealous of the lovely oranges I get to eat. Every once in a while I slip a piece to Denis and Michael who don't understand why they can't have one too. I check the cupboard at night to make sure they're still there and wonder if I should have my orange tonight or wait 'til morning. It's such a difficult decision to make.

About three weeks after the exam disaster Norah comes looking for me again.

"I've got good news this time, Patricia," she says. "My Dad pulled some strings with the government, and we can take the exam next Saturday."

"You're not serious?" I say, feeling like we've been graced with a miracle.

"Yes, I am serious," she says grinning. "My Dad has promised to make sure he's at the right school this time."

When I tell Mammy, I can't help beaming with joy.

"Thank God, Patricia," Mammy says with a smile. "That business was a wee bit of a worry, so it was."

I was all prepared to repeat fifth class again and this is a great relief. Of course, I remind myself before I get too confident, I still have to pass the test.

When Dr. Hudson drives us the second time, he stays in the car park until Norah runs in to make sure we're at the right school. She comes back out and waves him on. We even have time to spare.

We notice that there are many other boys and girls in the classroom. One boy is completely bald and others are in wheelchairs. Now we feel kind of out of place, and I say a prayer of thanks for my health. To think that I was full of self-pity about my stupid psoriasis and here these boys and girls have much harder crosses to carry.

After about a month we get the exam results. Norah and Angela failed, but luckily I passed. To think I was the only one with a chance to take the exam again, it's kind of ironic altogether. I feel badly for my friends, but at least their parents can afford the fee for high school.

Mammy says the government charges a fee to encourage young people who haven't passed the exam to go into a trade instead.

She'll be coming with me to sign up at Fortwilliam. Pauline and Irene are well along in the school and when I start my first year, Pauline will be in her last.

Chapter Fourteen

Aunt Marjorie is thirty years of age already. She's never had a boyfriend and I wonder if she'll ever marry. She lavishes all her love on Tom and Lucy's children, and our Denis and Michael. When she comes to visit she likes to take them for walks and give them sweets.

"I've a problem, Marjorie, all I can get that wee'un to put in his mouth is champ," Mammy says when Majorie stops by. "It's the same, morning noon and night, the only thing he'll eat." Mammy sounds exasperated. Our Michael is two-and-a-half already and all he wants is champ.

"Well, Bessie," Marjorie says, "if you look at it this way, he's getting potatoes which are a healthy food. They kept a lot of Irish alive when there wasn't anything else to eat. He's also getting the milk and butter that you mash into the potatoes. All in all, I'd say you shouldn't be worried at all. He seems healthy enough, so he does, look at those sturdy arms and legs."

"I suppose you're right, Marjorie. I shouldn't be concerned at this stage, but I wish I could get him to eat a bit of fruit or a vegetable now and then."

"Bessie, before I forget, we had a letter from Mari. She married that Minnesota Swede she's been going on about. He has a great job in an aircraft company. Not a labourer either... engineering or something like that. His name is Albin."

"Well that's good news, she just got in under the wire, if you ask me. She's thirty-five isn't she?"

"Yes she is, and she wants to have children before it's too late. Patricia, you might end up with real American cousins. Wouldn't that be something?"

I smile and start to daydream about what our cousins would look like being part Irish, and part Swedish, but all American.

"Eileen likes her secretarial job in Los Angeles," Marjorie says. "And she's still living in the apartment she shared with Mari on Mariposa Avenue."

"I know what Mariposa means, it's Spanish," I say. "Mari told me it means butterfly. Don't you think Mariposa Avenue sounds a lot better than Butterfly Avenue?"

Marjorie laughs, "I hope Eileen can meet someone too, she's no spring chicken."

"I know," Mammy says, "and you're not either. What about yourself meeting someone?" Mammy asks, and Marjorie blushes.

"I'm too self conscious...wouldn't know how to talk to a man."

Michael is pulling on Marjorie's skirt and she lifts him up to put him in the tansad.

"C'mon, Denis, we're off now." She looks at Mammy. "Now *these* wee'uns I can bring back to you at the end of the day." She walks down the pathway singing one of her many songs.

Mammy reads the letter from America that Marjorie left on the table.

"Mari says the sky is blue and you never see a single cloud all summer long," Mammy says. "Here all we see are clouds."

Sometimes I sit at the foot of our bed and gaze out the window at the Divis Mountain. If I squint I can make out the cows and sheep, and the ribbon of road that is the upper Springfield.

Shadows of the clouds drift across the mountain like a parade of ghosts. I enjoy the clouds though, and think if the sky were forever blue it could get monotonous.

Lately the weather has warmed up, with sunshine between sparse clouds. It seems like the doctor was right about the sun because my psoriasis has subsided, and is only on my knees and elbows now. I can live with that, even if it never goes away completely.

***

Mairead and Agnes's daddy, Mr. Cafferty, owns his own company down the Falls Road.

They're very well-off and have purchased the first television set in the whole area.

The neighbourhood children have gathered at their house, and are watching a man climbing the ladder with a thing called an aerial on his back. There's a constant chatter as he hammers a metal plate on the roof, then positions and attaches the aerial.

"What's that thing for?" Denis wants to know.

"It's for picking up airwaves," Mr. Cafferty says. "So you can see the picture on the screen. It's 1953, Denis, and progress must go on."

"But how can pictures float in the air?" Denis inquires. "And how can they run down that metal pole into the television set?"

"You got me buggered, Denis," Mr. Cafferty says. "It's a complete mystery to me as well."

It's just an amazing thing to imagine. We thought it was a marvelous feat for radio waves to get inside the wireless, and now we are faced with an even greater achievement. Mammy was about my age when she saw her first aeroplane, and now we see them all the time. I suppose someday in the future everyone will have televisions in their homes. And who knows what other new inventions are waiting to be discovered.

Agnes says she has asked, and Irene and I can come over Saturday evening to watch a variety programme. We are so excited we can hardly contain ourselves. We'll be part

149

of the new ritual that has so many people in America enthralled.

When the time comes, we squeeze into their living room where the seven Caffertys are gathered, along with a squad of their cousins from up the Glen Road. The lights have been turned off and Irene and I are sitting in the back. The younger Cafferty's are sitting on the floor close to the television set.

When the programme starts it's mostly silly nonsense. People hitting each other over the head with blow-up hammers and one man tripping over another and falling onto a table filled with food. Background laughter is coming from people we can't see. There are also a few comedians. I find myself having more fun just watching the watchers with the light from the screen flitting across their faces, glowing on and off the way the flames leap and wane in the fireplace. The Cafferty's cousin, Geraldine is staring at the screen. Her mouth is wide open in complete admiration of the whole thing, and there's sporadic laughter from the youngsters around the room.

After the programme, Mrs. Cafferty invites us to return next week, when Johnny Ray will be a guest singer. We are finally going to see what the singer of "The Little White Cloud That Cried" looks like.

Mammy and Pauline are crazy about some other new songs, like "Unchained Melody" and "Stranger in Paradise." Pauline, being the terrific singer that she is, loves to sing while doing her Saturday housework. Sometimes Irene and I join in and we harmonize. It's funny how when people sing in this country, they always do it with an American accent. Mammy thinks it's probably because that's the way they've heard the song.

When our student boarders arrive, my assignment on Saturdays will be to clean up their room after they leave for the day. They're from Derry, in their final year at Trench House, and turn out to be very interesting fellows.

Niall is short with medium brown hair brushed straight back. Gerry is tall and lanky and has blond hair that is a wee bit unruly, and his skin is very pale. They're both talkative and intelligent, and are settling in well with our quiet, reserved household.

It's great having them around the fire after the evening meal telling stories about Derry, and such a pleasant change for our family, which lacks the art of animated conversation. The boarders dote on Michael and make him laugh, and they even try to bring Denis out of his shy self. Our meals have improved too, as Mammy is trying to make a good impression, and we have more desserts than ever. They really seem to enjoy her leek and barley soup after a long day.

"It warms the cockles of our hearts," Gerry says.

"Did you know, Mr. Owens, that Derry is over sixty percent Catholic?" Niall asks, as we sit by the fire.

"I knew they were in the majority, but I thought maybe a slimmer one," Daddy says. "They should have more say in what goes on then, but I hear you have the same amount of discrimination as we do here in Belfast."

"Despite the majority," Gerry says, "it's almost impossible for Catholics to get government jobs no matter how well educated they are."

"But wouldn't that cause a shortage of workers?" Pauline asks.

"It should, Pauline, but they just recruit Protestants from Belfast rather than use the local Catholics. It's a shame and frustration to the Catholics who can't get jobs," he says.

"But how can England stand for that, don't they know what's going on?" she protests. "Uncle Freddy says there's no discrimination against Catholics in *England*."

"There's a threat in Northern Ireland, Pauline. The solution is called divide and conquer. The British have been doing it for centuries all over the world.

"Like where?" Pauline wants to know.

"India and Pakistan, and Iraq and Kuwait used to be single countries. Many countries in Africa were split up. Different tribes would be forced together and that caused problems among the people. So they'd be easier to conquer. Even in Scotland they pitted one clan against the other."

Daddy has been listening to the conversation and shakes his finger.

"Speaking of unfairness, there's many an Irishman was shipped to Botany Bay in Australia for the crime of stealing a loaf of bread to feed a starving family. Would you call that fair?"

Every evening that the fellows sit with us, we learn more history and politics. It'll be dull when they leave at the end of the school year, and start teaching in Derry's Catholic schools.

"I think they're practising on us for now," Pauline says.

Niall and Gerry's college started last week and our school starts in three days. I've got my uniform hanging over the back of a chair in our room, all fresh, crisp and ready to go.

I'm sitting on the toilet reading a book, and when I stand up, I drop the book and scream. My heart pounds, and I start to tremble. Mammy comes bounding up the stairs looking concerned, and I show her the toilet full of blood.

"Am I going to die, Mammy, where did all that come from?"

"Don't worry, Patricia, it's perfectly normal, you're just a wee bit early."

"Early! Normal! What's happening to me, Mammy?" She leaves for a minute and comes back with a sanitary towel.

"Here, put this strap around your waist, and pin the towel to the wee tabs in front and back."

"Oh my God in heaven!" I cried, "Our Pauline sent me to the chemist's shop for these things several times."

"Is that so?" Mammy says.

"Yes, and all the time she made me believe they were for catching the perspiration under her arms. I'll kill her, so I will. If I'd known what they were really for, I'd never have agreed to get them for her! I'd be mortified to ask a man for such a thing. No wonder she gave me sixpence for sweets every time she sent me!"

"She was too embarrassed, herself, I suppose," Mammy says, and I notice she's smiling slightly.

"Now calm down, Patricia, let's go and sit on the bed and I'll explain about your visitor."

"Visitor? How many times is it going to stop here?"

"Every month, I'm afraid," she says.

"What? Oh no, it's just not fair," I moan as I throw myself on the bed. "Why did I have to be a girl?"

"Well, Patricia, if you were a boy you'd have to be worried about shaving every day and making enough money to support your family. That's something *we* don't have to worry about, now isn't it?"

"Patricia, this is what babies are made of. If you don't become pregnant it just comes away every month around the same time. It's called your monthly visitor, and it can last from two to five days. You know, in my day, we didn't even have sanitary towels. We had to use old cut up towels, and rewash them for the next time."

"Yuck, I'm glad this is the fifties. The old days sound awful."

"It was a bit of an inconvenience, I'll admit, Patricia. Just be happy you're living in modern times."

"I don't ever want to get married and have babies," I say, feeling sorry for myself, and wondering if now would be a good time to ask how they make their way out of your body.

"Don't worry, you needn't get married if you're not so inclined," she says.

When I go downstairs Daddy's coming in the back door, he has the bicycle pump in his hand and smiles when he sees me.

"It's a lovely day, Patricia, how would you like to cycle out to Lough Neagh?"

I burst out crying and start to run back up the stairs. "You'll have to talk to Mammy about it!" Daddy stands there looking bewildered, and goes back through the kitchen.

153

Mammy comes in and says I can spend the rest of the day in bed if I like. She'll get me something to read and I won't have to do my usual Saturday work.

"I'll go to McErlean's and get you some ice cream," Mammy says. "It should make you feel better."

Irene stops in on her way to do my Saturday job of cleaning up the student's room. "What are you doing, Patricia? You're not supposed to be having your visitor before me. I'm three years older than you."

"I'm sorry, Irene, but you should consider yourself lucky to have this mess for three years less."

The only good thing about this day is the ice cream, and Pauline and Irene doing my work. Now they can see what it's like, crawling under the bed for stray socks and dust balls.

On my first day at Fortwilliam I'm nervous and excited at the same time. Irene shows me where to go for my first class. Her building is away at the back of the property and Pauline is in the middle building.

"Don't worry, Patricia, after a few months it'll be old hat to you, like you've been going there forever."

The school is run by Dominican nuns who wear white habits with black head covers. Stiff white collars start right under their chins and go as far as their chests, just like giant bibs. They look extremely uncomfortable altogether, so they do.

I'll be taking Latin, geometry, algebra, Gaelic and English Literature. I'm eleven and a half now, and because of what happened two days ago my major concern is that they have a supply of sanitary towels in the lavatory.

I'm relieved when I check the washrooms at the school and find a container on the wall for monthly visitor needs. They cost an arm and a leg though, so I'll have to check the calendar like Mammy showed me and bring one in my schoolbag just in case.

Sister Charles runs the bookstore at Fortwilliam and she acts like a tomboy, with her loud voice and jovial personality. Everyone likes her, and the first time I go for school supplies, I'm impressed with her efficiency. The new books are perfectly stacked in neat equal piles. They look like they're patiently waiting for their new owners. She also has a great selection of pencils, biro pens, protractors, rulers and exercise books.

I think Sister Charles has the best job in the whole school. She doesn't have to correct papers or anything unpleasant like that. The girls in the upper classes call her Charlie, but not in front of her. I think she is aware of this, but she doesn't seem to mind.

I order used books as they're a lot cheaper, and splurge on a new pen. I select a different colour of exercise book for each class, so that I'll know which is which.

When we have our exams, I'm third in the class in English and Gaelic, but Latin and geometry are another matter. Latin is difficult with its *amo, amas, amat, amamos, amatis, amant.*

The book is about an ancient class of people, and is hard to apply to modern times. There are pictures of women wearing long dresses, carrying water jars on their heads. The men are dressed in togas, and all the conversation is about that time in Roman history.

The first play we do in our Shakespeare studies is *The Merchant of Venice*. I'm chosen to play the part of Portia, and learning the lines is not the problem for me. It's getting up in front of the class and acting the part.

Annie Quinn, who is Antonio the merchant, speaks her part loudly and with loads of flair. She's not the least bit intimidated and it makes me wish I could have an outgoing personality like hers. Someday, I think, she'll make a great actress. When she plays the role of Julius Caesar and says "Et tu Brute!" her emotions and movements help you imagine what Caesar must have felt knowing that he was betrayed.

There's a girl in my class called Rachel Byrne, whom I met on the bus going to school. We get along famously, just like sisters. I'm all excited when I realise that she lives just down the road from Granny's house. We decide to meet on Saturday afternoon in front of the Broadway Cinema where a film starring Fred Astaire and Ginger Rogers is playing.

Rachel has pale skin, short dark hair and blue eyes. She's quiet and easy to talk to and is the eldest of six children. She'll be happy to get out of the house on Saturday, and I can understand that, for she lives in the same kind of row house as Granny Owens. It's really crowded and she can't find a quiet place anywhere.

After a few months at the school, we become friends with about four other girls, but Rachel and I are the only ones who live up our way.

The school grounds are beautiful, like a large estate, which I think it must have been at one time. There's a kindergarten building that is really a lovely old house the gentry used to own. Around the house are large stands of pampas grass at least eight feet tall, and the lawns are beautifully manicured. At the East side of the grounds is a driveway lined on both sides with tall rhododendron bushes. Most of the year they are covered with large pink blooms.

Rachel and I have become more daring. Now, after school, we use this driveway to reach the street. Because it's so far from the convent and hidden from view, we stop and pull off our ugly, thick, lisle stockings and replace them with white ankle socks that have been cleverly hidden in our school bags.

"Hurry up Rachel," I say. "I think someone's coming."

"Hold your horses, Pat," Rachel says. She likes to shorten my name. "I'm still trying to tie my laces," and our hearts are in our throats until the sound from the other side of the bushes dies.

"It was probably the gardener," Rachel whispers, "and he's almost deaf."

We have now acquired the desired effect, the modern look for our long bus ride home.

Most days we go down Fortwilliam Park to the Shore Road where we get a bus to the city centre. Hardly any of the girls go home in this direction, as it's a mostly Protestant area, so we are never noticed in our ankle socks. It's exciting to be taking a chance of getting caught out of uniform, but we feel it's worth it.

Our uniform consists of a bottle green jumper with wide pleats that have to be ironed. A white blouse is worn under the jumper, and a silver and green striped tie. We wear a green blazer in summer and a trench coat in winter. The thick beige stockings are by far the worst feature although they're nice and warm in winter. It took quite a few tries before I could get the tie done right, but now it's always done to perfection. The first time I tried to make a knot I wound the wide side around too many times and it looked like a skinny snake hiding its head behind a fig leaf. The second time the tie was so long that the knot ended up too small to fill in the space between the white collars on my blouse.

When Rachel and I board the bus at the Shore Road, we like to go upstairs on the bus so that we have a better view of the shipping channel and all. We are usually very uncomfortable as the emblem on our top pocket gives away our religion. When girls from Protestant schools get on they sit on the opposite side and glance over at us and whisper together. Then mean looks come our way and we usually busy ourselves looking out the window, pretending we don't notice.

Because of some strange, cultural hostility that has been going on for centuries, we can't speak to, or feel comfortable around each other, even though we look the same, speak the same, and probably have all the same feelings. It's like we're in two different worlds, side by side but apart at the same time.

How can they feel Irish when they are so pro-British and anti-Irish? How can we feel Irish when we have been robbed of our nationality because everywhere we look we see British influence? We feel unwanted in our own land, and we would be thrown in prison if we dared raise an Irish flag. Someday, please God, things will change for the better.

Rachel and I have decided to ride the same bus to school in the mornings. I will sit upstairs in the front seat, so that when it reaches the Springfield Road stop, she can just look up and see if I'm on it or not. They come every three minutes, so it won't be a long wait. If I haven't shown up by a certain time, Rachel will get on the bus and go to school. You never can tell if I may be sick or something.

We both have Latin first, and we're sitting in class going over the declensions of yet another verb. Sister Assumpta is writing on the board and her stiff collar has shifted so that we are getting a glimpse of her neck and throat area underneath. Everyone is glancing around and rolling their eyes at each other. We feel the same way about seeing her throat as we would if someone saw our underwear. It's strange how it seems immodest to look under her collar just because she's always covered up to the hilt.

There's a tap on the door and a prefect comes in. She's one of the upper-class girls who keep order in the hallways and the grounds.

After they have a few words, Sister Assumpta looks over at me and motions for me to come up to the front.

"There's been a call from your grandmother, Patricia. You and your sisters are to go to her house right away."

I collect my books with an awful feeling of foreboding. My heart is racing as I rush outside. Pauline and Irene are standing in front of the convent looking as concerned as I feel.

"What on earth has happened?" I ask.

"I haven't the foggiest," Pauline says, with a worried look. "They said that Granny didn't give any reason when she rang."

Irene has started to weep as we walk toward the Antrim Road. Sitting on the bus together our minds are visualising all sorts of disasters.

"Maybe Daddy's bus had an accident," I say.

"Maybe Mammy lit a match and blew up the stove again," Irene whispers.

"Maybe something happened to our Denis..."

"Or our wee Michael," Pauline blurts out, and we sob quietly in unison.

The ride home seems endless. So many people getting on and off causing the bus to move in the most sluggish fashion. The second bus is even slower and our apprehension increases as time drags on. People seem to be moving in slow motion as if they have all day. As we sit in silence with our anxious thoughts, the Springfield Road comes into view, and we rush toward the back of the bus to disembark.

We run past Nurse Peale's house, the first butcher's shop, the linen mill, Hughes Bakery, the second butcher's shop at the bottom of Dunmore Street. Now, out of breath and worried sick, we knock on Granny's front door and wait.

Patricia

Aunt Mari

Patricia, Irene, Pauline

Irene, Granny, Pauline,
Mammy and Patricia

Granny and Denis in Ballyhornan

First Communion

Daddy

L to R. Mammy with Angela,
AnneMarie, Patricia, Denis, Irene,
Marjorie with Thomas, Lucy.
Front. Michael, Vincent.

Patricia with Mari's boys,
Tim and Kevin

Neil

Chapter Fifteen

The front door opens and Granny is standing there wearing her hat and coat.

"Good, I thought you'd never get here," she says.

"What has happened, Granny?" Pauline inquires with a trembling voice. Like Irene and me, she's expecting the very worst.

"Happened? Whaddiye mean happened?" Granny asks.

"You know, the school said you rang and wanted all three of us to come here right away," Pauline says, looking more than a little frustrated.

"Oh that!" Granny says with a smile. "I've a surprise for you. You know the way your Uncle Frank gives me money every year to buy you each a new pair of shoes? Well, he just gave it to me this morning. We're going shoe shopping."

Our mouths hang open in amazement. A feeling of relief courses through my body and hits my brain. I start to get dizzy and feel like I'm going to faint. Pauline runs through the hallway, and up the stairs to the bathroom.

"May I have a drink of water, Granny?" I ask, "I'm so thirsty my mouth feels like cotton wool." Irene follows and we drink the water slowly, trying to regain our normal composure.

"This is unbelievable," Irene whispers as she rinses her glass and dries it. "I wonder if Granny realises what she's just put us through."

"I suppose she meant well," I say as I follow her back to the open front door where Pauline is talking to Granny.

Sitting on the bus to town, Granny starts reminiscing about the war years when so many things were rationed.

"I remember we used to go by train to Dundalk, just over the border in Southern Ireland. We always wore large overcoats when we went."

"Why was that, Granny?" I ask.

"Because you could get bacon, ham, butter and all sorts of things that we couldn't get up here. The women wore contraptions under their dresses with big pockets. When we came back across the border the customs inspectors would confiscate anything they could find. I just know they brought the booty home to their own families."

"Did they inspect under your dress, Granny?" Irene inquires.

"No, just our coat pockets and bags. I never in my life saw so many fat people crossing back into Northern Ireland who were skin and bones on the journey south."

We laugh, and I'm imagining people waddling up the streets of Dundalk with hungry dogs in close pursuit, sniffing the wonderful aroma of fresh bacon under their dresses.

"I remember going with Mammy once, when I was just a wee thing," Pauline says excitedly. "She bought a bolt of material and wrapped it around my stomach."

"Did the inspectors find it?" Irene asks in awe.

"No, they didn't, but Mammy declared the butter in her bag, and they took it from her. She cried all the way home on the train. In fact, most of the women in our carriage were sniffling."

"Poor Bessie, she never was any good at lying," Granny says with a faraway look in her eyes. "I've never known her to lie about anything."

The bus is reaching the city centre now, and we're more relaxed than we've been all day. We head down High Street toward the big shoe store, Granny leading the way with a sense of purpose and the three of us trailing behind in a single file.

164

When we reach the store, Granny marches toward the back where there's a display of men's and boy's shoes. Fourteen-year-old Irene has stopped to gaze at a lovely pair of ladies shoes with narrow straps and wee flowers engraved around dainty cutouts over the tops of the toes.

Granny looks at us with exasperation, because we're dawdling inside the entrance and holding up progress.

"What are you looking at, Irene?" she calls.

"Oh, I was just thinking it would be nice this year if we could have girl's shoes for a change." Irene then mutters under her breath, to no one in particular, and reluctantly makes her way to the men's section with Pauline and me following.

"These have to last you a whole year, Irene," Granny says, "and in this climate you need good, sensible shoes." Irene sits down with a look of resignation. Pauline and I know better than to wish for Cinderella shoes in a rainy climate, but our Irene is a bit of a dreamer, so she is.

When the clerk winds his way through the store to where we're sitting, Granny is very businesslike. "We need three pair of sensible shoes that will last."

"Let's see what size you need, Love," the clerk says.

He asks Pauline to stand on a long ruler that measures her foot. Then he walks over to the display and selects some plain shoes with laces and thick soles.

When he kneels down to slip the shoes on Pauline's feet, the flap of hair that was covering his bald spot shifts and falls over his left ear, exposing his naked scalp. My hand automatically starts to move to retrieve it, but Granny grabs my wrist and gives me a warning look. Pauline and Irene are glancing sideways at each other without moving their heads. They look like they're ready to break out in a fit of giggling any minute.

"These are well made shoes," the clerk says, tightening the laces. "The soles should hold up under any kind of weather."

165

He thrusts his head back, then jerks it forward again with a quick twist to the right, causing the wayward flap of hair to land on top of the bald spot, right where it belongs.

Pauline is beside herself now. She looks like she's going to choke and Irene has turned her head away and it's bobbing up and down. I think she almost broke down completely but she's fantastic at keeping it under control. Just looking at her makes me giggle and I have to put both hands over my mouth to keep from laughing out loud. Then I hold my hands between my legs to keep from wetting my knickers.

The man motions Pauline over to the wee X-ray machine and now there's an outline of the shoe with her toes inside "This way we can be sure if they're a proper fit," he's saying. "Sometimes youngsters say they fit when they really don't."

"I'm no youngster, I'm sixteen," Pauline says, her eyes looking up to heaven indignantly.

The whole process is repeated with Irene and myself, and the clerk does his head jerk, hair flap replacement in front of us as well.

I'm happy with my shoes on the whole, mostly because they have round toes, not pointy ones like most men's wing tips. But the day has taken its toll on the lot of us, and we still have to go back to Granny's to collect our school bags before we can go home.

We thank Granny profusely and tell her to pass it on to Uncle Frank. He's always been so generous, and Mammy probably appreciates not having to put out all that money every year. Shoes are frightfully expensive and most people have to save for six months or more just to buy one pair.

The next day at school Sister Assumpta calls me aside.

"Is everything all right at home, Patricia?"

"Yes, Sister," I say nervously, "nobody's sick and no one died or anything."

"Well, thank God for that," she says and I walk back to my desk.

Irene tells me at lunch that she said about the same thing. I wonder what they'd have thought if they knew that we were all pulled out of school for a shoe shopping expedition.

The next Saturday is wet. "It's coming down in buckets out there," Pauline says. "I won't be able to practice netball at the park." She turns on the wireless and dances to one of the top twenty songs.

I'm glad of the new shoes when I set out for my music lesson. Afterwards I stop and Uncle Tom and Aunt Lucy's and play board games with Anne Marie most of the afternoon. Lucy asks if I'd like to spend the night so that I can attend Vincent's school programme. I have to ring the Cafferty's to relay the message to our house. They're the only ones I know with a telephone.

Once our Pauline sent me to downtown Belfast at seven in the evening. I was to meet her girlfriend from Fortwilliam in front of the cinema, and tell her that Pauline couldn't go to the pictures like they'd planned. It would be so handy if everyone could have a telephone in their home the way business people have. I'm sure it would save lots of time and money.

This time I just have to go to a call box down the street from Anne Marie's house. I make the call, and rush back to Tom and Lucy's, splashing through puddles all the way. Lucy is holding their new baby, Thomas whose head is covered in curls that remind me of Uncle Freddy who went off to Birmingham. I wonder if we'll ever see Freddy again. He has four children already and writes to Granny once in a while. Anne Marie and Vincent are big enough to help Lucy, and they run for clean nappies whenever she needs to change the baby.

The school programme is really funny, although I don't think it's supposed to be. Some of the children trip over their costumes and upset pieces of scenery, causing howls of laughter from the audience.

When Vincent's class finally comes out on stage, they are dressed up like sailors with wee paper hats and all. The piano player begins and the children sing. I catch snatches of the song between my giggles:

> .....nice girls love the sailors
> ..... nice girls love the tar...
> something about a sailor
> you know what sailors are...
> Free and easy, bright and breezy
> ......the ladies pride and joy.
> .... something about a sailor
> Ship ahoy... sailor boy!

Vincent waves shyly when he sees us and everyone claps and cheers. On the way home, he is being bombarded with compliments and praise. Although he is shy about all the attention, I know that inside he must be thrilled to death. We all hold hands and sing the song until we reach their house.

Lucy puts on the teapot and brings out a sponge cake, sprinkled with powdered sugar, that she has made for the occasion. Anne Marie and I sleep in the same bed and talk for hours. We discuss how great Ballyhornan is and she says she heard her parents talking about renting the old boathouse for a few weeks next summer. I tell her about the new houses that are being built right across the street from our house.

Before we know it morning has come and the sun is pushing through the dark clouds. Dust particles float lazily in the wide bands of light beside the bed.

When I get home after going to Mass in Tom and Lucy's parish, Mammy is cooking potato bread. They all went to late Mass and are just now eating breakfast. Michael loves the warm flat slices of potatoes mixed with flour and rolled out thinly, then fried in hot bacon fat. At least he won't starve to death now that he's eating potato bread as well as champ.

Agnes comes looking for me and we wander through the streets of partly finished houses. The walls are composed of two rows of brick with a space in between. Daddy says that even with the double bricks, they still don't know how to build a warm house. The houses look just like ours and we wonder how many new children will be living in our neighbourhood when they're finished.

There's a night watchman who comes to work just before dark to guard the houses and materials. He sits in front of a drum that has a fire in it.

"Let's go over and talk to Mr. Shoebridge," Agnes suggests when it begins to get dark.

From a short distance you can see the warm glow of the fire shining through the holes in the sides of the drum. He sits there all night and I feel sorry for him, for the fire couldn't possibly keep out all the cold. The box he sits in looks like a privy without a front door.

He will never die from loneliness though, because someone is always going over to chat with him. Early in the evening it's the children, and later it's the men coming home from the late shift. In the wee hours of the morning, he'll have the company of the few men on the street who frequent the pubs, or so he has told us anyhow.

The stuff he burns in the drum is called coke. Unlike the coal we use in our fires at home, it burns without flames and seems to last longer and burn hotter.

"Hold your hands over that if you want to warm them up," he says, when we stop in front of him. "I have a wee girl myself by the name of Maisie, almost your age. Poor wee thing has a disease that has made all her hair fall out, even her eyelashes."

"Oh, I'm sorry," I say.

"She has to wear wigs to keep other children from making fun of her, a terrible state of affairs. Will you say a prayer for her if you're so inclined? I'd be forever grateful to ye."

"I'll mention her every night in my prayers," Agnes says sadly.

"Me, too," I say, "I promise."

We see Denis coming and call him over. Mammy is standing by our gate and waves.

"Patricia, can you keep an eye on him for a while?"

Denis runs over to join us by the watch house, he's shy and holds his head down when Mr. Shoebridge looks at him.

"I've a wee lad about your age, Denis," he says. "Are you six?"

Denis nods his head.

"Well, my wee Philip is a holy terror, so he is. He doesn't pay attention to a thing his mother or I tell him."

"Denis is very good," I say. "He only got in real trouble once. It was last year when he was only five."

"And why was that?" Mr. Shoebridge asks. "What did he do wrong?"

"Because he told a lie," I say. "He was slapped across the face, when he was completely innocent of any wrongdoing." I go on to explain to the watchman what happened last year.

I tell him how Peter Fitzgerald, from up the street, came over to see if Denis could play. He had two wee plastic boats, and Mammy gave them permission to run some water in the bath so they could float them. When I passed by I could see them leaning over, chatting away and pushing the boats around. Later while I was lying on my bed reading, I heard Daddy talking to them. His voice suddenly rose in anger, and when I looked, I could see Peter fleeing to the security of his own home.

"But I didn't do it, Daddy," Denis said in a low voice.

"Tell the truth!" Daddy yelled.

"But I am telling the truth, Daddy."

"Tell the truth!"

"But I didn't..."

"Tell the truth and I won't hit you!"

"Okay, I did it," Denis lied.

Whap across the face anyhow. Denis came running into our bedroom crying and I tried to comfort him. When he finally stopped weeping, I asked him what had happened to make Daddy so angry.

"Peter Fitzgerald scratched my name on the wall next to the bathtub and I had to take the blame," he sobbed.

"I can't even spell my name, Patricia. Peter is seven. He wrote my name, so he did, but Daddy thought I did," he said sadly.

"I thought Denis was very brave to finally tell a lie so that Daddy could be satisfied and dish out some punishment," I say, and I ruffle my brother's thick gold hair.

Mr. Shoebridge throws more coke on the fire and shakes his head. "It's a shame that your Daddy didn't believe you were telling the truth," He says as he pats Denis's arm. "I'll remember that the next time I'm angry at my wee lad."

***

It's been four months since Granny surprised us, and our new shoes have held up well through the wintry weather of rain, sleet, and slush. The new houses are finished now and four new streets have been added to our neighbourhood. The main one, Gransha Avenue, runs between the top end of Gransha Park and the Glen Road. Gransha Drive, Parade, and Crescent run off the avenue. The three streets have taken away part of the field with the swamp.

Uncle Frank is finally married, and he and his wife, Mary, have been looking at the houses in hopes of buying one. It would be nice to have them so close. Maybe they'll have children someday, cousins for Denis and Michael to play with.

I'm in the parlor practising the "Minuet in G." When I stop and have a look out the window I notice Michael sitting on the front step. He's watching some older boys in what's left of the field. They've fashioned a flag from a pole and some old blue material. They're acting like warriors, or knights, and one boy holds the flag high and walks with great strides through the weeds, while the rest follow behind.

They shout all sorts of commands, and Michael looks like he's dying to join them.

Later when I take another break I see Michael walking toward the field. The boys seem to have left their flag lying there and gone into one of the houses. He picks it up and starts to play the same game the boys were playing. He marches through the weeds holding one hand on his hip and his elbow stuck straight out by his side just like he saw them do.

"Hey, wee fella," I hear one of the boys yell, just when he's getting the knack of it, "give it back, now!" Michael runs toward our house with the flag, and the boys are close behind. I rush out to meet him.

"Michael, that doesn't belong to you. You'll have to give it back."

"But I want it, Patricia." His bottom lip starts to tremble and he looks so sad. I have to think fast. "Give it back Michael. I'll make you one of your own." Being only four, he hasn't yet learned right from wrong.

I poke through the linen closet and find an old pillowcase that has seen its last days, and check the rubbish pile in the back garden for a pole. The stick I find is a wee bit short, but with a few holes in the pillowcase and some string I have a homemade flag in no time.

Michael is tickled pink. He's already walking up the street waving it like he's King Arthur. I'm sure it will keep him occupied for the next few days. I just wonder if Denis will be wanting one too.

Down the street there's a nice young couple called McKeown who don't have any children yet, but their nieces from Dublin have come to visit. The neighbourhood children love to listen to them talk, and most of us are jealous of their real Irish brogues.

The Dubliners, Monica and Grace, have invited Irene and me to sample the fresh peas growing in their aunt's back garden, and after asking if it's all right with Mrs. McKeown, we stuff ourselves with the delicious, crunchy treats. One of the best things about this experience is breaking open the pods and seeing the plump green peas lined up so perfectly. Monica shows us how to check the pod and make sure it's puffed up and the peas inside are fully grown before we pluck them off the vine.

"I think we should eat them this way with our dinner," Irene says. "They're so much tastier, and it would save boiling water and all."

"Why don't you come up and meet our Mammy," I say, and the girls go in to tell their aunt where they'll be.

The McKeowns are one of the few families on the street who own a car. Theirs is a new car from Germany called a Beetle. It does look like a big black bug, too. The back window is so small that I wonder how they can possibly see out of it. It's said that these cars are so well made, like most German inventions, that they hardly ever break down. I suppose if you didn't have too many children they'd be great. On the whole there's hardly a family I know who could fit into one except newlyweds like them.

When we go in our back door to find Mammy, she has just finished scrubbing the linoleum floor in the living room. Denis and Michael have already taken off their shoes to participate in the Saturday routine. I ask Mammy if we can join in and after introducing the Dublin girls there are six of us skating on the floor.

"We'd better all go in the same direction," Irene suggests, after bumping into Grace. We pretend we're on a skating rink, and when the floor is gleaming we're ready to go out to play again. Just outside the back door on the kitchen window-sill, Mammy has placed a bowl of custard and one of jelly to cool and set.

"Away outa that wi you!" she shouts, when she sees greedy fingers dipping into the bowls. "Yi'll have some soon enough, when it's ready, and not before. Have a wee bun if you're that hungry." She's getting a head start on our Sunday dessert, and it's going to be difficult for us to look at it all day tomorrow, and have to wait 'til after dinner to taste it.

At the front gate we meet Mairead and Agnes Cafferty who look like they've been crying. "Our cousin, Olivia, died last evening," Agnes says sadly.

"What happened?" Irene asks.

"Her wee heart just gave out on her," Mairead says, wiping a tear from her eye. "Remember she got rheumatic fever when she was small? Well, it left her heart permanently damaged, so it did. She's always been weakly because of it."

"Poor wee thing," Irene says. I think of how pale little Olivia always was and now I know why.

"Aunt Rose would like you to come over and see her and pay your last respects, if you want to, that is." We go back inside to ask, and Mammy tells us to clean up a bit first. She's sad about Olivia, and asks about the funeral.

The Logans live up the Glen Road and Agnes tells us that Pauline is already over there helping out. Ann Logan is her best friend and they are trying to help her parents get through the pain.

At the front door we notice the usual sign of mourning, a black bow has been tied to their door knocker. Tomorrow at the funeral, all the men and boys will be wearing black armbands out of respect.

We enter the house where the blinds have been drawn, and only candles light up the parlour where Olivia is laid out. She's in a pale blue gown like the one Our Lady wears. The few men that I've seen laid out have had brown gowns like those worn by St. Francis of Assisi. Olivia looks peaceful. Her skin has a translucent white glow, and there's even a look of contentment about her, probably because her troubles are over. As we kneel and say a prayer for her I can hear the quiet murmuring of the neighbours and friends who are there for moral support.

"I'm grateful for the nine years that we had with her," her mammy is saying.

"It's good to think of the positive things at a time like this, Rose, or it would be unbearable for you," her sister, Mrs. Cafferty replies. With rosaries dangling from their hands the women are saying "Hail Marys." The last sentence of this prayer is very appropriate for this time. "Holy Mary Mother of God pray for us sinners now and at the hour of our death. Amen." We kiss Mrs. Logan on the cheek, shake Mr. Logan's hand, and leave with heavy hearts. You never know when your time will come, they say, and it's true. I only hope it's the last time I have to do this. Olivia is an angel now, but she had too few years on this earth, so she did.

Chapter Sixteen

Our boarders Niall and Gerry have completed their final year at Trench House Teacher's College. They're leaving for Derry tomorrow and will apply for positions in the Catholic school system. I'll miss them, so I will. They brought an exuberance to our household that was badly needed.

Daddy was great fun when we were small, but now that we're growing up he's not as jovial as he used to be. He's grown cynical and is a bit of a loner. If you bring up a subject with which he disagrees, he simply flies off the handle. Sitting by the fire when Daddy's there, and having a lively discussion about certain subjects can be like walking on eggshells. He has also become very dogmatic, and you dare not say a word against the church or the Bible. It's all taken very literally. I can't imagine anyone believing that Jonah sat in a whale's belly for an extended period of time, and not take it as an example rather than the naked truth.

Mammy never complains. No matter what happens, or how tired she becomes, she's very careful to keep things steady and doesn't make any waves. Married at twenty-one, she's been taking care of the house and children ever since.

I think she misses the chats across the back hedge with Mrs. MacCarrick, and now that two of her sisters have gone to America she must feel even more lonely. The poker games at Granny's have slowed down now that the families have expanded and everyone is off in a different direction. Mammy always enjoyed that, too. She and Daddy hardly ever go to the pictures any more; he says there's so much objectionable material that a Chicago gangster would be embarrassed.

I remember, once I started school, the feeling of utter panic I would feel if I came home and found that Mammy wasn't around. I'd run and find Irene, who always beat me home, and ask, "What happened, where's Mammy?" She'd just be down at the shop every time, and there was no need to worry. Irene told me that she got the exact same heart-pounding feeling of alarm as well, when she came home to an empty house. We didn't realize how much we depended on our mother emotionally as well as physically until we went to school.

Today when I come in from Agnes's house, Mammy tells me the good news that the carnival has come to Andersonstown. When I tell Agnes she's ecstatic. Tomorrow is Saturday, and we can go after our household chores are done.

It's in a field on the Falls Road just up from the dump where I had my unforgettable rat encounter. The gypsies seem to be running things, and their caravans are lined up along the edge of the field near the rides and game booths. Agnes and I discover a very good-looking boy of about fourteen, called Joe Foster. He has blue eyes and platinum blond hair and there's something fascinating about him that we can't resist.

He's trying his luck at the roll a penny game, and we just can't take our eyes off him. When we ask some children if they know where he lives, we're told his house is over in the estate across from Roger Casement Park, where Gaelic football is played.

We follow him around for a while until he notices us. Then we saunter off non-chalantly. We discuss how we can borrow some babies next week, and push their prams over that way to get another look at his gorgeous face.

While we're making the plans, we notice a gypsy woman with long dangly earrings, standing on the landing at the top of her caravan stairs. She's wearing a bright red cloth wrapped around her head, and her skin is dark and leathery.

We can't help but stare and take in her unusual clothing style. Her long skirt is a brilliant shade of yellow, and her shawl is orange.

Suddenly, she's standing with her legs spread apart and her hands on her hips, staring us down with a harsh, evil look. We realize how rude we've been and start looking for somewhere to hide. She must be thinking we are insolent youngsters without manners. Or then again, she could be putting a gypsy curse on us both.

Clearing quickly out of that area, we run over to the swing boats. You sit facing each other and each grab a long rope that is attached to the back of the boat at your partners side, then flung over their top bar, so that the ropes are criss-crossed in the middle. When you pull with all your might on the rope, the swing starts to move. When you're up in the air your partner is down, and when she's up you're down. It's completely self-propelled, so the stronger you are, the harder you can pull the rope, and the higher the boat will go. The only bad thing is the feeling you get in the pit of your stomach when you're up, but it's such a thrill that it's worth it.

Mammy told me that when I was three years of age, she put me on the hobby horses at Bundoran. When my horse came back around the carousel, she was dismayed to see me sitting backwards, holding on to the horse's tail, with a look of glee. It was the start of my love of exciting rides, and I've never lost it since.

The carnival will only be here for two weeks and three weekends, so we have to make the most of it. They'll visit a different area after this, and our lives will suddenly seem dull after such excitement.

Agnes and I spend a good part of the summer walking Michael and our next door neighbour's baby down to Joe Foster's neighbourhood. We get a glimpse of him only once, but at twelve years of age that can sometimes be enough to make everything worthwhile. Of course, we're too shy to start up a conversation with him and he doesn't even glance our way.

When the new student boarders arrive in the autumn, they turn out to be only in their second year at the college. This time there are three. Mike is a tall gangly fellow, a comic in the making. Conor is plump, red faced, and extremely self-conscious. The third one, Sean, is perfect in every way. He's tallish, good looking, and has a lovely country lilt to his voice, unlike the broad accent we have in the city. Actually, he could easily pass for that new American heart-throb, James Dean. I notice Pauline looking at him with longing when he's unaware. Now Daddy will need to have eyes in the back of his head. The boys are settling in and I notice that Irene is very uncomfortable when they sit with us by the fire at night. She's fifteen now and I see Mike throwing occasional glances her way. I think he should be looking at a girl his own age, and not someone so young.

The only problem I have with the students is with Conor. He spends ages in the lavatory.

"Do you think he's squeezing pimples in there?" Irene asks.

"Maybe he's just a slow, careful shaver," I say.

Pauline has heard our conversation and sets us straight right away. "He's taking ballroom dance lessons and goes in there to practise," she says with an air of importance.

"How do you know that, Pauline?" Irene asks.

"Well, Sean told me about the lessons, and I've heard the tapping sounds on the lino when he does the fox trot."

"But, why our lavatory? Couldn't he find a more suitable place to practise?" I ask.

"You know Conor. He's very shy, and it's nice and private in there," Pauline answers with a smile. There are ten people in our house now and one toilet doesn't seem to be enough as it is, without people using it as a ballroom. Now, when he's in there for a long time, Irene and I sneak up to the door and listen. Sure enough, Pauline was right, so she was. He's humming a Strauss waltz and we can just imagine him whirling his imaginary partner round and round under the sparkling globe in the romantic ballroom in his head.

Our student boarders are creating an interest for the older girls in the neighbourhood, but the girls don't get far, for the boys stick to their studies most of the time. It was nice when they left for their own homes at Christmas and we had the house to ourselves.

Tonight when I come up from Cafferty's and go down our pathway toward the back door, I'm stopped in my tracks. There through the kitchen window, I see Pauline and our boarder, Sean, standing in front of the sink. They're locked in a passionate kiss, and they don't see me. I tiptoe back to the front of the house, slam the metal gate shut as hard as I can and start singing at the top of my lungs while clattering my feet all the way back. When I pass the window the second time, I notice they've separated.

As I enter through the back door Pauline is diligently washing the dishes and Sean is drying them looking like sweet Mr. Innocent James Dean's double!

"Oh, hello, Patricia," Pauline says when she sees me, and she throws Sean a secretive look. I wonder what Daddy's reaction would be if he'd been the one to catch them in an embrace like that. *Thank God he's at work,* I'm thinking. The three of us girls seem to be saying that more often now, and we sigh with relief when we come home and Daddy's not there.

Pauline and Sean seem to be always taking long walks up the road now. I think they're madly in love for it's spring again, and romance seems to be in the air at this time of year.

As May has arrived, we've set up a wee altar on our bedroom dresser in honour of our Blessed Mother. Every few days Irene goes plodding through the back field to gather fresh mayflowers to decorate our shrine.

Every evening during Mary's month, crowds of people flock up the Glen Road to St.Theresa's for devotions. By the time the service starts there's usually standing room only. When we have a visiting priest it's always more interesting and enjoyable. Their amusing stories even cause laughter to break out in this otherwise devout and straight-laced congregation.

Tonight we sing my favourite hymn, "Oh, Mary, we crown thee with blossoms today, Queen of the Angels and Queen of the May." It gives me such a feeling of love for this regular lady who became the Mother of Jesus and didn't let it go to her head. We know that God would never deny his mother anything; look at the wedding feast at Cana. When they ran out of wine Mary asked her son, Jesus, to do something, and he obliged by changing the water into wine. So if we ask her to intercede to her son for us, the chances are excellent that our prayers will be answered.

Fortwilliam has its annual May procession through the school grounds, where we move very slowly and devoutly, singing in Latin. We sing verse after verse of "Salve Regina," Irene's favourite hymn.

The waves of song reverberate from the front to the back. Because the procession is so long the sound takes a while to catch up, and the girls in back are always a word or two behind those up ahead. The more we sing the more spiritual 1 feel. The music builds with emotion and reaches a crescendo before going back to a softer tone as we sing "Amen."

Sometimes the sun appears from behind a dark cloud throwing wide bands of brilliant light to the earth a short distance away. I feel like the Blessed Virgin is sure to appear before us any moment, because we are showing such piety and putting love and feeling into the words.

Maybe it's because the spring flowers are starting to bloom and the farms are dotted with new lambs, but there's just something about this time of year that warms the soul. Pauline is fortunate to have her birthday during this special month. She says it's her good fortune because she is so exceptional herself. She's kidding of course, for she's just as insecure as Irene and I are, and she has feelings of inferiority like us.

On the first day of my second year at Fortwilliam I'm happy to see Rachel again after the summer holidays. We have new teachers and find Sister Veronica to be very strict. She is far too prim and proper and hardly ever smiles. We take turns reading aloud from Charles Dickens or Emily Bronte's books, and her face reddens and her eyes blink wildly when we come to a passage where love or passion are described plainly. It's as if we shouldn't hear such things, but after all, we have to live in this world. We're not shuttered and sheltered from it all like she is.

When the bell rings, Sister Veronica leaves and Miss McSparran sweeps into the room wearing a long black cloak over her dress. It looks like the kind of clothing judges wear in the British films. She's one of the few lay teachers in the school, and geography is her forte. Wearing her sandy coloured hair in a thick plait twisted round and round on top of her head gives her a severe look. She's really very kind though, and seems to enjoy teaching.

She quickly rolls a large map of the world down over the blackboard and starts with an overview of the book.

"We'll be studying the continent of Europe this year, girls, including the physical features such as mountains, rivers and plains; the crops and livestock, and the natural resources, such as oil, coal, gas, and precious metals," she says, and smiles, seeming to hope we will have as much enthusiasm as she has. "We are interested in the type of government as well," she continues. By this time she's rubbing her eyes as if they itch. Later, while showing us the mountains on the map she balls her fist and is rubbing them even more vigourously than before. After a short time they begin to look red and painful, and I feel sorry for her. She needs to see a doctor about the problem. The more she talks the more she rubs, to a point that she even has her hand flat on her face and is poking her lower lids with her fingertips. It's getting difficult to concentrate on the lesson with all this going on, and I feel like running out of the room screaming, and I'm sure everyone else feels the same way. We're relieved when the bell finally rings and Sister Loretta comes in with her quiet, easy manner, and her unusual tolerance for fidgeters. It would be great if only we could have this lovely nun for all our subjects.

My stomach is growling and I watch the clock. Finally the bell rings and we file out quietly, then let loose once outside the building. My sandwich is made with raspberry jam. It has become very soggy and now has a deep purple hue as the jam has seeped into the bread. It looks awful, but I'm famished and eat it anyhow.

On the other side of our playground wall is a beautiful old house with a very large apple orchard behind it. The wall separating it from the school grounds is only about five feet tall. As we're eating, Rachel suggests that we take the plunge, and sneak into the grounds next door.

Mary McCartney and Phyllis Bingham want to join in the effort, and after watching the apples grow since our first year at the school, we finally decide to try our luck.

After checking for prefects who may be in the area, Rachel and I give Mary and Phyllis a heave-ho over the wall. It's crumbling in spots on the other side, so they should be able to get a good foothold on the way back.

The fruit in the orchard turn out to be crab apples, and, after throwing plenty to us, the girls are helping themselves when we all hear a low growling sound. I see a look of fear on their faces and suddenly a bulky dog, that looks an awful lot like Winston Churchill, comes into view. His drooping jowls and muscular body give him a ferocious look. The girls start running with the dog in close pursuit, and they scramble back over the wall as if propelled by powerful engines.

We sit down on our side of the wall while Mary and Phyllis regain their composure. Their startled looks gradually change to smiles, and then we laugh so hard we spill all the apples. They are quickly retrieved, just seconds before a prefect walks by and gives us a look of disdain. She probably wishes giggling could be a punishable offense.

"Now I know how the Germans felt," Phyllis says.

"Whaddiye mean?" Rachel asks.

"Well, once they saw Churchill coming after them, they must have been petrified. That dog looked just like him, and we were turned to jelly at the sight."

We laugh and start to eat the apples as fast as we can before the bell rings. As we're indulging ourselves, I'm thinking this is a good venial sin for my Saturday confession. Maggie McCotter sees us eating the apples. "You pinched them from the Bishop's garden?" she says in amazement. We look at each other and bless ourselves. This could have turned out much worse.

The next day we're paying the price for our misdeeds. Our stomachs are aching and swollen, but we come to school anyhow so that our parents don't get suspicious about what we've eaten.

"I'm never doing that again," I say, when I see Mary and Phyllis at lunch time.

"You're not the only one, Patricia." Mary is holding her stomach, "I had to be excused four times already to go to the lavatory."

"I only had to go three times so far," I say, and we laugh as we look over the wall at the orchard that has lost its magnetic charm in a single day.

As I get off the bus to go home my stomach is still hurting. I'm not sure if it was only the crab apples or a combination with that raspberry sandwich causing the pain, but I don't think I can ever eat another jam sandwich like that as long as I live.

Going in the back door, I see Daddy balancing one of the glass, kitchen cupboard doors on his knee. He's washing them for Mammy. Just then Pauline comes in from the other room looking concerned.

"Daddy, could you put that window down a wee minute, I've got something important to tell you." He sets the window down and Pauline doesn't waste any time. "Your easy chair's on fire, Daddy!" She rushes into the living room with Daddy close behind, and a minute later he's running back through the kitchen holding the chair out from his body.

"Make way, make way," he shouts. "Patricia, the back door, quickly!"

I do what he says, and he's soon running the hose over a smoldering spot on the side of the chair. When Mammy comes up from the shop with Michael she can't understand why it's sitting outside.

"Good Heavens...What on earth...?"

"The wee electric heater came on, Mammy, and it was too close to the chair, so it was." Pauline says, looking like she's about to cry.

"We're lucky the house didn't burn down," Daddy says. "It's well the blackened side is by the wall and can't be seen. When it dries off I'll carry it in, but we're going to have to keep the heater away from the furniture after this, since it's automatic and can come on at any time." He shakes his head. "Sometimes I think these new-fangled gadgets are more trouble than they're worth."

Suddenly my sore stomach doesn't seem so important. I have this profound feeling that even though we've had a few close calls so far, God seems to be taking especially good care of our family.

Chapter Seventeen

Pauline was lucky to get a civil service job. She said her Protestant-sounding name helped. I think her brown eyes helped too. They just asked to see the results of her A Levels, which is an exam that the government gives to all students during their final year of secondary school. Her exam scores were excellent, so they didn't check anything else. Her job is with the Ministry of Finance, and she says a lot of the work is related to agricultural products.

She gives her earnings to Mammy and gets back enough for bus fares, incidentals, and clothes now and then. She went downtown and bought herself a T-shirt for summer. It's sleeveless, and is that new colour we hadn't seen until Mari sent us the paper dolls. It's called turquoise, and looks very attractive with her dark hair. This is the first piece of outer clothing she's ever owned that Mammy didn't make, and she's already eighteen, five years older than me.

She's still dating Sean, and he's always giving her expensive presents. The last one was a beautiful makeup kit. Yesterday I met them coming down the Glen Road from one of their long walks. Michael was with them, and he held out a little yellow dump truck for me to see. He said Sean bought it for him.

Our Michael is showered with so much love, being the youngest. When Aunt Marjorie is over she goes upstairs and lies on the bed with him while he has his naps. Too bad she never got married and had children of her own.

Denis is eight and hates school. In fact, he gets stomach-aches just thinking about it. I thought it was hard for girls being whacked with the cane, but when I ask Denis why he's so afraid of school, he says, "Mr. Mackey lines us up against the wall to ask us our times tables. If we hesitate for just one second, he pokes us in the chest or stomach with his stick, and it really hurts. I'm always so nervous of getting one wrong, that I can't help but hesitate, so I get the stick in the stomach every day."

Last week he was caught skipping school and hiding out in the back field all day. He was just too scared to go because of his nine times tables. Poor wee man. I feel so bad for him. Thank God summer holidays are almost here. Maybe he'll have a nicer teacher next year.

Michael is only four, and doesn't know what's ahead of him when he goes to school. At the moment he's enjoying his friends who live in the new streets.

We hear news from California that Aunt Eileen is married. Her new husband's name is Jim Doolin, and he's Irish-American. They had a small wedding with Mari and Al as witnesses. Eileen's best friend Rosaleen and her husband, Barney, who is also an Irish-American, were there as well.

Uncle Frank and Aunt Mary have moved into one of the new houses near us, and are expecting their first baby.

On my first day of school holidays I'm having a nice sleep-in. I'm awakened suddenly by Uncle Frank's voice downstairs. He talks to Mammy for a short time then leaves. I go down and ask Mammy what he was doing here so early.

"Mary's been ordered by the doctor to complete bed rest for the rest of her pregnancy," she says. "Otherwise she's in danger of losing the baby." She wipes her hands on her apron and brushes some strands of her thick brown hair out of her eyes.

"Who will cook her meals?" I ask. "Frank has to work, doesn't he?"

"He's taking the rest of the day off, but needs someone to stay with Mary every day after this. Pauline and Irene are working, so that leaves you, Patricia. I've got Denis and Michael and this house to take care of."

"What will I have to do, Mammy?" I ask.

"Frank can give Mary her breakfast before he leaves in the morning, so all you need do is give her lunch and cook the dinner for the two of them. Anything that she'll need during the day you can get for her, and you can tidy up and wash the dishes as well."

"That's all right, Mammy. It's the least I can do. Uncle Frank paid for our new shoes every year for so long. I just hope my cooking is good enough."

"Don't worry, Patricia, you know how to boil potatoes and throw a bit of meat on the pan. You'll do fine. It'll be good for you. Frank wants you to go down today and get acquainted with the electric cooker. It's a lot different from the gas we use, and he'll show you where everything is as well."

I'll do my best for them, and pray that everything turns out all right. I know our Frank would make a great daddy, he's so generous and kind to us who are only nieces and nephews.

The cooker takes a bit of getting used to. It's slow to warm up and when you turn it off it stays hot for a long time. Mary must be tired of lying in bed all day, but it has to be done for the baby's sake. She's being very cheerful, although deep down inside I know she must be worried sick.

It's been five weeks since I began helping, and I feel very comfortable in Frank and Mary's kitchen. I'm sure she's having too many cups of tea, because I enjoy doing that. She has such a pretty delft teapot with a fancy tea cozy to keep it warm.

I'm in bed now, in our house on Saturday morning, watching the rising sun throw splashes of light on the mountain, and I hear Uncle Frank's voice downstairs. When I step into the kitchen he has his head down on the table and Mammy is gently rubbing his back.

"I'm so sorry you had to lose your first baby, Frank," Mammy is saying in a soothing voice. "Please God the next time will be successful."

"It's much worse for Mary," he says. "She tried so hard despite the odds. She wanted this little boy so badly." He stands up to go.

"You'd better get some sleep, Frank," Mammy says. "You look exhausted."

"Hello, Patricia," Frank says, when he sees me standing there in tears. "Would you like to come to the hospital tonight and visit Mary with me?"

"I'd be happy to, Frank, and I'm sorry for your trouble. It's just not fair!" I say.

"It was God's will, Patricia," Mammy says. "They have their own little angel now."

I climb up the stairs and get back into bed. I wonder why this could have happened, when that wee baby was fine up until now. It doesn't make sense. I can imagine how awful Mary must feel. She'll surely be sad for a long time to come.

When Frank picks me up, we stop at the greengrocers near the Royal Victoria Hospital to buy a bunch of red grapes for Mary.

"You can try a few, if you like," he says as I hold them.

"They're sweet and juicy," I say. I had no idea they'd be so good."

When we walk down the hospital corridor, I can see women, three or four to a room, with their new babies in baskets next to the beds. Mary is in a room by herself. I'm glad they didn't put her next to a nursing mother, or it would have been unbearable.

She's trying to be cheerful, but a sadness fills the room. "We'll have to try again," she says. "You can't always know why bad things happen."

Frank bends over and kisses her, and she wraps her arms around him and weeps. I go out and take a walk down the hallway.

Later, after Frank drops me off, Mammy tells me about her own stillborn child.

"It was a girl between Denis and Michael. We named her Dorothy."

I'm shocked and saddened that Mammy lost a baby, and we lost a sister. If she'd only survived, things would be so different, she'd be around six years of age now.

It's well Mammy had four other children at the time, or it would have been worse for her. Mary has nothing to keep her mind off her loss.

A few weeks later, Irene, who has kept her wee altar going weeks beyond Mary's month of May, asks Michael, Denis and me if we'd like to go up the mountain loney with her to gather the tall daisies that grow in the farmer's fields.

"They'd look very graceful on the altar," Irene says. "Besides we need a change from the mayflowers."

Michael seems upset when we go into a field that is occupied by a bull. We're at the opposite side though, and stay close to the fence. The tall weeds give us lots of cover. As we walk toward the daisy patch Michael starts to sob. Irene asks him what's the matter.

"Denis told me last week that a bull will charge at anybody wearing red, and I have my red cardigan on."

"Don't worry Michael, I think that's just an old saying," Irene replies, looking warily toward the grazing bull. "Just stay quiet, and there'll be no reason for him to charge us." She's trying to make Michael feel better, but I've begun to get a wee bit nervous myself, and sure enough, before we can gather the flowers we came for, the bull looks toward us and begins to move steadily in our direction.

We only sustain a few scratches while scrambling back through the barbed-wire fence, but I think we learned a lesson today; Denis was right. Bulls are indeed attracted to the colour red. Poor wee Michael was just terrified, and said he will never again go into any farmer's field as long as he lives.

Michael's nerves seem to be shattered by this afternoon's fiasco, and we're still trying to appease him. Mammy and Daddy are off to see "Ben Hur" at the Broadway, and we three sisters have promised Michael and Denis some homemade potato crisps. You'd think they were made of gold, they cost so much and we could never afford to buy them.

"You're pulling our legs," Michael says, "you don't really know how to make them."

"Just you wait," Irene says with a sly grin.

Pauline drops lard in the big pot and turns on the heat.

"Michael, you'll have to help peel the potatoes if you want to have any," she warns. When the spuds are peeled, Irene and I cut them so thin, that they're almost transparent.

"What's keeping the fat?" Michael asks impatiently.

"We have to wait until it's hot enough," Pauline says. "Just hold your horses."

Denis pulls Michael back from the stove for fear of an accident. After the blue smoke finally rises, Pauline slides the potato slices off the plate into the hot fat, and they sizzle and spatter for a moment before slowing to a steady bubble.

Michael is thrilled a short time later when Pauline extracts the thin, brown crisps. I don't think he believed we actually knew how to make them. Denis remembers us doing it once before. We all enjoy it when Pauline makes toady in the evening. She mixes onions with left over mashed potatoes then fries the patties in the pan. I know she'd just die if she didn't get her potatoes every day. But Michael is more impressed with the crisps, and he and Denis dig in like it's their last meal.

Today Agnes and I have been sent to McErlean's for three Woodbine cigarettes for Mammy. She's short of cash and can't afford a whole pack until Daddy's payday. Just outside the shop we notice our Irene, and Agnes's sister, Mairead, leaning against the low wall by the telephone box, and Mairead is laughing her head off.

"What's so funny?" I ask.

Irene looks warily at Mairead, who leans over and whispers in my ear. "We were just talking about what a dirty old man Mr. Conway is."

She points across to the Conway house and covers her mouth with her hand.

"Why do you say that?" I ask.

Mairead speaks out of the side of her mouth. "It's because they have twelve children. That means he's done it at least a dozen times."

"Done what?" I ask.

"Oh, Patricia. Haven't you ever seen two dogs doing it?" Mairead says, looking smug. "Or do you always cover your eyes and walk the other way?"

I feel my face flush, knowing she got it exactly right, and she starts laughing. My heart is racing and I feel just awful. Now I know for sure I'll never get married. It all seems so disgusting. How could God have possibly thought up this terrible method of filling the earth?

Mairead stands thinking for a while, then smirks and says, "Do you know how you can tell how long a man's mickey is?"

"I don't know," her sister Agnes says sharply. "Since you're such an expert on the subject, why don't you give us the answer."

"By his shoe size, dummy!" Mairead says. She starts to cackle like a hen in a barnyard being invaded by a fox.

"Why don't you just shut your gob, Mairead!" Agnes says with disgust, and she marches into McErlean's with her nose in the air.

Irene has started to look uncomfortable now. I don't think she had imagined the original conversation could take this kind of turn. She's looking around to see if anyone else has heard us. I follow Agnes into the shop. We buy the Woodbines, and when we leave, Mairead and Irene are standing outside. "Sorry, Patricia, I wasn't thinking, I forgot you were so naive," Mairead says. "Let's talk about something else."

She points to the field just up the Glen Road between St. Meryl Park and Fruithill Park.

"Do you remember the time they found a wee dead baby in that field, years ago?"

I shake my head and Irene says, "I do! I was coming home from St.Theresa's school and the peelers were all over the place. They had the area blocked off. Even that constable, Tig McFeeney, who tries to keep us Catholics under his control, was in on the action. I think he hoped to solve the case, and make a big impression on the rest of the Royal Ulster Constabulary. I heard later that they assumed it was a gypsy baby because it was wrapped in a bright yellow cloth, and the caravans had moved out of there just days before."

"I'm glad I didn't find the baby," Agnes says. "I would have died."

"Do you remember the Aeroplane crash near the airport? It was so close to the runway too, all ready to land. The woman who lived in that house was killed." Mairead points to the big house down the road.

"Her wee boy is lucky to be alive, but it must have been terrible for him to lose his mother like that. Now there's just his Dad and himself."

"He was thrown right out of the aeroplane," Irene says. "God must have been looking out for him."

Agnes and I say goodbye to Irene and Mairead, now that we've gained so much knowledge, both shocking and sad. We climb the hill and discuss what it must be like to be born into a gypsy family.

"One good thing about being a gypsy is you wouldn't have to go to school," I say.

"Yes, but think how awful it would be to be cramped into a little caravan when it's pouring down rain," Agnes replies. "And sitting around a campfire all winter would be dreadful."

We're interrupted by our Denis who has been sent down to hurry me along.

"Mammy's waiting for her cigs," he says. I feel in my pocket to make sure they're still there. One is a wee bit bent, but it shouldn't affect the taste.

"Here, Denis, why don't you take them to Mammy, and tell her I'm stopping at Agnes's for a few minutes." He takes the Woodbines and gently places them in the top pocket of the corduroy jacket that Mammy made. It's army green, and looks so nice on him. He likes the pants she made to match because the material is so soft on his legs, unlike the heavy tweed shorts that boys usually wear.

As we go up Cafferty's path, I ask Agnes if she heard what happened to Irene last Saturday.

"What was that, Patricia?" she says with interest. "It better not be anything dirty."

"Don't worry, it's nothing like that," I say.

"Our Pauline and Irene went down to St. John's church for confession," I say. "Irene went into the box and started into the 'Bless me Father,' and her whole list of sins, when she noticed the priest's area suddenly getting brighter. You see, *he* had been listening to someone on the other side while *she* was rambling on, and he had just opened the wee door to Irene's side. He said, 'Start over again,' so Irene started to say, 'Oh, my God, I am sorry and beg pardon for my sins...'

'No, start at the very beginning,' the priest said, 'I haven't heard anything yet' She had to start again with the 'Bless me Father' her whole list of sins again, and she was embarrassed and annoyed. When she came out she asked Pauline why she hadn't told her there were two sides to the confessionals, and not one, like those at St. Theresa's. Pauline just laughed and asked her if she had eyes in her head."

By this time we're up in Agnes's room sitting on her unmade bed, something that wouldn't be permitted in our house. We have to make our beds as soon as we get out of them.

"Do you want to hear about Pauline's experience down at Clonard church near my Granny's?" I ask. She smiles and nods so I continue. "Pauline went down there because all the

194

priests up here know her voice, just like they know yours. The priest asked if she was courting. She told him she was. You know our student, Sean. They go to the pictures now and then. Anyhow, the priest kept asking her questions and yelling at her. Finally she was so distraught that she fainted and fell out of the box onto the marble floor outside. A few people stayed to help her up, but most of them fled to the queue in front of the confessional on the other side of the church. I suppose the long wait across the way was worth it to avoid that awful Father Quigley.

Well, the following week she went to the other priest and told him about her experience and he said, 'I heard about it. Don't you worry yourself. Father Quigley yells at everyone.'"

"Well, it's nice to know in advance," says Agnes. "I must remember about that if I'm ever telling my sins in Clonard. Do you think we'll have to confess about listening to our Mairead and your Irene going on about S-E-X?" She spells out the word as if there were a wee child present.

"I think we will," I say. "We're supposed to avoid the occasion of sin, and I think that would qualify."

"Shoot!" Agnes says, "I'll have to go to St. John's next time, so I'm glad you told me about the confessional boxes on both sides of the priest. I'd hate to have to repeat everything like your Irene did. I'd most likely leave something out on the second go-around."

We go downstairs just as Denis comes to the door and says, "You're wanted for your tea, Patricia, right away."

After tea I'm ironing my white blouses. It's almost time to return to school. The six week holiday goes by so fast. Several pair of my lisle stockings have ladders, so I'll use this rainy night to darn them as well.

Pauline's at the pictures with one of her school friends, and our parents have gone down to Granny's for a rare poker game, so Irene and I are minding the boys.

"I beat you two times in a row, Irene," Denis says with a grin. Irene gives me a wink. She knows the routine. Let him win at draughts, and he won't get into any tussles with

195

Michael who loves to wrestle at every opportunity. Irene has set up Daddy's chess board and lets Michael play by himself. He likes the kings and also enjoys putting all the horses in a row.

Irene wants to sing and play a duet with me on the piano to entertain the boys:

Oh I can wash my Daddy's shirt
Oh I can wash it clean.
Oh I can wash my Daddy's shirt
And hang it on the screen.

The boys end up banging on the piano and causing an awful din, so we try to get them interested in colouring. Just this afternoon the *Beano* and *Dandy* were shoved through the letterbox, and Denis has been in his element ever since. These comics are his favourite thing so today Irene and I don't fight over them. We let Denis read them first, besides the *Girls' Crystal* is more our style, and that arrives next week. Once Denis and Michael are in bed the *Beano* and *Dandy* will be all ours.

196

Chapter Eighteen

"They're looking awfully happy this evening," Irene whispers when our parents return from the poker game. It's only nine o'clock and still daylight.

"Maybe they won the pot," I say.

"I suppose we'll know soon enough," Pauline says, while tidying up the comics and newspapers. She's become extremely domesticated lately. It must be her age. You'll be just after setting something down a minute, and before you know it, she's picking it up and putting it in it's rightful place. You can't even finish a cup of tea when she's around.

Daddy says, "Good night," and goes up to bed. He has to work tomorrow.

"Run upstairs, Patricia, and get Denis and Michael," Mammy says.

She brings a cup of tea into the living room and she's beaming from ear to ear. We watch her take a sip and wonder when she's going to come out with it. I'm sure she must have won big this evening.

"How would you like to go and live in America?" she says finally.

"Get on with ye,' Mammy! You're codding us, aren't you?" Irene says, and her eyes dart from Mammy to Pauline to me.

"How could we afford it, Mammy?" I ask, my fingers crossed behind my back.

"Your Granny suggested that we sell this house and move in with her for a year," she answers. "Daddy will go first in a couple of months and send for us when he has enough saved for our fares."

"I can't go, Mammy. I just can't!" Pauline says. She's raging at being put in this predicament.

"Ach, why not, Pauline?" Mammy asks. "We can't leave you here. Daddy would never agree to it." She looks alarmed and tries to pacify our distressed sister.

"I can't leave Sean, and anyhow, I'm eighteen. By the time you go I'll be nineteen!"

"Why not come with us, Pauline," Mammy says, "and if you're not happy you can return later?" She goes to the kitchen to pour herself another cup of tea. While Mammy's gone, Pauline plops herself in Daddy's easy chair, throws her head back, and closes her eyes.

I go to the kitchen and ask if I can have some tea as well. Mammy reaches for another cup.

When we're back in the living room sipping our tea, I say "I want to go, Mammy. I'd really love to." Irene paces the floor.

"Will we be going to California?" she asks.

Mammy smiles and nods. "We will indeed, Irene. Mari has offered to sponsor Daddy and put him up for a year. She'll help him find a job, a house, furniture, everything. We'll have to start over from scratch. We'll probably be able to bring only one big trunk with our clothes, pictures, and a few keepsakes."

"You mean we won't be able to bring the parlor lamp with the tassels?" I moan. Mammy stares into the fire. She's probably thinking of all the other things we'll have to leave behind as well.

"I still would like to go, so I would," I say.

Irene starts to mention some of the good things about living in America. "There's great opportunity there, and the weather's warm. They don't care what religion you are, but I think I would really miss this place and my friends, if we were to go."

"I still don't want to go!" Pauline complains. "Why are you making me?" She walks upstairs like she's dragging a heavy weight behind her. "Good night everyone."

Our student, Sean, with whom she's in love, is already in bed in the student's room. He's going to a Gaelic football match in Dublin tomorrow and needs to be up at the crack-of-dawn to catch the train.

Mammy looks sad about Pauline's dilemma, but Irene and I sound a bit more enthusiastic, so she continues to explain.

"Mari said there's a place near Torrance called Artesia. It's miles and miles of dairy farms. She thinks Daddy could easily get a job there milking the cows. If the American Embassy agrees to let our family immigrate into their country, he'll go up the hill to the farms on the upper Springfield Road, next week. Maybe they can teach him how to milk the cows, and that way he'll have some experience."

I just can't see my daddy working on a farm. He was born and raised in the city, and now they're trying to make a farmer out of him. Driving a bus would be more his style, but then I heard they drive on the other side of the road over there. This could get very complicated with one thing and another.

"How will we get there, Mammy?" Denis asks. Michael sits waiting for the answer with interest.

"By ocean liner, Denis. A very big one with a dining hall and everything." Michael smiles and gazes out the window. He's probably thinking of the adventure ahead of him. Denis doesn't look as happy as I thought he'd be.

"Granny's going to miss us, isn't she?" Irene says.

"Aye, she will indeed," Mammy replies. "Actually, she was the one who originally discussed going over to help Aunt Eileen out."

"What's the matter with Eileen?" I ask.

"Her husband's a drinker, and he's mistreating her, so he is," Mammy says sadly. "He has her scared out of her wits."

"Oh no," Irene says. "Eileen's awful nervous as it is, without having to live with someone like that."

Mammy pokes the fire, and new flames leap up, then die in the pink ash that turns gray and then white as the coals begin to cool.

Pauline is asleep when we go up to bed, so Irene and I can't discuss how this great move will change our lives forever. There's so much depending on what the American Embassy says, whether we can sell this house, and if Daddy can find a job in America. Maybe we should just take one thing at a time and not get our heads all muddled with unnecessary information.

I'm lying in bed thinking of Aunt Eileen being mistreated. Irene's right, Eileen was always a bundle of nerves, and now she must be very unhappy altogether.

In the morning when we get up, Daddy has already gone to work. Sean left at seven for Dublin, and Pauline says she didn't get up in time to tell him her bad news.

At breakfast, Mammy tells the other students, Mike and Conor, that they'll probably have to be looking for new digs next year, as we'll most likely be living at Granny's and then going to America. They're very surprised and look at Pauline sadly. They know she's in love with Sean. She and her friend Ann had their first dates with Mike and Sean less than a year ago. They went to see the film *Three Coins in the Fountain*. She said she'll always remember her first date. Now we're wondering how our Pauline is going to leave Sean.

"I'll have to take things as they come," Pauline says. "It's a long way down the road. Anything can happen. I'm just not going to bother my head about it right now."

Irene is in her last year at Fortwilliam, and will be looking for a job soon, so she shouldn't mind moving. Once she's working, there won't be so much time for hanging around with friends anyhow.

Denis, who is eight, is not too thrilled at the prospect of starting all over again in a strange country. The only good thing he learns is that the teachers are not half as cruel over there.

Michael is four, and the thought of sailing across the ocean on a big ship like has him all excited. He's never met his Aunt Mari, as she left before he was born. Now she has two wee boys of her own, new cousins for Michael to play with.

Our house is buzzing and we have a hard time concentrating on getting ready for Mass. So many questions are tumbling out of us. Once we're in Mass, I glance at Irene and Denis now and again and notice they are distracted like me. I feel like jumping up and shouting. "We're going to America! We're going to America!" It's almost impossible to keep my mind on the the priest's sermon.

On the way home from Mass, we meet Mairead and Agnes. They aren't happy with our news, and say they wish they could emigrate as well.

After school on Monday, our parents have good news. They visited the American Embassy and have a pile of forms to fill out. Daddy must go for a complete physical, probably the first in his life. He'll need vaccinations, and they'll check for any criminal record. There shouldn't be a problem on any of those accounts. Daddy hasn't missed a day of work in his life, never visited a doctor, and wouldn't do anything criminal in nature.

The rest of us will be required to do the same, only they said we should wait until our departure time is closer.

When I tell Rachel about us moving to Granny's for a year, she's all excited. "You'll be just up the street, Pat. We can hang around together after school and on the weekends. We may move ourselves, in a few years," Rachel says. "My parents have been contemplating a move to Manchester, England, where we have relations. My Daddy could get a much better job there," she goes on. "With our big family, we're having a hard time making ends meet."

"I think we are too," I say. "and, England for you, wouldn't be much different than living here, as they have the same flag."

"Yes, but in England we wouldn't have to contend with the Orange parades and all that nonsense," she says.

"It'll be the same in California," Rachel. "We can say goodbye at long last to those bloody Orangemen, their tin whistles, and their 'Kick the Pope' songs."

Chapter Nineteen

Irene has herself a job in a Catholic solicitor's office doing typing and shorthand. She seems happy enough. Our house is in the process of being sold, and Mammy has contacted an auction company about taking all the furniture. I hate to see the piano go, but Granny already has one and won't be needing another. As soon as the sale is finalised, the company will come for the furniture, and we'll move to Granny's.

We've been in this house only three years, but we'll miss the countryside and the freedom to wander the fields and mountain loneys. Irene will miss Mairead and I'll miss Agnes, but life is full of changes and we may make new friends in the Clonard area before leaving the country altogether.

On the day we move, to Granny's, Denis is upset. He doesn't want to leave his best friend, Peter Fitzgerald. Denis and Michael are great friends though, and at least they'll still have each other.

Daddy has passed all the requirements, and he's leaving soon. He pays a visit to his parents to say goodbye, and plays a last game of chess with his friend John.

On the morning of Daddy's departure, Denis and I go to school as usual, and Pauline and Irene go to work. Daddy insists that no one should even think of taking a day off. Mammy is sad. I think she draws a lot of strength from Daddy and she'll miss him. A year is a long time to be separated. We say our goodbyes as we leave for work and school in the morning.

"Now take good care of your Mammy for me, and behave yourselves," he says. "I'll write often." Mammy starts to weep when she sees us crying. We run out the door after saying our goodbyes until we meet again in sunny California.

At the bus stop, Rachel notices my swollen eyes, and I explain.

"He's really gone?" she asks. "That means it's getting closer to your going." I don't want to think of that.

"Since we have money from the house, he's going by aeroplane." I tell her. "One of the O'Hare boys has offered to drive him to the airport." I glance at the sky, trying to imagine what it must be like to be up there above it all, looking down at the wee dots on the ground, that are really people with complicated lives, some of them happy, others in pain.

Denis still goes to St.Theresa's school and has to take the bus now because the Springfield Road is quite a distance from the school. He says he won't miss Daddy yelling at him all the time. I think it's sad. Denis is such a good child and he really didn't deserve to be constantly put down like he was.

Now I'll go right by Rachel's house on the way to school in the morning, and we'll walk together to the bus stop near St. Paul's.

"You can come to the pictures with us every Sunday evening," she says looking tickled. "I usually go with Joanne who lives a few doors down."

"What kind of pictures are you talking about and where are they shown?"

"Right here, in St. Paul's church hall." she says. "It's mostly always cowboys and Indians, but once in a while we see an English thriller."

"I'm looking forward to it, so I am," I say.

***

203

I'm having mixed feelings lately. I've been thinking about all the things I'm going to miss when we leave and it makes me sad."

We have no idea what lies ahead in a new land. What are the people going to be like? Irene and I have already discussed the possibilities.

"I just know I'm going to feel inferior to the Americans," Irene says.

"Me too, they seem so knowledgeable and sure of themselves, the ones in the films anyhow. It all seems a bit scary now, doesn't it Irene? I wonder what the schools will be like over there."

"Well, at least that's not one of my concerns," Irene says. "I have to worry about what it'll be like in an office."

Pauline, Irene and I are sleeping in the attic room right above Granny's bedroom. It's the same size as Granny's but has a sloped ceiling. The stairs creak on this floor and the bannister moves slightly when you hold on to it. I feel like it's going to collapse under me, causing a three storey fall. I've had a few dreams already about this house and its squeaky stairs, where the whole business collapses and I'm falling down... down... and I'm relieved to wake up in a cozy bed.

In the older houses in Belfast the kitchen is called the scullery, and the living room is called the kitchen. In Granny's kitchen there's an unusual pulley system. The contraption is made of four long wooden slats joined together, like the seat of a long park bench. You hang your washed clothes on the slats when it's lowered. Then you pull on the rope and raise the whole kit-and-caboodle up toward the high ceiling. Mammy says the heat from the fire rises, so the clothes have a better chance of drying when they're higher up. This way they're out of sight as well.

When someone comes to visit, I'm usually hoping they don't look up and see Granny's oversized knickers and brassieres hanging there. This worry usually takes all the pleasure out of their visit for me. People like Lucy or Frank's wife, Mary, are not a problem, but occasionally one of the

O'Hare boys, who are in their twenties and thirties, will stop by. In this case I try moving the undies by telepathy to the back of the rack, behind the dresses where they won't be seen.

This evening, when I'm coming back from Rachel's house I'm surprised to see a large crowd of children in front of Granny's house. Getting closer, I observe the cause of all the excitement. Parked next to the kerb is a long, sleek, American car.

"It's a new '55 Cadillac," says a boy I've never seen before. He has an air of importance about him "I saw one of these in an American film last week. Look at the length of that thing, and the colour. Did you ever see anything like it?"

"Where did it come from?" I ask.

"It only just arrived here a few minutes ago. Driven by a classy woman," he says.

I'm wondering where the owner is, and find out as soon as I reach Granny's kitchen. There sits a short, stout woman with dark curls and makeup the likes of which you'd only see on a film star. She's wearing a beautiful blue suit made of a shiny material. On her wrists are gold bracelets and a very big diamond shines from a gold ring on her finger.

"This is my late brother's wife, Maisie," Granny says. "She lives in America, in Montana. They emigrated ages ago." This is the first time Granny has mentioned this brother. The lady looks over, smiles at me, and keeps on talking in a rapid fashion. One thing I notice about her is the way she talks. "I this" and "I that." She sips her tea and goes on talking without stopping for air. "I this and I that." Never asking after any of Granny's clan, or how life is treating them, and not giving anyone else a chance to get a word in edgeways.

I wander into the parlour because there isn't any place to sit in the kitchen. I wonder if anyone else notices Maisie's unusual speech pattern. When Irene comes into the parlour, she whispers that she noticed the same thing.

"I was hoping she would tell us about Montana; the scenery, the cities, the weather. But she seems to have a one track mind, doesn't she?" I ask. Irene nods.

"I hope all Americans are not this talkative, it almost makes me dizzy," Irene says. "I told Mairead I'd be at her house at seven o'clock, so I'd better be going. See you later, Patricia." The woman is still talking a mile a minute. I feel that the long, shiny car outside is an attempt to show us lower classes how important and successful she has become. A vehicle of this proportion is a complete oddity to the people of this city, and she's certainly receiving lots of attention. Even the steering wheel is on the opposite side of the car from the ones here.

When she's walking out the door at the end of her visit, she hands me two pounds. I'm flabbergasted. Two pounds! That's what Irene earned working for a week at the Belmont Photo Works. I try to give it back to Maisie, but she won't have it.

"Not at all, love. Buy yourself some candy and ice cream." Now I feel guilty for having negative feelings about this Irish-American lady.

She has to shoo away the crowd that's grown considerably around this beauty of a car. It'll be the talk of the town all over Ireland, and wherever else she may travel.

After she's gone, Granny, Marjorie and Mammy have a lot to talk about.

"It must have cost a small fortune to transport that vehicle all the way across the Atlantic," Granny says.

Mammy nods in agreement "It seems a wee bit pretentious. The country roads here would hardly accommodate the size of it, if she plans to do any sightseeing."

"I suppose she must have shocked her own people as well," Marjorie adds, "Driving that grand car through her old district."

When Irene returns from the Cafferty's later in the evening, she sees the money I was given and wishes she'd stayed at home.

"You can save it and get some nice underwear to wear to America," Mammy suggests.

"Ach, Bessie," Granny says. "It'll burn a hole in her pocket long before that."

Mammy smiles and releases the pulley to drop the clothes down from the drying rack.

***

There's a wee shop called Frank Stewart's right behind Granny's house. It's the first building on Oranmore Street, so to run a message for groceries, all we need do is step across the entry outside Granny's back gate, and we're there. Denis and Michael like to go in and get penny sweets, and it's very handy when Mammy needs cigarettes. She said when she was a child she used to buy sweets at Stewart's for a farthing, which is only a quarter of a penny.

Our Michael is very close to the Stewarts' wee boy, Paddy, who lives above the shop with his parents. The boys spend a lot of time peeking through the window of the pub. I'd be too embarrassed to do that. What if someone saw me? But they have no fear of such things, and seem to get a lot of pleasure out of watching the men inside spin yarns and tip the bottle. They also like to take turns on Michael's wee pedal car that was passed on from one of Granny's friends.

Denis comes in while we're cleaning house this afternoon. He seems nervous, and says he was looking up the entry and could see Paddy and our Michael driving the pedal car away down at the other end, over near Clonard Church. They disappeared around the corner and he kept waiting for them to come back, but they never did.

"How long ago was this?" Mammy inquires.

"Around twenty minutes ago, Mammy," Denis replies.

"Patricia, go with Denis and see if you can find them. They're probably on their way back right now."

Denis and I walk up the entry behind the houses on Oranmore Street and down another one. We get farther and farther from Granny's house, and as we round the bend in one entry we see the two of them away off in the distance, minus the toy car. When we reach them they're both crying and Michael has a skinned knee.

"What on earth, Michael?" His tears make two clean channels down his dirty red cheeks.

"They hit us and chased us...called us Micks, and took the car."

"Why did you let them?" I ask, getting mad at the injustice.

"They were big boys, older than our Denis. We were scared. They threw stones at us as well."

"Poor wee fellas," I say. "I'm sorry about the car, Michael."

"We can go and get it back, Patricia," Denis says starting to run down the entry.

"No, Denis," I shout, "it's a Proddy area, and they don't want the likes of us over there. They'd probably come out in full force."

I turn back sadly toward Michael and help him to walk home on his hurt leg. I doubt if we'll ever see that wee car again. When we get home, Mammy rages at the cheek of those big boys taking the car.

"It's just not fair, Mammy," I say, my fists clenched. "Michael and Paddy had such adventures while driving it." I think they are more devastated by the loss of the toy than being chased and called Micks. They promise never to go near that neighbourhood again, and I don't think we'll have to worry about them breaking their pledge.

Hughes's Bakery is just a few hundred yards down the Springfield Road. The aroma of fresh-baked bread and pastries keep wafting up toward Granny's, making our mouths water. They have vans that load up early in the morning after the men work all night, baking. Sometimes we are sent down to get three or four fresh baps for breakfast. They're small round loaves that are light, airy, and delicious. My favourite pastries are Paris buns that are dry and cakelike, but not too sweet. You have to eat them right away because they get stale quickly.

Next to the bakery, is a fish and chips shop, and on Friday evenings they do a roaring trade. Granny likes to send us over for dinner that night, as we can't eat meat. It's a treat we never had in our own house. The man wraps the hot chips and deep fried fish in a few sheets of newspaper, shakes salt and vinegar over them and tells us to bless the cook and enjoy the meal. Usually, by the time you get across the street to Granny's house, the grease has soaked through the paper. Plates are laid out on the table, the family is waiting patiently for the delicious meal, and never a word is spoken, except for an occasional, satisfied "umm" to prove that everyone is enjoying the food. I fear this is one of the things we'll really miss now that we've had the satisfaction of the experience.

Rachel lives on Harrogate Street, not far from the bakery. When I go down to her house in the evening, there's usually a group of boys standing around at the corner. Rachel has introduced me to all of them and they seem to be very nice.

There's one fellow whom everyone calls Horsey, although his real name is Barry. He has carrot-coloured hair and freckles, and I figure out why he got the nickname. His jaw is rather square and long, that's all. Actually, out of the whole group, I find myself attracted to him the most. Such a gentleman, he always reminds the others that ladies are present when they use certain words. He has my heart, but doesn't know it. Rachel gets upset with the others.

"Pat here, is not used to such language. She comes from the Glen Road, and she's going to America in a year, and I'm sure American boys would never use such awful words."

"You're right, Rachel," I say as we walk on down the street. "That's the first time I've ever heard those words spoken. I bet American boys are clean-cut and wouldn't talk dirty. From what I've observed in the films they all seem to be perfect."

Rachel's younger brother is very handsome but he's only about eleven, and we're thirteen and a half already. He has taken to teasing me in a playful manner, but on Saturday morning when I meet him in one of the shops, he gives me a mischievous grin and says. "Hello there, eight six."

"What are you talking about Gerry?" I ask.

"You know, Pat, eight stone, six pounds. Isn't that what you weigh?" I'm mortified and tell him I'll find a way to pay him back for his cheek. I wonder how he found out what I weigh. Just because I'm on the plump side doesn't give him the right to make fun of me.

When I see Rachel again, I complain about Gerry.

"Sorry, Pat, I let it slip, and didn't know he was listening," she says. "I'll have a talk with him, I promise."

As we're walking down the street from her house, the wee old woman who lives at the corner asks us to run over to the shop and get her snuff tin refilled.

"Her sister usually gives us toffee-apples for doing her messages," Rachel says. "She'll say, 'Here, you can chaw on that,' when we bring back her groceries, and they're delicious, so they are."

"What on earth does she do with this stuff," I ask when we pay for the powder.

"Lots of older people use it," Rachel replies. "They sniff it up their nostrils. Don't ask me why. I'd imagine it would make you sneeze." But the woman is thrilled when we bring back the tin, and she even gives us each tupence for our trouble. I had thrupence in my pocket, so we go back to the shop to see what we can get for sevenpence.

"Look at this, love. It's brand new, from England," the owner of the shop says. "It's called shampoo, makes such a great lather with no work at all. Your hair will fairly shine after using it."

It doesn't take long to convince us. We always use bars of hand soap to wash our hair and it isn't any fun. With anticipation, we buy the tiny, three-inch bottle of shampoo. Rachel will use it first, and I'll have what's left tomorrow. "I wonder if this'll really work like she says," Rachel says as we walk toward her house, "or is she pulling the wool over our eyes? I do take a dim view of people trying to take advantage."

"We'll know soon enough, so we will," I reply, as she puts the shampoo in her pocket.

Later when I mention the snuff business to Irene, she says,"Sure, Granny Owens uses it. Didn't you notice?"

"I never did see her do that, Irene. I suppose it's because I usually keep my eyes averted when we're in her company," I say.

Living in the Clonard area is a whole new experience for me, and every day is different. On Sunday evening we go to St. Paul's hall for the cowboy film. The story is quite good once you get involved in the plot, and everyone cheers when the bad men on horseback are chased down and shot by the sheriff's posse. Of course a few of the good men have to die as well in the process. The hall is always filled with shouts of glee and jeers at the bandits, and it's a very enjoyable experience altogether. A few good-looking boys even turn around and make eyes at us, to our delight and embarrassment, although they seemed to be looking at Rachel more than me. The best part of all is we don't have to stand and sing "God Save the Queen" when it's over. As we walk up the street on the way home, we don't want the weekend to end. "School tomorrow," I whine, and Rachel breaks into song. "It's almost tomorrow but what can I do, you're kisses all tell me that your love is untrue." We laugh and finish the song before we reach Rachel's door.

I leave Rachel's at about ten o'clock. It's a dark Autumn night, and as I walk home past the butcher's shop at the bottom of Dunmore Street, just a couple of hundred feet from Granny's, I hear a man's voice calling me.

"What do you want?" I ask. I see a fellow leaning against the shop window. The chickens, with their feathers still adorning them, hang by their feet in a row above his head, on the other side of the shop window.

"How would you like to have five shillings, love?" he asks. I walk over with my hand out, thinking, *if he wants to part with it, I can always use it.* "You'll have to give me a wee present in return if you want the money," he says wearing a crooked grin.

I have just begun to realise what's going on, and I turn heel and run as fast as I can, letting myself in through Granny's front door. I'm shaking as I bolt the door behind me and rush up the stairs, hating myself for being so stupid. *After that nasty fellow up the mountain loney, Patricia, you'd think you would have learned something.* I scold myself. *Such a bloomin' eejit, stupid, stupid me. What if he saw which house I went into? He knows where I live now. Maybe he'll try something again, Sacred Heart of Jesus protect me.*

I think I've grown up tonight. With that encounter comes the realisation that, even here in "Holy Ireland," there are people who are up to no good, taking advantage of children, and thinking only of their own perverted needs. From now on everyone will be suspect in my mind.

I wonder, will there be people like that in America, who are sick, demented, and a danger to children? Why does God allow such people to do their dirty work? Why doesn't He just strike them down like he did in the Bible stories? With that I slump into bed and try to change my thoughts to the fun we had at St. Paul's hall instead. It'll be something to look forward to every Sunday evening until we sail away to a brand new land.

Chapter Twenty

The winter season this year has been bitter. It causes my heels and knuckles to bleed, costing Mammy a small fortune in elasto-plasts. Those on my heels fall off after a short time because my shoes are always rubbing on them.

We have an enjoyable Christmas at Granny's, though it's strange not having Daddy here. I think Mammy misses his help with the decorations, preparing the plum pudding, and cleaning out the turkey.

We've received many letters from him in the past months, and when he finally sends a picture we're shocked. He looks downright skinny, and his cheeks are sunken. His complexion is as dark as the Indians in the cowboy films. On his knees sit Mari's two wee boys who look very pale next to Daddy. Mammy says he must be lying out soaking up the sun when he's not working.

He never got the dairy job, but works in a factory in Torrance called Standard Brands Paint Company. He drives a forklift, and hauls big pallets of paint cans from one place to another and helps to load trucks that go out to the different stores around Los Angeles. I think a driving job is more his style anyhow, even if it is indoors. He just doesn't look much like the cow-milking type. He said that when he filled out the application at Standard Brands, they didn't care about his religion, they were only interested in whether he had transportation.

The job is only a five minute drive from Mari's, but would take close to an hour to walk, so Daddy bought a car.

It's a '39 Chevrolet, and we're trying to decide how to pronounce that name. We settle on Shev-row-let, and wonder what it means, if anything.

He said it was over seventy-four degrees Fahrenheit on Christmas Day, and the house was hot from Mari cooking the turkey. I can't even imagine weather so warm at that time of year, and we're wondering how hot it could get there in the middle of summer.

This afternoon when I get home from Rachel's, Granny's house is in a bit of a uproar. Michael looks like he's been crying and Denis is trying to comfort him.

"What happened, Mammy?" I ask, and Mammy relates to me the goings on of the last few hours.

"Michael heard Granny complaining about the price of coal and saying she didn't know if she could afford the new higher prices. He and Paddy Stewart decided to take matters into their own hands. They got a sack and went down the entry ways collecting several lumps of coal from each family's coal pile." She rolls her eyes up to heaven and continues. "I caught them emptying the full sack into Granny's coal shed and told them that they had to return every piece to its rightful owner. Reluctantly they went round the back yards returning several lumps to each pile, but one wee woman caught them in the act." Mammy pokes the fire and shakes her head. "She wouldn't believe that they were *returning*, not stealing the coal. I had to go over to explain things to her, but of course she was still upset that there had been a theft in the first place. Michael said he was trying to help the family, but now he knows better than to take what doesn't belong to him."

I look at Michael and he smiles sheepishly at me. I just want to howl with laughter, but I keep a stern face. I shake my head at him. *Thank God Daddy's in California,* I think to myself and go into the parlor to practise my new Beethoven piece.

Rachel and I enjoy walking up to the Falls Park on weekends and we even venture out to Bellevue on Sunday. It seems to have shrunk since Aunt Mari brought us here when I was five. We decide to trek up the trails on the side of the hill, to get a better view of Belfast Lough and the surrounding area. By now we're out in the back-of-beyonds and discussing the different boys in Rachel's neighbourhood, when we notice a man behind us who seems to be keeping at a certain distance all the time, not overtaking like most men or boys will do.

"Take that wee path to the right, Rachel," I whisper, and when we do we are dismayed to see that the man has followed.

"All right, Pat, it could be just a coincidence. Let's take the next side path that we come to, no matter which direction." We are slightly agitated now, and sing a song to keep our minds off our dilemma. I don't really want to turn around for fear he may still be following us. My heart is thumping so hard that I imagine Rachel can hear it. When I glance over at her she has a pinched look, like she's scared as well.

"Sneak a look back, Rachel," I say. "If he's there, we'll take the next path to the left." When we do he's behind us still, so we decide we'd better start running as fast as we can back down the hill toward civilisation. It seems to take forever. When we're halfway down, Rachel turns her head slightly. I don't have to ask her if he's still there. Her face says it all.

"Quickly, quickly!" Rachel says. I've slowed down as I'm out of breath.

We make a sharp turn and start to run like we've never run before, leaving the man behind to do his evil on some other unsuspecting females. By the time we're back down the hill near the big pavilion we're exhausted. Our shoes are covered in damp mud, but we're relieved that the man is nowhere in sight.

We leave Bellevue on the first bus that comes along, making sure that the man on the hill doesn't get on as well.

"He was too old and heavy to catch up to us," Rachel says with relief as the bus winds its way back to the city. We sit, breathing hard, trying to calm ourselves, hoping to forget the awful possibilities of our foolish trek.

"Pat, after what you told me about the man up the Mountain loney, the one by the butcher's shop, and now this, I'm beginning to think we're living in a terrible place."

"You're right, Rachel, but they must be people who don't go to church. They don't seem to have any conscience."

"Let's not ever go there again, Pat. It's too dangerous."

"But, Rachel, it happened to me a few hundred feet from my Granny's front door," I say, and we sit in silence the rest of the way home. I find myself looking at men with distrust, unless I know them. It's a sad state of affairs altogether.

"What do you think of the Teddy Boy craze, Pat?" Rachel asks when we get off the bus. We've been sitting across from a couple of them most of the way home.

"I think they look ridiculous," I say. "Don't you?"

Rachel puts her hands behind her head and strokes the back of her hair, until it looks like the ducks arse the Teddy Boys are famous for.

"I think their tight blue jeans and thick soled shoes look just as bad as their duck tails," I say. "I wonder why on earth they wear such strange clothes."

"They're just looking for attention as far as I can see," Rachel says patting her hair back down. "Thank God we don't have too many here. But England is supposed to be swarming with them."

"I know. Daddy said he thought it would be just a passing craze, but the people in England are worried about them. They don't seem to show any respect for authority."

I'm glad we changed the subject to take our minds off the Bellevue incident, but now we have a new thing to worry about. What if every child growing up becomes a Teddy Boy? Who will be put in charge of running things?

The following week we're sitting in English class, and I'm looking out the window dreaming of my future. The big day of our move is getting close, and I'm a bit nervous about the whole thing.

"Patricia! Why aren't you paying attention?" Sister Veronica says. Her voice hits such a crescendo that I jump, and anyone who was dozing is now wide awake.

"You have become extremely lackadaisical in the past few months. I can't imagine what your problem is. Up until now your marks have been excellent. Maybe you can explain yourself, young lady."

"Sorry, Sister. I've been thinking a lot about America lately."

"I'm sure you'll be needing your education in America, so why don't you buckle down and keep your marks up as long as you're here."

I look at her and my face feels flushed. It's my last year at Fortwilliam, and somehow, I don't feel like putting all that much effort into my studies.

As Rachel and I walk up Cavendish Street in the pouring rain on our way home from school, she says she doesn't blame me for slacking off. "Who knows what school in America will be like. You may be ahead, or you may be behind but you won't really know until you get there. Come over after your homework, all right?"

Later, on the way to Rachel's, I meet our Irene coming up from work. The rain has stopped momentarily, and I notice that she's wearing a very attractive pair of shoes with heels.

"I was so embarrassed today, Patricia, wait'll I tell you about it," she says.

"What happened?" I ask, still admiring the lovely cream coloured pumps.

"You know how it rained all day?" she says. "Well, I've been looking at these shoes in the window for months now and I was determined to get them today. I had these big holes in the soles of my other ones, and had to stuff newspaper in to protect my stockings? Well, the shop clerk was a very good-looking young fellow, and when I took my old shoes off to try on the new ones, my feet were covered with muck from the rain going through the holes. I was absolutely mortified and thought of running out of the shop and never going back. He was real nice though and said, matter of factly, 'You're bound to get holes in your footwear in this dreadful climate.' Then he gave me a big smile that helped relieve some of the embarrassment."

"Did he ask you out?" I ask.

"Gosh, Patricia, he's probably married, with half a dozen wee'uns."

"Oh, well, you wouldn't want to meet someone right now anyhow, since we'll be leaving soon. You'd just end up being unhappy like our Pauline. I really love those shoes, though. See you later, Irene." I run across the Springfield Road toward Iris Street.

By the time I get to Rachel's, it's pouring again and we end up standing in her wee hallway between the inner and outer doors, waiting for the rain to stop. There's no way we would go into her house filled to capacity with people, and this is the only dry place. All over the city there are probably hundreds of hallways occupied with young people like us, waiting out another shower.

There isn't much to do tonight so we pool our money to buy another bottle of shampoo. We were really surprised at how much lather the last bottle gave, and our hair felt so squeaky clean after using it. It had a delicate fragrance too, almost like the sweet peas Mammy grew in our garden in Gransha Park.

Everyone at Granny's was impressed with the results of the last bottle. It's so simple and easy compared to the soap bars. They said my hair felt really soft as well as shiny. This time I get to use the shampoo first, and tomorrow I'll bring the remainder to Rachel when I go by on my way to school.

Ever since winter my psoriasis has exploded in great blobs all over my joints. It seems to affect the areas where bones are close to the surface, like my shins, elbows, and the back of my hands. Even though it's the end of May, the itch is as bad as it was in winter, and Mammy decides I need to see a special skin doctor.

"We've been doing a bit of experimentation," the dermatologist says, when we're sitting in his office. "I'd like you to be a test subject. All you have to do is stay in bed for two weeks and see what kind of results you get."

"You mean it may be a cure?" Mammy says with interest.

"There is a possibility." He looks at us over his horn-rimmed glasses. "We figured out that sunlight is very helpful, so now we would like to look at warmth, be it from sunshine or just staying undercover for an extended period of time. When does your summer holiday begin?"

"She has three more weeks, Doctor," Mammy says, "before school is over for the season."

"Well, why don't I write a prescription so that she can finish early at the end of next week, and then she'll still have her six weeks of holiday after the experiment." He gets his little pad and writes in a scribbly fashion, and hands it to Mammy.

"What I want you to do, Patricia," he says, "is stay in bed for two weeks without getting out. Have your mother give you a chamber pot so that you will be out of bed only for seconds at a time to use it. Stay under the covers for two solid weeks and report any change at the end of the fortnight."

I look at Mammy, wondering if she'll go along with my getting out of school for the summer two weeks early. I haven't really begun to imagine what this "cure" is going to be like. Outside the office she tells me she's willing to try anything to relieve me of the terrible discomfort I've been suffering.

When I tell Rachel about the experiment she says, "I'm jealous, Pat. You'll have two weeks less of school!"

"Yes, but it's not like I'm going to be having loads of fun or anything. I'd better move the bed over to the attic window, so I can at least look out and see what's going on in the world. "Why don't you come and wave at me sometimes, if you're not busy," I beg.

"All right, agreed, keep your eye out for me. I'll stand at the bus stop right across the street after the evening meal." Mammy has suggested to us that since Granny has allowed the lot of us to live with her for our last year in Ireland, we should respect Granny's privacy and not bring our friends into her house.

It's a strange feeling to be spending my last day of school in Ireland. There's a certain amount of relief, but waves of sorrow move across my mind, as I look at all the girls I'll probably never see again.

Will they remember me? I know I'll always remember them, especially the ones who made going to school fun and enjoyable.

Mari writes and warns us not to expect America to be a bed of roses. Most people who come seem to think that it will be. She also mentions that in America when you leave secondary school, there's a big ceremony where you dress up in a gown and a flat cap with a tassel. You parade down and get a certificate telling all the world that you're a success.

When Pauline and her classmates left Fortwilliam, all they did was say goodbye to their friends and the teachers that they liked. No ceremony or anything. Here that stuff is reserved for people leaving the university.

I walk down the rhododendron-lined driveway of Fortwilliam with Rachel for the last time. Now that's something I'm going to miss.

"I'll be sad next year when I'm coming here by myself," Rachel says.

I feel a lump growing in my throat now, and turn away so that she won't see the tears trickling down my cheeks. "Oh, I'll miss you too, Rachel," I say, and I start to bawl.

She hugs me and I let it all out. I'm certainly not the most gregarious girl in the school, and my personality is actually quite somber. I come from quiet parents who don't like to make spectacles of themselves. Now as we reach the street, I find myself attracting unwanted attention from passersby as the tears flow on and on.

"We'll have to sit in the front seat of the bus, Rachel, so that no one will see my face when they get up to leave," I say.

"All right, Pat, but don't worry, no one will notice."

When we board the second bus on Divis Street to go up the Falls Road, I've calmed down.

Mrs. McCann from Andersonstown Crescent gets on at the next stop and sits across from us. "You're an Owens girl, aren't you?" she asks and smiles. I nod and try to act cheerful.

"Is it true what I hear, that your family is leaving for America soon?"

"Yes, it is indeed, Mrs. McCann. My Daddy's already there, working to bring us over."

"That sounds wonderful," she says, pulling her scarf back up on her head and tightening it under her chin. "I doubt if my family could ever get enough money aside to take the plunge. How do you feel about leaving, love?"

"I'm betwixt and between," I say. "I'm thrilled and excited in some ways and afraid and sad in others. It'll be a big change in our lives I'm sure." I'm trying to act natural and hope I don't start blubbering again, or that will be the next rumour to make its rounds in Andersonstown.

"Ach, I'd be thrilled to be going," she says. "I'm sick and tired of this constant rain, and my wee'uns are always sick from the dampness. I heard you're going to the Los Angeles area. You won't see too much stormy weather there, now will you?"

I smile and shake my head, no.

As Rachel and I stand to get off the bus at the Springfield Road, Mrs. McCann grabs my hand, "You said you're betwixt and between, love. Well, those of us left behind will be betwixt and between the orange and the green. Isn't that about the size of it?"

I laugh and follow Rachel down to the back of the bus where we hop off to the hubbub that is part of the Catholic area; people coming and going with shopping bags, boys shouting out headlines of newspapers they're hoping to sell, throngs of children pouring out of the schools and an occasional ambulance screaming toward the Royal Hospital just up the street.

I'll have to make a trip to the library later and stock up on reading material for my fortnight of bed rest.

After three days of reading, dozing, being fed by Mammy like royalty, and even having my chamber pot emptied and washed out, I'm about to go mad.

Every evening around seven, I look across the street at the linen factory. It was raining the last two days, but tonight it's dry, and I'm delighted to see Rachel. I wave at her and she waves back.

It's more interesting later in the evening when Pauline and Irene get home from work. They come in and talk for a while and the time passes more quickly. Irene always wants to inspect the psoriasis to see if it's disappearing like we've been hoping it would. But there never seems to be any visible change.

"It'll probably take the two whole weeks to show any results," I say hopefully.

"After all this, it better work, Patricia. Look at all the fun you're missing."

"Don't rub it in, Irene. I know it more than anyone," I say with a sigh.

Every morning it's the same routine, Mackey's Linen Factory across from Granny's blows its whistle a couple of times to call the workers in. I look out the window and see latecomers jumping off the bus before it comes to a full stop, and running like mad to the factory gate. On this side of the road, the women walk swiftly toward the Blackstaff Spinning and Weaving Mill.

In the evening, after the whistle blows to end the workday, I can see the crowd of mostly men from the linen factory, waiting at the bus stop to head home. The ones who live closer step lively down the road to their homes. Mackey's was one of the German targets during the war, but they missed and hit a row of houses near Granny's instead.

On the thirteenth day of my confinement, Aunt Marjorie comes in and sits on the bed wearing a big smile.

"Looks like you're nearing the end of this ordeal. How does the skin look?"

"No change, Marjorie. It was an experiment, and it didn't work, so it didn't."

"Well, at least you've had a nice wee rest," she says.

"I don't know if I'd call it nice," I say with a sigh. "Since it's almost the end of my time in bed, I took the liberty of wandering around this top floor today. I was in the wee room at the back, the one with the skylight. I looked in a drawer and found a box with some army medals. Do you know who they belong to?"

"Yes, your Uncle Freddy was in the British Army, and that was his room," she says. "It was a job, wasn't it, at a time when very few people could find work?" She leaves and comes back with a picture of Freddy in his Army dress uniform. He looks handsome, with his shock of frizzy red hair barely contained under a smart hat. His jacket has stripes and he looks very solemn, but I detect a twinkle in his eye. Just like our Freddy to never really be serious.

"Patricia, since you're near the end of this trial period, I thought I'd let you know; my boss at Belmont Photo Works is badly in need of summer help. People seem to be taking more pictures now than ever before. How would you like to start on Monday?"

"It sounds great to me, Marjorie," I say. "Did you talk to Mammy about it?"

"I did indeed, and she says she can certainly use the money for your journey."

Mammy suggests that I get out of bed tomorrow, and take two days to hang around with Rachel. The bed rest did nothing for the skin disease, and since I'm starting work in a few days, I may as well have some time for friends.

Early on Monday morning, Marjorie and I, scaly skin and all, walk down the Grosvenor Road. She's smoking and singing, and seems to be very happy. I'm a wee bit nervous since it's my first job and I'm only fourteen.

"Don't worry, Patricia, the people are real nice there, and the boss is a kind soul."

She's right, and the boss seems friendly as he shows me where I'll be working. "This is Muriel, you'll sit next to her. She'll show you what to do." He walks back to his office and closes the door.

"Hello, Patricia," Muriel says. "Marjorie has told me all about you, and I remember your sisters who worked here last summer." She leads me over to a large table with two chairs. The one I'm to sit in is next to hers and facing a shallow vat containing developing solution. Marjorie is already sitting at her station right across from me. She's close enough to serenade us with her quiet songs.

A man from another room keeps bringing rolls of paper to Muriel. She puts them in the machine, cuts them and hands the squares to Marjorie.

After floating them in the solution until pictures appear, Marjorie sets them aside to dry then passes them to me. I count them, multiply the number of photos by the cost, and write the total price on the envelope.

They go to a checker after that, and if I make a mistake, I'll hear about it from her.

I enjoy the job and get used to it in no time. Once in a while, when there's a lull in the work load, I'm sent to the enlargement room upstairs. The fellow working there is extremely handsome, and I feel self-conscious around him. Later when I mention him to Marjorie, she tells me that he's married. He's a Protestant, like most of the people here, and the father of several children. He still looks great to me, even though he's older than he looks. Actually, he's the most handsome man in the whole place.

At the end of the week, I'm excited to be bringing Mammy my pay packet.

"You made two pounds two-and-six, Patricia," she says. "Good for you." The two and six is a shiny half-crown, and Mammy hands it to me. It's like First Communion all over again. I can get into the pictures five times with this amount, or buy five toffee bars.

The job lasts for the six weeks of summer holidays, and I enjoy walking home at noon with Marjorie for the dinner hour. At night I go over to see Rachel, and we usually take a walk up to the Falls Park. Now that I'm earning some money, we can buy ice cream or go to a film at the Broadway once in a while.

When Rachel starts school in August, I don't. Instead I spend the time getting ready for America. We go to the American Embassy, and the six of us visit a doctor's office for the physical examination and vaccinations we need. The doctor is in a Protestant area, and as we come to the dividing line we notice a large sign painted on the side of a Loyalist building saying: NO CATHOLICS ALLOWED HERE!

Right underneath it a Nationalist has painted in bright yellow: WHOEVER WROTE THIS WROTE IT WELL, FOR THE SAME IS WRITTEN ON THE GATES OF HELL!

We all laugh quietly, "How long do you think that'll last?" Mammy says. "You'd have thought it would be painted over already." We glance around to make sure no one has seen us laughing, and we're relieved later when we cross back into the Catholic area.

Today Michael and Paddy got into it again. They had so much fun watching the bonfire the other night that they got the idea to make their own wee fire in the back entry behind the pub. They spent the day collecting bits of wood and scraps of paper, and got matches from the house. They thought they were far enough from home that they wouldn't be found out. A nice fire was blazing in the entry when a woman hanging out her wash spied it and yelled at them. The pair of them ran 'round a couple of streets then walked back toward Granny's house from the opposite direction looking as innocent as newborn lambs. But the woman knew who they were, and they didn't get away with it.

If Daddy ever found out I don't know what he'd do, but thank God he's safely out of here enjoying the California sunshine!

"Sure they were only being wee boys," Marjorie says indignantly, after dinner. She's holding Michael on her lap trying to make him feel better.

"Yes, Marjorie, but they could have burned down the pub," Mammy says rubbing her hands on her apron. "Their fire was that close to it, so it was."

"Well Bessie, you'll all be gone this time next month anyhow, so you don't have to worry about him getting into any more mischief," Marjorie says sadly. "I'm going to miss the lot o' yis, so I am."

Excitement grows as the time passes, but Pauline is getting more upset every day about leaving Sean. Granny thinks we shouldn't force her to go with us, but Mammy says she'll have to go, because Daddy will just turn us all around and come back here if she doesn't.

Daddy has been sending us most of his salary. Mari refused to take anything for his keep, and there's lots of money left from the sale of our house.

Mammy and Daddy bought our house on Andersonstown Crescent when they were just newlyweds. They had it almost paid off when they sold it, and made a nice profit on the sale. The house on Gransha went up in value in the three years we lived there, and they did quite well on that sale as well.

Daddy has rented the house next door to Aunt Mari's. He'll be moved in there a month before we arrive. It already has furniture, bedding, and everything we'll need.

So many of Mari's neighbours have pitched in with generous donations of blankets, kitchenware and towels, that he had very little else to worry about. Granny put us up for the last year without charge and Pauline's and Irene's salaries helped feed us as well, and will help us get a good start in California, once they find jobs.

We'll be able to go by ship and then train. Mammy is happy that she'll be so close to her sister. It's amazing that the house next to Mari's became available just in time.

Since we have to wash all the clothes we own for our trip, Mammy has rented a washing machine for the day. It's delivered in the morning and we spend the whole day getting all the wash done. Denis and Michael are fighting over using the wringer. I'm afraid our Michael is mesmerised watching the clothes being pulled through. We have to warn him to keep his fingers clear of that area. It certainly does take all the moisture out of the clothes though, and they dry on the line so much faster.

Mammy has made me two new dresses for the journey and I love them. One is pale blue, gathered at the waist with wee dark blue stars all over it. The buttons down the front are even shaped like stars. The other dress is pale yellow, and the same style, only with red stars. She has enough material left to make a dress just like mine for Rachel, and Rachel is thrilled to pieces.

Irene and Pauline have new dresses also, and Mammy makes shorts and shirts for Denis and Michael out of a lightweight material, because Daddy said it's very hot in September.

The trunk has been packed and re-packed, trying to utilise every inch of space. Decisions have to be made about which pictures from the walls can go, and which will have to stay behind.

We make our last trip up Oranmore Street to say goodbye to Granny and Granddad Owens. They're sorry to see us go, but happy that we're going to a land where we'll have the chance of a better future.

Mammy doesn't really have any close friends to leave. She used to stop occasionally and talk to different neighbour women, on her way to and from the shops, but all the women are too busy cooking, shopping for food every day, and doing laundry to make close friendships.

Tom and Lucy throw a big party for us, and we're surprised to see most of the O'Hare clan as well as our friends and some neighbours. It's a happy and sad affair and everyone is wishing us well on our new adventure.

Lucy's new baby, Angela, has grown quite a bit, and is lovely, so she is. Thomas is only four and he still has his curls. There's a good possibility we won't get to see them grow big like Anne Marie and Vincent, and this saddens everyone.

As we leave the party at the end of the evening, I say goodbye first to our the neighbours and friends and then to the Limestone Road that I may never see again.

Two taxis stand outside Granny's front door. The drivers struggle to get the big trunk into the back of one vehicle. The suitcases will fit in the other. Marjorie and Granny are coming with us in the taxis, and Frank and Mary will come in their car. It's six o'clock on Wednesday evening.

When we arrive at the ship we're surprised to see again Mammy's cousins, the O'Hare clan. What a crowd they all make.

My friend Rachel is there, and Irene's friend Mairead Cafferty. Sean is with Pauline, as well as several of her girlfriends. Tom and Lucy, Frank and Mary, and Granny and Marjorie give us hugs after the rest of our relatives and friends have said their goodbyes.

"You will come, I just know it," Mammy is saying to Granny and Marjorie. It's almost more than I can bear to watch Marjorie saying goodbye to Michael and Denis. She doted on them both and they were a huge part of her life.

Mammy takes our wee Michael's hand, he's only five, so young to be going on this big adventure, and we climb the gang plank slowly, being careful not to slip because the tears make it difficult to see properly.

The six of us stand at the railing of the small ship bound for Liverpool. At that port we'll board a large ocean liner.

Rachel waves and I yell, "I'll write!" She nods her head and dabs her eyes with her hanky.

Once the men start casting off the ropes that are tied to the dock, the wailing begins as reality sets in for both those going and those staying behind. So many people are leaving home to live in distant lands.

The ship filled with people, both happy and sad at the same time, strains and pulls slowly away from the dock. Below, hundreds of hankies flutter like leaves on a tree as they wave in unison.

As we look sadly down at our relatives and friends, I glance with mixed feelings toward the town we have called home. *Goodbye, beautiful Ireland, Someday you'll be free.*

Chapter Twenty One

"Please God, we'll see them all again," Mammy is saying through her tears, and Pauline is weeping loudly, her body heaving, shoulders rising and falling with every sorrowful sob. Her true love, Sean, disappears from view as the ship moves farther up the Belfast Lough and reaches the curve where the Lough melds into the Irish Sea. She stands at the railing long after the rest of us have gone in to explore the small ship. When Pauline finally comes into our cabin, she says she met Liam McNulty from the Glen Road on board. His parents' house is just a couple of doors up the Glen Road from Gransha Park.

"He always had a notion of you, Pauline," Irene says, trying to distract Pauline from her loss of Sean.

"He's on his way to South Africa," Pauline says. "I didn't even know about his interest in me. Do you think he really did like me?"

"I know his sister, Pauline, and she said he sent you one of those secret Valentine cards you received this year," Irene says with a smile. "But you were too involved with Sean, so I didn't think I should mention it." Pauline cheers up a little at this new revelation.

We have beds for the night, and the boys are happy to be on the top berths. This is not a ship of leisure, so there's nothing to do but walk around the decks until dark. When we wake up in the morning we'll be in England. The slow roll of the ship from side to side has the boys asleep in no time, but the rest of us are so excited and nervous about tomorrow that we have a restless night.

The sun is rising when we disembark from the small ship on Thursday morning, and make our way toward another dock and the ship to Canada.

There she stands in all her glory, bigger than any of us could have ever imagined. We stand gazing up in awe at this thing of beauty. "H.M.S. SAXONIA" is painted boldly on her side, and I feel like a wee ant next to this monstrosity, with her tall smokestacks and beautiful railings. The people waiting to board are buzzing with anticipation. They say there's a theatre and a dance floor, as well as the usual deck games.

"It'll be another hour or so," Mammy announces.

"Then could the three of us take a wee walk around, Mammy, do you think?"

"All right, Pauline, but only for thirty minutes, we need to keep together when it's time to board."

We walk through the small streets around the dockside in Liverpool. There are stands selling vegetables and fish, and the people here have strange accents. When we pass a small cafe an unusual aroma floats out to greet us and I wonder what it could be.

"What on earth is that?" Irene asks, and Pauline and I lift up our hands and shrug our shoulders. A woman sitting outside the cafe has heard our conversation and notices us sniffing the air trying to place the aroma.

"That's coffee, luv." She smiles and lifts a cup to her lips and sips slowly, savouring every last drop. "'Aav you ever 'aad any?" she asks, and we shake our heads in unison.

"We've never even smelled it before now," Pauline says.

"We really must be going now, we're leaving on the ship for America very soon," I say, and the woman smiles.

"You'll ave a choice of tea or coffee on the ship, 'Am sure," she says. "It looks laak 1956 is a gointa be a record year. They bin leaving in droves lately." She waves to us as we move on.

Mammy looks relieved when she sees us making our way back through the crowd. Denis and Michael are restless and want to know why they can't get on the ship right now.

"What's H.M.S., Mammy?" Denis wants to know as he studies the tall ship.

"It means Her Majesty's Ship," Mammy replies.

"Why is she letting all these people on her ship?" Michael asks.

"All British ships are named like that, Michael, in honour of the Queen," Mammy says. "But that doesn't mean that they're just for the use of the royal family. Just think, it was probably built right downtown at the Belfast shipyards," she speculates.

"Just like the Titanic," Denis says quietly. "I hope it gets farther than the Titanic, all the way to Canada, I mean." He looks at Mammy for assurance.

"I don't think we'll need to be worrying about icebergs, after all it's September," Mammy replies, and Denis looks relieved.

Our ship will sail up the St. Lawrence River to Quebec, then on to Montreal where we get off. From there we'll travel by train to Detroit, then to Chicago. We'll spend five days and nights on the rails across America to our final destination of Los Angeles.

The luggage has all been loaded on the ship, and people are starting to line up to board this magnificent vessel. We're lucky the weather has held up. It hasn't rained even once.

"Thank God all our goodbyes are behind us," Mammy says, as we move slowly toward the gangplank of our floating home for the next five days. Mammy has told Pauline if she really wants to return that Daddy has agreed she can save her money for the fare back. She does seem a little happier now, and excited like the rest of us to be taking this great trip across the Atlantic.

We've been assigned a large cabin and our own table in the dining hall. Waiters dressed in black pants, crisp white shirts, and black dickie-bows bring our meals, and we feel just like royalty. The tables are covered with beautiful white tablecloths that give them a look of elegance. We're served four-course meals, on delicate China dishes, crystal goblets, and more cutlery than we know what to do with. We've never been treated so well.

Denis and Michael have discovered the table tennis area, and spend a lot of time learning the game. It's nice that they're kept occupied and they've made friends with several other children.

In the evening there's dancing, and Pauline has noticed this fellow who's been giving her the eye all day. When the music begins, he asks her up to dance and she accepts. When Pauline comes back she tells us he's a Dutchman, and moving to Canada.

Mammy, Irene, and I stay at the back of the room and watch. Every once in a while one of us goes to the cabin to check on the boys. We notice something completely different about both the American and Canadian women, especially on the dance floor. They're very outspoken, not in the least bit withdrawn, and don't care who can hear their whole conversation. We've been raised differently and are very reserved. It must be great to be so uninhibited. I don't think, with our upbringing, we could ever be that jovial in public.

Just from sitting here, we practically know where everyone is headed, and their complete family history. Many are Canadians and Americans returning home from their summer holidays. The more reserved ones are probably emigrants like ourselves.

When we're leaving to go to bed, Mammy warns Pauline not to stay up too late. When she finally comes back to the cabin, she whispers that the Dutchman asked her to walk out on deck with him, and she said she couldn't. "I don't know what came over me," she says, "but I had an eerie feeling he might throw me overboard."

"Where did you get that idea from, Pauline?" Irene asks.

Pauline gets into her bunk and says, "I don't know, but I need to follow my instincts."

On Friday afternoon, we all go to the pictures, and as we sit in the dark watching the film I can hardly believe that we are on the great Atlantic ocean. Beneath us, are millions of fish swimming around in a magical underwater world in the midst of forests of seaweed and castles of coral. They exist in this different world, completely oblivious to our existence above them, and we to theirs.

We've slept here two nights and when I wake up on Saturday morning the ship is rolling back and forth. The boys are awake, and when we go on deck the ocean is churning, and the waves look ten feet high. When we try to walk around to the table tennis area, it's hard to stay on our feet. It takes great strength and determination to get there. Our hair is blowing in all directions, and I have to keep holding my coat down, for it wants to fly up around my waist. Some people are trying to play table tennis, but the balls keep rolling off the tables. The ship tilts forcefully from one side to the other. It reminds me of Denis and Michael playing with little boats in the bathtub on a wet day, and splashing their hands wildly in the water to make them rock. While we hold on to the handrail for dear life, our stomachs are churning like the water surrounding us. We make our way slowly and carefully back toward the cabin, the boys faces turning a sickly green.

Passing the dining hall, I glance in. The early breakfast crowd is only about one-quarter of its usual number. Most of us are sick to our stomachs for the rest of the day, and the cabin and its commode is our refuge. I'm hoping the storm won't last all the way to Canada or we'll be awful hungry when we get there.

"Wake up, Patricia, pleeez!" Michael is shaking my arm. He runs to the small porthole where he squeezes his head in next to Denis's larger one. Together they gaze in awe through the round window at the ocean beyond. "It's like glass, isn't it?" Denis whispers. They turn and smile at me with pride at their exciting discovery.

"Oh my goodness," I say when I finally get them to move away from their favourite spot. "I wouldn't have thought the ocean could ever look like this after that wild storm yesterday!"

Mammy and the girls are awake now and take turns looking at the ghostly ocean, still and flat as far as the eye can see. It's as smooth as an ice rink, not a breeze nor a ripple.

"Well, thank God for that," Mammy says as we hurry to get dressed for breakfast. "I suppose this must be what they call the calm after the storm. Yesterday was the sickest I've ever felt."

"Are you all as famished as I am?" Pauline asks.

We are, and this morning the dining hall is filled to capacity. If the kitchen crew had an easy day yesterday they'll surely make up for it today. Later as we march in a single file past the tables, Americans keep telling Mammy that she has a very large family.

"Not at all," Mammy says, "sure I only have a handful where I come from."

We go to Mass in a small chapel, and wander the decks for a few hours. A strange game is being played in the dance hall. There are small wooden horses lined up on a miniature track and people bet on them. They're attached to some kind of metal rods in slots underneath. The man throws a switch when all the bets are placed and the horses move in a kind of rickety fashion around the track. The first one over the finish line is the winner.

I've never seen real horse racing, but there's a greyhound track in Belfast, and I remember passing men walking their dogs up the Falls Road for exercise in the evening. At the greyhound races, those poor dogs chased down rabbits that weren't even real. There were bookie offices all over the city where you could place bets. Maybe betting on horses and dogs is the reason some families in Belfast were so hard up most of the time. I thank God Daddy never took an interest in that sport, or we wouldn't be on this great ship watching wee wooden horses galloping round the track.

"I feel so spoiled, being fed all this rich food, and no dishes to do afterward," Mammy says after dinner. She is really enjoying this part of the trip. The next leg of the journey may be more difficult for her, when we have to pass through several train stations.

On the fifth morning, as we get closer to the Canadian coastline, we are treated to the sight of several icebergs in the distance. "Don't worry Denis," Mammy says when she sees his look of concern. "Those things are miles away. There's no chance we'll come anywhere close to them." But Denis keeps a sharp eye on them nevertheless as we travel closer to the white islands floating in the sea. They seem to grow larger and closer as the day passes.

We're approaching the eastern coastline of Canada now, and as the ocean blends and merges into the St. Lawrence River, the ship slows down considerably. The river is very wide in this area, but it's still difficult for me to imagine that a ship of this enormous size can go through the channel without scraping its bottom.

Lush hillsides grace both sides of the river, and the soft green blaze of trees is a welcome sight after five days of looking at nothing but water. For the rest of the day we enjoy the dazzling scenery along the St. Lawrence, and late in the evening when the sky darkens, the stars come out in the millions, as if welcoming us to this great land.

Suddenly the people leaning on the railings hold their breath in awe. When our eyes follow theirs, the most amazing apparition appears before us in the northern sky. Great bands of light waft through the heavens like silken, pastel webs. Floating above us like ghostly visions, they create a silence among the watchers, and I can hardly believe this is real.

"It's the aurora borealis," the man next to us says. "A phenomenon that can be seen in the Northern Hemisphere. The farther north you go the better chance of viewing it."

"It's almost like a giant waving a flag in the sky," Michael says, and we agree with silent nods.

"It reminds me of the banshee legends in Ireland," Irene says. "I always imagined the banshee would look ghostly like that, only dark and scary."

If I live to be a hundred I'll never forget this experience, I think, as I gaze on this wondrous sight. So many people stand here in wonder, quietly watching. I'm sure they feel like me; insignificant under this vision of God's presence in the heavens.

On Saturday evening, the lights from Quebec city come into view. It's long past our bedtime, but there's an excitement in the air as many of the passengers prepare to disembark. Joyful sounds are heard from the docks far below, as people shout each other's names, and families greet their relations and friends.

The next morning because of the exodus in Quebec, the dining room has fewer people, and it's a strange feeling to be coming to the end of this delightful stage of our journey. Our next stop will be Montreal, the final destination on this long sea voyage.

When we finally disembark in this French-speaking city, Michael keeps turning his head and looking back at the Saxonia. I don't think he wants to leave her behind. Mammy has to hurry him along in order to get to the taxi stands. We are taken to the train station, and our luggage is supposed to follow. Mammy is a wee bit nervous about all the connections being made correctly, and I feel sorry for her all alone here with the five of us to worry about. Pauline and Irene are a big help, though.

No one is of any help, however, when we sit down at a cafe in the Montreal train station. The waitress brings us menus in French. We look at the strange words and try to decipher them. Mammy asks the waitress if she speaks English but she just gives us a look of annoyance and refuses to utter a word.

Since communication is impossible, we have to get up and parade over to a wee snack stand at the other end of the station. Mammy points to what we want and holds up six fingers. We're given ham sandwiches with moist white stuff spread on the bread.

It costs a small fortune for the meal, and Mammy is concerned about traveling for five more days on trains where we'll have to buy all our food.

"Mammy, since the wait is so long for the train to Detroit, do you think Patricia and I could take a wee walk around Montreal?" Pauline asks. "Irene says she'll stay and help watch the boys."

"Yes, but you must be back in two hours," Mammy replies "Don't get lost, or we'll all be in trouble."

The city is very pretty, at least what we can see from this area. We circle several long streets and look in shop windows along the way. It's funny that we're in Canada, and everything is written in French.

"Why did we have to take Latin in school, Patricia?" Pauline says. I agree that French would have been really handy at a time like this, but it wasn't offered.

We return to the station with lots of time to spare, and listen with interest to the loud-speaker blasting in French.

"We must listen for the word Detroit," Mammy says. "It's boarding on track four, according to the schedule posted over there. I just wish I could get a decent cup of brewed tea. They have hot water and wee metal balls filled with tea leaves, but you can only steep it in the cup."

"Don't worry, Mammy," Irene says. "When we get to Torrance, Daddy will have a real teapot and everything we need." Mammy smiles and tries to relax. She should feel much better once we're on board.

We watch our suitcases being loaded on the train, but the trunk is nowhere in sight. Mammy is a little concerned, but the train leaves in five minutes so she'll have to inquire about it when we get to Detroit.

When we enter the train, we are disappointed to see that the carriage is open rows of seats on either side. On Irish trains, you have separate little compartments with doors on them, so a family could sit in one of these with complete privacy. We must sleep sitting up using each other's shoulders as pillows. We have been given blankets, and that helps. I'm afraid we've been spoiled by having beds on the ocean voyage. It's been a long day and we sit quietly now on the speeding train, and watch the evening sky fade from bright red to burnt umber, slowly pulling its cloak of darkness over the peaceful Canadian landscape.

The night has been a restless one and sleep intermittent. It's Tuesday and outside, the blackness is being slowly painted over with deep shades of purple, then blue, and finally pink. We stretch and stand, trying to get the numbness out of our legs. Speeding past small Canadian towns, we notice names like Hamilton, London and just before our American point of entry, the final Canadian town of Windsor.

Chapter Twenty Two

ENTERING THE UNITED STATES OF AMERICA
PLEASE HAVE PAPERWORK READY

This sign greets us in Detroit, our port of entry into the United States. We're queued up waiting for paper clearances and permission to enter. The inspectors spend a long time with each family, and Michael is getting restless. They ask questions, look at the children, if any, and then stamp the immigration papers.

When our time comes, they go over our papers, check the number of children, compare our green cards with our faces. After glancing through our medical histories, an inspector asks, "Which one is Patricia."

"She's the third from your left," Mammy says. She looks agitated when the man wants to lift my skirt above my knees to check my legs, and then ask me to take off my cardigan. My heart is pounding, and I'm feeling extremely self-conscious. Little beads of sweat pop up on my forehead, and my scalp feel tingly and moist. They're asking Mammy all sorts of questions about my skin disease, and the people behind us are watching.

Is it contagious? How long have I had it? Is there a cure? I'm waiting for them to pry open my mouth to see if my teeth are all there as well.

Pauline and Irene look nervously at each other, and when the papers are finally stamped and we're allowed through, we breath a collective sigh of relief. I have a splitting headache now and just want to go and sit down.

"My God, Patricia," Mammy whispers. "I thought we were going to be turned away for a minute there, so I did."

I smile and act nonchalant in hopes of calming her, as we drag our bags across the floor of this great station. We now must wait for the train to Chicago. I notice that when the man on the loudspeaker says the word Chicago he uses a CAW sound in the middle. Mammy has been calling it Chicago with a AH sound like in flat. It's in her head now, so there'll be no changing it, even with a quiet hint about the man on the loudspeaker's correct pronunciation.

There's a great hustle and bustle in this American city of Detroit. The train station is crowded with people and we're happy the language is back to English again. We each have a sandwich at the snack bar, and since the train to Chicago doesn't leave for another couple of hours, Pauline asks if we can walk around this city to see the sights.

"Remember my earlier warnings," Mammy says, and I think she is worried that our trunk wasn't unloaded from the Canadian train. When she inquires, the man behind the counter gives her a form to fill out.

"This should have been filled out in Montreal, Ma'am," he says. He's being very patient and helpful. "We'll do all we can to make sure your trunk arrives in Los Angeles with the rest of your things. But if not, you will be apprised of the situation."

Pauline and I walk past the tall buildings in this part of Detroit. We try to take note of the street names so we can find our way back. After a while we come to a large park and walk through it, admiring plants and flowers we are seeing for the first time.

We notice a group of boys dressed in tight white pants, and shirts that are all blown up at the shoulders. They're wearing helmets that almost obscure their faces, and they seem to be in the middle of a game of American football.

Pauline and I stand watching, enthralled at the whole scene.

"Imagine these young boys of thirteen or so, being able to afford all that stuff," I say. "Such elaborate uniforms and all. Everyone must be rich here."

The game doesn't make any sense, however, because they circle into a wee group like they're telling secrets, and then the ball shoots out of the heap, and, before you know it, they're in another heap, except one team seems to be trying to smother one or two boys from the other team. The coach keeps blowing the whistle, and the tangle of boys comes off in layers, kind of like peeling an orange around the sides.

"Jesus, Mary, and Joseph, did you ever see the likes of it?" Pauline asks. "I wonder how the wee lad on the bottom could just get up and walk away after all that."

"They must be awful tough," I say. "Maybe the stuffing in their uniforms protects them from the mob on top. I wonder how they keep score at all."

We've been standing here so long enjoying this new experience that when Pauline checks her watch she looks at me in alarm.

"We'd better hoof it, Patricia. We don't have that much time."

We run as fast as our legs will take us through the streets we remember, hoping it's the right direction. Back at the train station, we find we have fifteen minutes to spare.

"I was hoping you were going to show up," Mammy says with relief. "We've had a bit of a problem here ourselves. Our wee Michael was attacked by his first escalator, so he was."

None of us has ever seen an escalator before today, and Irene starts to tell Pauline and me about Michael's experience as we walk toward the platform, and the Chicago bound train.

"I was taking Denis and Michael up on the escalator to the confectionary shop, and just as we got near the top, Michael decided to sit down," Irene says breathlessly. Her eyes grow bigger, and her spectacles make them look enormous.

"His short pants got stuck in the cracks between the metal steps, and he couldn't stand up. It was awful. Denis and I were pulling and tugging and Michael was howling, and finally a big man behind us got him free, but not before the steps took a bite out of his pant leg. It could easily have been his thigh."

"Oh my goodness, I'm glad we weren't here to see it happen," Pauline says. "Are you all right, love?" Michael gives her a weak smile, and she picks him up and holds him.

"Well, we've all learned one thing from this," Mammy says. "You can't ever sit down on those moving steps."

Pauline pats Michael gently on the back as we pick up the pace to the waiting train. "Poor wee man, you'll be all right. You must have had a dreadful scare." Michael lays his head on Pauline's shoulder and she strokes his hair.

Mammy is going to be relieved to reach the safety of the train, I'm thinking. We're all tired and in need of rest. I would just love to soak in a warm bath right now, but that'll be impossible for the next four days.

"All aboard! All aboard! Last call for Chicago, leaves in five minutes. All Aboard."

We have two long seats facing each another, so we'll be together in our little nook. Again there are no footrests, so we try out several different sleeping arrangements, before coming up with a solution. When it's time for bed, Michael can curl his feet up next to him. The rest of, us being much bigger, will have to sit up, and leave a space next to us for the feet of the ones on the opposite side. Of course we remove our shoes.

Later, I wake. It must be the middle of the night, for it's pitch black outside. The train is rocking forcefully because of its high speed. I'm a little nervous about whether it can stay on the tracks at this rate. People are slumped over on one another's shoulders, and at some point I fall asleep again. In the morning my neck is stiff from leaning so low against Michael. At daybreak it takes forever to get our hands and faces washed, because so many people have to use the cramped toilets. The train rattles and shakes as I try to make my way down the aisle, and when I finally get in there, the place is a mess. The floor is wet and scattered with little papers. It's probably because the motion of the train makes you sway and lose your aim. It's a relief when we reach our destination.

In Chicago, we sit close together in the station, and eat more ham sandwiches. We're a bit tired from the activity of the past few days. And as we wait for the train, Pauline and I tell everyone about the football practice in the Detroit park. It's late evening when we finally board the train to Los Angeles. We find the space that will be our home until Saturday morning. Again, it's two seats, one facing the other, and it doesn't take long to get in position hopefully, for a good night's rest.

When morning arrives, I discover to my horror that my monthly visitor has paid an un-expected visit. Thank God I make it to the lavatory in time. The only problem is that there aren't any pads in the box, and I have to use those wee squares of thin toilet paper instead.

"What am I going to do Mammy, the box is empty in there?" I whine when I return cautiously to our seats.

Mammy saves the day. Before long she has a collection of paper serviettes. We hear people call them napkins when requesting them from the porter. Walking through the train, she'll bend down occasionally and pick up any wayward drifters, and I find myself doing the same. Michael and Denis think I have a cold or something and go with me from one carriage to the next searching for serviettes. As to why, I let them imagine what they want.

I'm wearing my new pale yellow dress with the tiny red stars, and I'm worried sick that it'll end up with a bigger red star on the back if they don't refill those visitor-needs boxes in the toilets. The chance of discussing it with any train personnel is slim, however, because they're all men, and none of us would dare breach the subject.

When the porter comes around with his wee push cart at breakfast time, the only kind of food he has to offer is doughnuts. They're small round cakes with holes in the middle. We have two each, with milk or tea and we're so hungry that we eat them quickly. I'm watching Michael to see if he's going to finish all of his. If he isn't, they won't be going to waste. Mammy hasn't gotten up the nerve to try coffee yet, for fear of not liking it and wasting the money.

We had the doughnuts at six in the morning, and by twelve Pauline's stomach is growling with hunger.

"Do you think we could have lunch now, Mammy?" she asks.

"Sure we're just after having breakfast, Pauline," Mammy says. "The longer we can hold out the better." We eat ham sandwiches for both lunch and dinner. I just know Mammy would love to have the roast beef, but it costs so much more. The man who comes around with the sandwiches doesn't seem to have any variety: only fancy roast beef on beautiful rolls, and the ham on soft bread that has the texture of cotton wool. There's hardly any meat, and no lettuce or tomato, so a few of these don't really fill us up. We're used to much heavier bread that you could live on if you had to.

Several army lads wearing spiffy dress uniforms sit a few seats ahead of us. Irene and Pauline are the object of some sly looks and occasional grins from them. The soldiers are extremely handsome and look so strong and brave with their badges, stripes, and sparkling shoes. Irene is embarrassed by their glances, but I think Pauline rather enjoys it. It's been about eight days since she last saw Sean, and she must miss him. She probably thinks a little flirting will do no harm. On the outskirts of the big cities that we pass, huge car parks are filled with sleek, shiny cars of every description. Every adult in America must own one. When the train whistles through towns and over crossings, we notice long lines of vehicles behind the lowered barriers waiting to cross the tracks. The colours turquoise and salmon seem to be popular in cars, as well as powder blue and pale yellow.

Even the houses are painted different colours. We see countless square homes, in every shade imaginable with gardens surrounding them. Mile after mile, it's the same scene. All we're used to is brick, brick, brick.

Further out, the farmland seems to go on forever. This country is so vast. What a difference from the Auld Sod which is approximately 300 miles long by 200 miles wide. It's hard to imagine we're only at the beginning of our long journey across this country.

By the time we get to Kansas, the soldiers are gone, and there's a monotonous sameness to the flat land. Mile after mile, hour after hour, the same scene passes before us. Acre after acre of yellow grain shines in the brilliance of the sun and sways gently in the breeze. So much open land has been cultivated and planted. No wonder it's said that America is the bread-basket of the world.

Unexpectedly, the train grinds to a stop in a quiet station outside Kansas City, Kansas. We are told that there will be a delay. Gradually, the cool interior of our home on wheels begins to sizzle. After fifteen minutes, the air is sweltering, and we feel the need to escape.

"In Heaven's name, what possessed them to turn on the heat!" Mammy moans, while wiping her brow, and using the newspaper to fan her now beet-red face. The rest of us are feeling the same discomfort, and a woman from across the aisle laughs at us.

"They haven't turned on the heat. They just turned off the air conditioning," she says.

"You don't say?" Mammy replies. "It feels like a heater is blowing hot air at us."

We flock to the end of the carriage with the rest of the passengers as fast as possible, searching for a source of fresh air.

Once outside, our family is in shock. The temperature must be in the hundreds. We've never experienced anything like this. It feels like we're in an oven, or maybe the Sahara Desert. People stand in the sizzling heat fanning themselves with the daily newspaper and we wonder why the train has stopped at this remote location.

The delay lasts about an hour. Finally, when our air-conditioned train moves forward, gradually picking up speed, a marvelous coolness floats over our clammy bodies. We appreciate being inside on the train like never before.

Traveling through the southern end of Colorado and into northern New Mexico, we notice many beautiful dark-eyed people coming on board. The women have long, black, shiny hair, and their skin is the colour of milk chocolate.

"I heard someone back there say that they're Mexicans," Pauline informs us, and we can't help but glance at them from time to time, and admire their difference. The trouble is, as more people board the train, it becomes more difficult to get into the toilet, and the toilet paper keeps running out.

After another night of fitful sleep, I walk with Denis and Michael from one carriage to the other, trying to keep occupied. At one point the train climbs slowly and almost painfully up a steep grade. Shrub-covered rolling hills give way to high mountains and tall pine forests. As we climb, the mountains get higher and the canyons deeper.

Irene comes through to where we are standing and she's excited. "The man on the loudspeaker says we're going through the Rocky Mountains. If we watch carefully at an area not far from here, we'll be able to see the front and back of the train at the same time."

We lean over the little half-door in this bumpy area between the carriages. Soon Pauline and Mammy join us, and we just stand quietly watching this beautiful scene unfold before our eyes. The clickety clack of the wheels is almost drowned out by the occasional scream of a large bird with huge outstretched wings seemingly calling out with the joy of it all.

The locomotive rumbles higher and higher, through trees and rock-covered hillsides along this green fertile canyon. At long last, we have the thrill of seeing the front and back of the train at the same time, and cheers break out in all the jammed connector sections like the one in which we're standing. We're close to the middle and we wave to people in the other parts of the train.

Many ham sandwiches later, we pass from New Mexico into Arizona and travel for hours through rocky terrain and vast desert landscape, where nothing but cactus seems to grow.

"I wonder how people could live out here in this barren wasteland," Mammy says, as she gazes out the window. Michael is asleep with his head in her lap. I think the excitement of the Rocky Mountains was too much for him.

"There are many Indian Reservations out this way," the lady across the aisle informs us.
"They're usually away from the noise and grime of the big cities."

"Aye, it must be a very different life for them, so it must," Mammy says and looks dreamily out the window.

The scene changes quickly to pine trees and pretty mountains again, as we sweep into Flagstaff. People are saying it's the gateway to the Grand Canyon, something we know little about. Maybe, someday we can return to this area and see that great sight. The people on the train say it is truly magnificent.

Somewhere west of the Flagstaff station, before the train picks up speed, I see a group of people in an open courtyard not far from the tracks. An American Indian woman opens the heavy door of a round clay oven. I stretch my neck and watch as she slides a long pole with a flat end into the oven, removing a beautiful loaf of bread. It makes my mouth water. At this point, the lot of us wouldn't care if we never saw another ham sandwich, but some fresh baked bread would be wonderful.

There have been so many new experiences for us on this journey. If we'd flown to America the way Daddy did, we'd have missed them all.

It's Friday evening, and when we wake in the morning we should be close to Los Angeles. Mammy suggests we take sponge baths if possible, and change our dresses before going to sleep. Tomorrow, we'll be seeing Daddy again after a whole year.

At dawn, the train is snaking along in a vast barren desert. Only a few shrubs can be seen here and there. We pass an area called Barstow, and from there the scenery gradually begins to liven up with an occasional green shrub. Just before the train starts to descend through the hills toward a place called San Bernardino, we enjoy the view of some distant mountains.

The vegetation is more lush now, and, as we slowly wind our way down the steep grade, we enjoy the sight of large yellow boulders sticking up out of the ground, like some giant just threw them up in the air and let them drop there.

By the time the skyline of Los Angeles appears, the railroad tracks have increased and seem to be running in all directions. Mammy is extremely excited and nervous at the same time. She's lived in Ireland so long, and I only hope she'll be happy with her new life.

Chapter Twenty Three

"Union Station, Los Angeles. Everyone must exit the train!" A mans voice blares through the loudspeaker. When we get off, there are so many people milling around that we can't see Daddy. Irene and I walk right by and don't even recognise him.

"Irene, over here!" We hear someone shout, and when we look, we see a tall, skinny, dark brown man with sunken cheeks rushing toward us. He bears a slight resemblance to our father and we're shocked that it's him.

"Where's your mammy?" he's asking, and we point behind us to where Mammy, Pauline and the boys are being carried along in the crowd. After everyone hugs Daddy, taking in the great change in his appearance, he says he can't believe how Michael has grown in a just a year. We comment on his dark colour, and he laughs and says it's caused by the lovely weather. We're introduced to Aunt Mari's husband, Al Swanson, who helps us find our luggage. The trunk didn't arrive with us, but will come later and be sent to the house.

Union Station is very elegant with its marble floors and great square seats in the waiting area. The ceilings are high and rounded, and out in front are beautiful palm trees, the first we have seen up close.

Daddy and Al tell us to wait out by the kerb while they get the cars. Two nice metal benches sit empty in front of this impressive building. When Denis and Michael sit down they shoot up again so fast that it looks like they sat on something sharp.

"That seat is so hot, it burned my legs!" Michael cries out. He and Denis are wearing shorts, and when we feel the bench we find the metal is too hot to touch. No wonder they were empty.

"I wonder what the temperature is today," Mammy says, wiping her brow. When Al and Daddy drive up, they tell us it's in the nineties. "After all, it's the middle of September," Daddy says, "one of our hottest times of the year." He sounds like a native Californian already.

Al has a beige coloured car, and Daddy's is light gray with a Chevrolet insignia inscribed on the back. After squeezing the suitcases and bags into the boots of both vehicles, there's a discussion about who should travel with whom. Pauline, Irene and I end up in Al's car, and he gives us a running commentary of the Los Angeles skyline as we travel along the Harbor Freeway.

"They spell harbor without a letter u here," I say, thinking out loud.

"You're going to be spelling a lot of words differently from now on, young lady," Al says. "You'll have to learn all over again."

We are fascinated with the speed and straightness of the freeway. There are no stop lights, no people crossing, or anything like that. Al thinks it's funny that we are so excited about things he takes for granted. When we first left the station, I thought we were on the wrong side of the road, until I remembered they drive on the wrong side here.

After twenty minutes or so, a sign up ahead says, "Rosecrans Avenue. End of Freeway." The lanes merge into one, and the traffic flows onto the street. We travel for quite a while making turns to the left and right and soon we're on Cranbrook Avenue, the street that I only imagined up until now. It's slightly different from my daydreams, but better.

Mari runs out to greet us, and she's as lovely as I remember from so many years ago. She hasn't changed and still has her bubbly personality.

She introduces us to her two wee boys, and tells us that she had a baby girl just two weeks ago. There's no way we could have known because we've been on the go for the last ten days. The baby, Terry, is really beautiful, so she is. She's all pink and powdery, and smells like delicate roses.

The oldest boy, Kevin, is extremely smart. He knows the name of every car he sees. He also has a huge collection of car keys in a wooden box, and he can tell which key matches which car type. He's only two-and-a-half, and when I ask him about the large box in their kitchen, he says it's a re-frig-er-at-or, sounding out every syllable. We all laugh and are amazed at this child who knows so much for his age. His brother, Timothy, is around eighteen months old and still quite shy of strangers.

Mari tells us to sit and relax, and she disappears into the kitchen. She returns with a tray filled with unusual glasses that seem to be made of shiny tin, each one is a different color; my second new spelling word. They're full of Coca Cola and little squares of ice float on top, something else for us to be amazed about. After much questioning from us, she goes out to the kitchen and brings back what she calls an ice cube tray and explains how it works. I'm hoping we'll have some of these in our house.

"You should be sitting down, Mari, not catering to us," Mammy says. "If you were back in Ireland you'd be just getting out of bed after the birth about now."

"Oh, not here, Bessie," Mari says. "Over here, they have you on your feet in three days, and it seems to be the best method, overall." We all look at Mari with admiration.

She's wearing a pair of great looking pants that stop right below the knee, and I ask what they're called.

"These are pedal pushers, Patricia," she tells me. "How do you like them?"

"They're great," I say. "I can see they'd be perfect for riding a bike. You wouldn't have to worry about the oil from the chain getting on them."

"Who wants to see *our* house?" Daddy asks when we finish the Coca Cola. We all jump up. "It's right next door," he says. When we walk over toward the house that Daddy has rented, we can see that the side garden runs right down into a very large park with a baseball field. Farther over are swings and see-saws, or teeter-totters, a funny name that Daddy says the children here call them.

"This is a great location, Danny," Mammy says. She's looking at the park that seems almost like part of our garden. "Denis and Michael are going to love it."

The most interesting feature of the two-bedroom house is the shower. It's something we've never seen before and a cause of great excitement. Daddy turns it on to show how it works. "You'll probably still want to give Michael a bath," he says. "He could get scalded if he turned on the wrong tap. C'mere 'til I show ye," he says with a mischievous gleam in his eye.

We follow him into the large kitchen at the back of the house and see a refrigerator like Mari's. He opens the top door, and produces a cardboard box that says vanilla ice-cream on the outside.

"Ice cream in your own house?" Pauline says, and we all sit down at our new Formica table to eat ice cream out of our new dishes with our new spoons. He opens one of the cupboards and takes out a jar of brown stuff that is the same color as toffee.

"Try this on your bread," he says.

Mammy looks at him. "What on earth is that, Danny. It says peanut butter."

"Where does peanut butter come from?" Denis asks. "Surely not from cows?"

"No, they grind up peanuts. Try it Denis." Daddy spreads some on a piece of Wonder bread and the bread can hardly hold up under the assault. We each take a bite and Michael and Denis like it, but I'm not so sure. It leaves a kind of sticky dry sensation in my mouth.

"Lets look at the rest of the house," Mammy says, I know she's excited about it, and a bit perturbed by this long interruption.

Our room has a set of bunk beds and a single bed as well. A wee table is attached to the bottom end of the lower bunk and drops down when not in use. "This will be perfect for your homework, Patricia," Mammy says. The other bedroom has two double beds, one for Daddy and Mammy, the other for Michael and Denis.

"Someday we'll buy a house with more rooms," Daddy says, and Mammy smiles. "I'll drive you all down to the beach, next Sunday," he says. "It's not all that far."

School has already started so Aunt Mari takes me across the street to meet a girl called Donna. She goes to North High, where I'll be going, and has already told Mari she'd be happy to show Mammy and me how to get there on Monday.

Donna is very pretty. She's tall and her hair is swept back off her face, Teddy Boy style. It's light brown with little wisps of blonde at the ends. She's fifteen years old, just six months older than I am.

She asks if I'd like to watch television with her family, and I'm all for it. I'm fascinated with the witty, musical commercials. Donna's father enjoys watching me laugh at them. He tells me the commercial tunes are called jingles. I also enjoy seeing how a real American family looks and acts. Her mother is washing up after dinner, and her brother is putting stamps in his collection. I promise I'll bring him any stamps I receive from overseas as soon as Rachel writes.

Sitting on the side of Donna's bed, in her stylish room, I'm admiring the pink curtains and pretty flowered bedspread. When I look down at the deep pink carpet, I notice that she's wearing a pair of tennis shoes with writing all around the sides in bold black letters. I read what it says: I LOVE ELVIS PRESLEY.

"Is he your boyfriend?" I ask.

"Is who my boyfriend?"

"Him, the name on your shoes, Elvis Presley." I point to the shoes.

"You mean you've never heard of Elvis?" She's tittering and then starts to laugh, bending over holding her stomach and almost falling off the bed, and I feel confused.

"Who is he?" I ask, trying not to show my embarrassment.

"He's just America's number-one heart throb, that's who." She runs into her kitchen to tell her mother that I never heard of this stupid Elvis person, and I feel like crawling behind the sofa. *It takes time forAmerican entertainers to become known in places across the water,* I'm thinking, and I feel a bit better when her mother calms her down and says, "Patricia is from another country, Donna, thousands of miles from here. Next time Elvis comes on television, be sure and ask her over, so she can watch him perform."

On Monday, Mammy and I walk with Donna to the high school. It's just three blocks away. That's another new word I've learned, blocks, instead of streets. It should be easy enough to remember. She shows us where the office is so I can get my schedule. I'm put into 4th-year Latin, American history and American literature. When they ask about science, Mammy tells them I've had domestic science, so for some strange reason they put me in physics. And then there'll be a gym class as well. Mammy tells them we have five years of high school in Northern Ireland and I've completed three of them. They tell me I'll be a junior and that's fine with me.

On my first day in the school, I feel completely out of place. Never before have I had boys in the same class, and it's nerve-wracking. Some boys turn around and give me glances, and I don't know where to look. The kids (another new word) are very outspoken.
They talk to the teacher like she's one of them, and not an important person who should be revered, like the teachers in Ireland are. Over there, teaching is one of the most prestigious jobs to have.

Out on the playground I'm shocked to see couples sitting at the picnic tables, necking. The girls in my junior class are wearing lipstick, and even brassieres. They're all at least sixteen years of age. Being fourteen, I feel weird, and out of place. I don't have any lipstick and have never worn a brassiere.

When it's time for gym class, everyone changes their clothing in front of one another and I just turn my head and wait. Outside, we walk to a large open area, where a bale of hay has a target painted on the front. We practice pointing arrows at the center of the circle, and shooting. Most of my arrows go miles away from the hay bale. It's almost like reverse magnets are steering them out of range, just for spite.

Back in the gym when the class ends, I'm in shock watching all these girls stripping down to nothing. They laugh and squeal as they run toward a long row of showers lined up on the wall with nothing to shield the girls from view.

I avert my eyes from this shocking scene of naked bodies and stare at my locker. Feeling lost, and on the verge of tears, I listen as echoes of their joyful squeals bounce off the tiled walls.

The gym teacher comes over. "You'll have to get some gym clothing from the book store for this class," she says kindly.

I nod and try not to let her see my troubled face.

"Aren't you going to take a shower?"

"Not today," I say, trembling at the thought.

"Tomorrow you should bring a towel, so that you can join the rest of the class."

When the girls are finished showering, they dry off, and I notice that they don't show the slightest trace of embarrassment. They take little plastic tube things out of their lockers and rub them under their arms before dressing. When I ask one girl what it is, she looks at me strangely and says it's deodorant.

"Haven't you ever used this?" she asks, trying to hide her smile.

"No, I've never seen anything like it. I'll have to look for some at the Best Foods store, I suppose." I notice that she doesn't have hair under her arms like I do. What happened to it, I wonder. It could be that disease that the night watchman's daughter in Belfast had. But then again I rule that out, because this girl has a beautiful head of hair and two dark eyebrows.

"Are you new?" she asks, beginning to get curious about my lack of knowledge.

"Yes, I just got off the boat," I say. I turn to hide my tears and walk quickly out of the gym.

After school, I begin to weep when I tell Mammy about my terrible experience in gym class. "I can't wear those gym shorts, Mammy. My psoriasis is terrible, it's all over my knees. I'd be so embarrassed, and I'd rather die than take a shower in front of everyone like that. I just can't!"

Mammy looks bewildered, and thinks for a bit. "Don't worry, Patricia, I'll figure something out." She runs her fingers through her thick hair. "I'm going over to Mari's for a minute. Will you mind Michael, and watch the potatoes? I've put them on low, but don't let them get soggy." She returns with a notepad, sits at the table and begins to write:

To whom it may concern,
My daughter, Patricia Owens, was raised in Ireland.
She had a very different upbringing, and as we are
extremely modest, I request that she not be forced to
take a shower in front of everyone. It would cause
her a great deal of embarrassment and anxiety.
             Sincerely
             Elizabeth M. Owens

"Mari's going to lend me her sewing machine, Patricia, and I'll make you a pant skirt for gym, so that your knees and shins will be covered." She looks at me hopefully. This makes me feel a wee bit better.

The shower problem has been solved with the note from Mammy. The skirt pants are accompanied by another note the following day. The gym teacher raises her eyes to heaven when she reads this second note in two days. The culottes come way below my knees and cover the worst of my lizard skin, but they actually bring more attention to me just because they look so different, which adds to my self-conscious feelings as well. This whole high school experience is becoming a bit of a nightmare altogether.

Physics class is mostly boys, only three girls. The teacher is talking about sound waves and I am completely lost. I can't understand a thing he's saying and I feel like it's a foreign language. When I read the book it still doesn't make any sense, and on the first test I get a D-. What a mess. This is the worst grade I've ever received.

My new life in America is not going so well.

Chapter Twenty Four

On the first Sunday after our arrival, we come home from Mass, and load sandwiches and blankets into the car for a trip to the beach. That's what they call the strand here. The seven of us squeeze into our 1939 Chevy and head for Manhattan Beach. It only takes about fifteen minutes, and when the car reaches the top of the hill, we are treated to a panoramic view of the blue Pacific. Daddy lets the old car coast downhill the rest of the way.

When the lot of us parade across the thick dry sand, wearing our Sunday best, we notice people looking at us, snickering and whispering to each other. After we sit on the blanket and take off our shoes, we look around and notice that no one is dressed like us. The women are all wearing shorts or bathing suits. God, we must look completely out of place, sitting here, for their scrutiny and enjoyment. We're even wearing our petticoats, and Daddy is wearing his suit.

People here don't get changed into their bathing costumes under towels, like they do in Ireland," Daddy says. "It's so warm you can wear your suit under your clothing, and it'll be dry enough to put your clothes on over it before you go home. We're just here to look today. We can shop soon for bathing costumes for the lot of us."

Denis and Michael try to make sandcastles to no avail. The sand is too soft and dry, and they end up digging a great hole instead. The rest of us lie on blankets and soak up the warmth of the sun. The waves lashing on the shore have a hypnotic effect, and before long Pauline, Irene and I doze off. When I wake, Pauline and Irene are walking along the sand, their feet in the water at the edge of the waves. When I run to join them, Pauline is talking about how she misses Sean, and wondering how soon she can find a job and start saving for the fare back.

When we've all had our fill of the beach, and the Chevy is going up a steep hill toward home, the traffic light at the top changes to red when we're halfway up. Daddy, not being accustomed to the gear shift on hills, is cursing under his breath. The car begins to roll back, and he keeps putting one foot on the brake and the other one on the clutch. When we glance back, we notice that the cars behind us have to roll back every time we do.

Suddenly Pauline opens the back door and says, "I'll meet you at the top of the hill." Irene is next, and I follow closing the door behind me. We walk quickly to the top of the hill where the road is level, and when Daddy arrives in that spot we open the door and get back in.

"What did you do that for?" Daddy asks.

"We were too scared to stay in the car," Pauline says boldly.

"Well you didn't have to embarrass me like that," Daddy replies. "Next time we'll go to Redondo or Torrance Beach. They don't have hills to contend with and they're just as close."

I wonder why we didn't go there today. Maybe he wanted to impress us with the beautiful ocean view at top of the hill.

Pauline and Irene go to Los Angeles by bus every day, looking for work. They are beaming when they come home one day and tell us that they've both been hired by The Telephone Company on Ninth Street. The money they'll be making is more than they ever imagined they could earn.

Mammy lets Pauline save part of hers for her fare back to Ireland. She gives them both a nice amount for clothing, bus fare, and lunches, and the rest will be used for the household. We're saving for a television and look forward to having one.

Mari comes over after dinner tonight. She's carrying a large box, and Daddy helps her in with it.

"The folks on the street donated these kitchen utensils and dishes that they didn't need," she says, and her dimples show when she smiles at our reaction.

"The neighbors (another new spelling word) are far too good, so they are," Mammy says.

The most interesting dishes we receive are oval glass plates with a round etched section to hold a cup. "You put cake and ice-cream on the plate along with your coffee cup," Mari says. "The housewives use them when they have their friends over for coffee and a snack."

"It's strange to think that people have time on their hands to be having friends over," Mammy says, with a look of wonder. "And I can't imagine eating ice-cream and drinking coffee at the same time, either."

"Well, you know Bessie, with washing machines you save an awful lot of time that in Ireland you'd be spending scrubbing clothes. Another thing, when you put them on the line you don't have to take them off several times because of the rain." Mammy laughs, and Mari continues. "The glass plates can also be used at baby or bridal showers, something I'll explain to you later."

Our house is at the curve in the cul-de-sac next to the park. There's a boy named Randy who lives at the other end of the short street. His mother is good friends with Mari, and I really like him. He's quiet, good-looking, and has freckles that make him look like the perfect American boy of my dreams. He's fifteen, and we have a great time climbing trees in the park and flying our kites together as well.

Mari's next-door neighbors have a couple of girls around Denis's age, and when we're in the park, I ask one of the girls what she's called.

"Darling," she says, and I'm puzzled. I can't imagine someone naming their baby Darling.

"I've never heard of anyone with a name like that," I say.

After a few days of playing with her and calling her Darling, I ask her, "How do you spell your name?"

"D-a-r-l-e-n-e," she spells out, and I laugh.

"I thought you were saying Darling all this time. Still, I've never heard that name either."

She laughs, and we talk about how things can be unfamiliar to people from other countries.

"You probably never heard the name Mairead, Emir, or Seamus," I say and she laughs and shakes her head.

I've been at North High for six weeks now, and physics is still a complete mystery to me. I've made only one friend in the same grade as me. She's a quiet French Canadian girl with fine elfin-like features and long thick hair the color of wheat. She feels as out of place in this school as I do, and for the same reasons. She moved down from Canada with her mother and grandmother.

As we're leaving class today, I tell her about our experience in Montreal trying to order food and she laughs. "That waitress could easily have spoken to you in English," she says. "I feel bad that she didn't. Why don't we sit together for lunch tomorrow." We're a couple of misfits, it seems, and more than grateful for each other's company.

During my sixth week in school, Mari comes over when I get home. She tells me that she's heard about a Catholic school that would be just right for me. Some of her acquaintants at St. Catherine's Church send their kids there.

"It's called St. Mary's Academy, Patricia, and I think you'd be much happier there."

"I feel so out of place at North High, Mari," I say. Anything would be better.

The next morning, Mammy and I take a bus down to Crenshaw and Slauson Avenue. The school is a lot like Fortwilliam in Belfast, and seems to be part of an old estate although not as grand. We sign papers and get a class schedule. I'll have science instead of that dreaded Physics. The school is all girls, taught by nuns, and just perfect. I feel bad that I'll be leaving my French Canadian friend however. I didn't even have enough time to really get to know her.

The new school costs money, but Mammy says with Pauline and Irene's salaries coming in, there shouldn't be a problem, and it's only for two years anyhow. We go by bus to the uniform company and purchase my school clothing. Each class has a different colored tie, so when you see a girl on the campus, you can tell which class she's in. I'm to be a gold tie.

Next year when the green tie seniors graduate, the incoming freshmen will take their color, and the gold ties will be the new seniors.

I really like the uniform shoes; they're navy and white saddle shoes, and we get to wear them with white ankle socks, just like in the movies. I'm supposed to use that word instead of films, another new word to add to my collection. If Rachel could only see me in my ankle socks she'd be jealous. I remember us having to sneak after school to change out of those ghastly lisle stockings.

When we get home from signing up at St. Mary's, Mammy calls North High and tells them I'll be going elsewhere. I was never so happy to be leaving a place as I am that school. It's not their fault, just a clash of cultures, I suppose.

Mari sends me down to meet her friend's daughter who goes to St. Marys. Her name is Katy, and she's very nice. She shows me where they catch the bus right behind the church, across from Alondra Park.

"I'm a blue tie," she says. "That's a freshman, and I'm fourteen like you. My Aunt Deanna, who's my dad's baby sister, is a junior, or gold tie like you. She lives round the block. Would you like to meet her?"

I nod thinking I'll need all the help I can get in this new school. We walk round the street to Katy's grandmother's, where Deanna is working on her homework.

"You're Katy's aunt and you're only three years older?" I ask.

She nods and laughs. "I was what they call a change of life baby. My mom had me when she was old and she had Katy's dad when she was very young." She asks me about my homeroom, and I tell her I'll have to check when I get to school. I don't have a clue what a homeroom is. In Ireland, we stayed put, and the teachers came around to us. Maybe that's what she's referring to.

"Don't forget, the bus leaves here at seven thirty." I do a calculation in my head to realize she means half past seven.

Daddy says it'll be perfect, he works at 190th Street near Prairie, so he can drop me off on his way to work in the morning. It's only about two blocks out of his way.

"Mind you, it's not that far for you to walk, Patricia," he says. "When the bus leaves you off in the afternoon, you'll have to walk home."

Next morning the bus is full of noisy boys and girls. After about fifteen minutes, we arrive at Serra High school in Gardena, where the boys are dropped at their Catholic school. It's a long ride from there to our school in Los Angeles, and Deanna and Katy introduce me to a few of the other girls.

When the boys are gone, the girls start to sing songs, and I'm really enjoying the one about rowing your boat down the stream. The next one they sing is a whole different matter:

Give a cheer, give a cheer
for the nuns that drink the beer.
In the cellars of old S M A.

I'm surprised, and wonder if there's any truth to it. Probably not. It reminds me of the girls at Fortwilliam calling Sister Charles, Charley.

Homeroom ends up being the first class of the day, where attendance is taken and prayers are said to last us the rest of the day. It's also my French class, and when filling out a questionnaire, I find that I've made an error.

"Do you have a rubber I could borrow?" I ask of the girl sitting next to me in class. Her eyes shoot open and she looks at me in amazement, and hisses under her breath. "You want to borrow what?"

"A rubber." I point to the brand new pink rubber that she has in the hollow of her desk.

"You mean an eraser," she squeaks under her breath, and I'm glad we're near the back. Sr. James is glancing around trying to figure out where the hissing sound came from.

"You rub things out with it, don't you?" I whisper, feeling hurt and confused. "Why can't you call it a rubber?"

"No, you erase things with it, that's why you call it an eraser."

"I'm sorry, I've never heard that word before," I say feeling stupid. I glance around hoping Deanna is somewhere in the room, but she's not. She must have a different homeroom, so I'll wait and see her at lunch. I don't understand why my classmate had such a weird reaction to me wanting to borrow her rubber. I don't think I'll ask again.

After school on this first day, I realize I forgot to ask Deanna where and when the bus picks us up to take us home. By the time I find the location, it's too late. The bus has come and gone.

I know the school is on Crenshaw, and I live about four blocks from Crenshaw, only in a different town about ten miles south of the school. I wait at a public bus stop, and when a bus pulls up, I ask the driver if he's going to Torrance. He nods his head, so I get on and put money in the box. As soon as the bus comes to Florence Avenue, it turns left and goes down that street for about a quarter of a mile. It's the wrong direction altogether, so I run up front feeling upset.

"I thought you said you were going to Torrance."

"I thought you said Florence, hon." He stops the bus. "Sorry 'bout that." He clicks the bottom of the box and gives me back my money.

I hop off, and now have to walk several blocks to get back to Crenshaw again. I start walking in the direction of Torrance, crossing countless traffic signals. I'm afraid to get on another bus for fear of really getting lost.

I pass movie theaters, stores, churches, schools, parks, and traffic light after traffic light until I finally come to Rosecrans. Then I know for sure I'm going in the right direction. It's now about two-and-a-half hours since I started, and when I see El Camino College I know that Alondra Park is right behind it. I sigh with relief, and start walking toward the park and St. Catherine's Church.

Katy yells out the window when she sees me pass her house. "I'm sorry you missed the bus today, Pat."

"Well, you can be sure I'm not going to miss it tomorrow," I say. "I think I should have nice tan, after *that* walk."

"I'd better finish my homework. See you in the morning." She drops the curtains.

After the long walk home, Mammy fusses over me. She gets me water with ice cubes, and tells me I should be proud of myself for finding my way back home. She doesn't seem to realize that I wasn't too swift about getting the information needed to catch the school bus home.

On the Friday of my first week at St. Mary's Academy, the whole student body is told to meet on the bleachers after lunch. The mid-day sun is blazing down, and I'm having a hard time sitting there in the sweltering heat.

"You know why you can't take it, don't you?" Deanna asks.

"I really don't, everyone else seems to be able to stand the heat better than I can," I say.

"It's because your blood is so thick, coming from a cold climate. It'll take months, maybe even years for it to thin like the native Californians," she says with an air of authority.

"That's why my daddy can stand it and we can't," I say. "He's been here over a year now and can handle the heat

266

much better than the rest of us. How about your mom, Deanna, isn't she from overseas?"

"Yes, but she's from Malta. It's in the Mediterranean, and the weather there is a lot like here." She turns and motions toward a girl who's standing in the middle of the small square volley-ball court surrounded by bleachers. She's holding a megaphone.

It's time for the rally to start, and I'm interested in finding out what it's all about it. Apparently there are basketball games every Friday evening. This pep rally is supposed to get the players all fired up to win.

The activities begin. Five girls dressed in short little outfits, shake giant pom-pons wildly over their heads, while singing cheerful songs about winning. I've never seen anything like this before, and I'm certainly enjoying it. One of the songs is really easy to learn, and soon I'm singing along with the rest of the girls:

Cheer cheer for St. Mary's bells
We've got the spirit we've got the yells.

And our team will do their best
They'll fight on and never will they rest.

We'll always beat you, we'll always try
And if we lose we'll never say die.

To our alma mater dear
We'll fight and we'll win for you.
Rah, rah, rah...

The song is repeated in a faster tempo, until the students are in a frenzy of passion to win. Now I know what loyalty is about. Tonight's game is being played far away though, and we have little chance of attending.

I feel so much better in this school, and when it's time for gym class, I'm happy to find that they have separate booths for changing clothes, and enclosed showers as well.

The following day at lunch, a girl from Deanna's home room is sitting with us in junior glen. She whispers something to Deanna causing her eyes to open wide with shock.

"He even lets me drive his car after school," the girl is saying. She's dumpy, very plain and has pimples all over her face. "Do your parents know about it?" Deanna asks. I sit there listening trying to imagine what they are going on about.

"They'd better not find out," the girl says, scowling, "I'd be in a mess of trouble."

After lunch as we walk back to the school building, I ask Deanna what that was all about.

"One of her neighbors, a married man with kids, has been taking her out, letting her drive and Lord knows what else." Deanna whispers.

I'm shocked. How could a seventeen year old deceive the man's wife like that. She knows it's wrong. That poor woman doesn't know what's going on under her very nose. This girl could end up being the cause of splitting up a family with children.

On Fridays they have confession in the chapel at school. Deanna has spoken quietly to her friend and asked her to confess the sin so that she will feel clean again and worthy in God's sight. I can see the girl in line at the other side of the chapel. She seems distressed, as if she's fighting with herself about what to do. When she finally goes in, she remains in the box for the longest time and when we hear raised voices we're not surprised. She finally comes out and kneels down. She looks angry and after a few minutes she walks out of the chapel in a huff.

I feel dreadful just knowing what another person has been confessing, without their knowledge, and feel I should confess that myself when my turn comes.

Outside, Deanna tells me that the priest told her friend she'd have to stop doing what she's doing. Right away, today. Never again to have contact with her neighbor in that way.

"I can't stop, I don't want to stop," she shouted at the priest. He refused to give her absolution for her sin. She had hoped to get forgiveness and then go on with her affair.

Deanna almost feels like going to the neighbor's wife and tell her what's going on but she doesn't know who she is. I'm afraid this girl is in for more trouble in the future because of her reckless behavior. You don't have to be a marriage and family teacher to know that.

We have a priest who comes once a year to the upper grades, to lecture us on marriage and family. "One thing to remember girls is that you may marry a man for his looks and or his money, but what you end up living with for years and years to come is his *disposition*. The most important part of the man is his *disposition*. Remember, that's what you'll be married to. And if he isn't that handsome you won't have to worry about other women looking at him or wanting him."

He has a real point there. I think out of all the information and advice he has given us this will stick out most in my mind. Not that I would ever have a chance with a gorgeous man anyhow.

***

Aunt Eileen's boss, Dr. Burby, has offered to give me free heat lamp treatments on Saturday mornings. Mammy can't believe it. Such generosity. I take the bus from Torrance to Los Angeles every week now, and the treatment seems to be working. The psoriasis is fading from my elbows and only remains on my knees.

Aunt Eileen is putting up with her abusive husband, and lives out in Rosemead, on the other side of Los Angeles. One evening, several months after our arrival, she drives over to Mari's house and asks if she can stay the night. She's very distraught. Apparently her husband Jim stuck his dinner fork in her buttock, because he wasn't satisfied with the meal she served. She had found liquor bottles earlier in the week; under the sink behind the cleaning stuff, and under a stack of blankets in the hall closet. Alcohol is probably the reason for his bizarre behavior.

The next evening, Irene, Denis and I are sitting in the park watching a night baseball game, when we see Aunt Eileen's husband, Jim, driving up our street. He gets out and bangs on Al and Mari's door. Eileen who happened to be in our house at the time, runs out our back door and into the park. Jim is causing a big fuss in front of Mari's house now, and it must be embarrassing for them. The neighbors are probably making remarks about the trouble with those Irish.

Thinking Eileen isn't there, Jim finally leaves, but early the next morning when I go out, I notice that Mari and Al's front porch is covered in a gooey red paint. It's even flowed down the steps to the walkway. Poor Eileen is so embarrassed about the problems she has caused, that by the afternoon she has left and gone back to that awful man.

Chapter Twenty Five

This evening Daddy comes through the front door with a wicked sparkle in his eye. "Mr. Martinez, a friend of mine at the Knights of Columbus has a good looking son who has noticed you in church, Pauline. Pedro would love to have a date with you, take you to the movies or something."

"Really?" Pauline says, looking slightly interested. "What does he look like?"

"He's handsome enough, but what's more important, he's from a good Catholic family. How would you like it if he came over to meet you?"

"I don't mind," she replies with a look of resignation.

I think Daddy has hatched a devious plan to make our Pauline forget about Sean. He doesn't want her to leave us and go back to Belfast.

On Saturday evening just before twilight, Pedro comes to the door. He's good looking, with brown eyes and dark curly hair about the same color as our Pauline's. There's an uncomfortable few minutes after the introductions and before they leave. No one quite knows what to say, and Pauline is shifting her feet around awkwardly. It's such a relief when they finally leave. I notice Daddy's smug look as he watches Pedro open the door of his lovely powder-blue Thunderbird for Pauline, just like a real gentleman.

Over in the park a baseball game has begun. The lights have been turned on, and Irene and I decide to go over and sit on the bleachers to watch. Denis and Michael are inside watching our new television with Mari's boys.

There's an autumn chill in the air, so we wrap our cardigans around us to keep out the cold. There's something magical about the whole environment. People in the stands are shouting encouraging words, and the players look so relaxed and sure of themselves. It's one of the scenes I imagined in my head before we came to this country. I figure I must have seen a movie with this same scene.

The teams have lots of good-looking boys around eighteen or twenty years of age, and this makes it so much more pleasurable to watch. One fielder in particular, keeps looking our way and smiling.

At the end of the game, he comes over and talks to us. I think he's probably smiling inside at how shy Irene and I are compared to American girls our age. We're told his name is Gil. He also tells us he's fascinated with our singsongy Belfast accents. "How would you like to get a bite to eat," he asks.

"All right," Irene and I say in unison.

He looks a little perturbed that I'm going too. I think he'd rather be alone with Irene, who's seventeen. He leads us to his car, which is a long DeSoto with fins in the back. The kind of fins that the girls on car commercials always run their hands over, like they're stroking a cat or something. His radio plays a doo-wop song as he drives, and he clicks his fingers in time with the music. Irene is sitting next to him, and I'm by the door, admiring his good looks from a distance. He drives to Hawthorne Boulevard.

Slowing down, he pulls into the parking lot of a closed store. A slow romantic song is playing on the radio, and almost before he has the car turned off, he's grabbed Irene in a tight embrace, and his hands are roaming to every forbidden place imaginable.

She tries to get out of his clutches, and as soon as her mouth is free, she shouts, "Take us back now, please!" She's very upset, so I start yelling at him as well. I don't think this is quite what he expected from two greenhorns.

His once handsome face is beginning to look downright ugly. He starts up the car and peels out of the parking lot, his tires screeching.

Irene and I hold on for dear life all the way back to our street and jump out the minute the car jerks to a stop.

"Jesus, Mary, and Joseph, that was close," Irene says.

"And I thought he was so cute," I say. "How could he have acted like that?"

Under the lights from the ballpark Irene looks ashen. We hold hands to comfort each other and walk down the street, away from our house, as he squeals off out of the area. After we've calmed down, we go back and enter our dark living room to watch television with the boys. Mammy doesn't even notice anything different, she's so engrossed in the Saturday night movie.

I wonder, are all men and boys the same? That fellow didn't even try to get to know Irene first. He's probably one of those people without any religion, and was just interested in his animal instincts. Tonight I lie in bed and remember lying in Granny's attic room not so long ago. Back then I had an image of American boys from the movies I'd seen.

Music plays in the background. Tall trees line both sides of the street and stretch out to touch each other. Dogs bark here and there seeming to compete with the birds in the trees. A clean-cut, freckled-faced Yankee boy, rides his bike, wobbling from one side of the street to the other.

The bike is the heavy Schwinn type, and from each handlebar hangs a large cloth bag. The word Tribune is printed on the bags, and every so often the boy reaches in and takes out a newspaper. He flings it with precision, and it sails gracefully through the air, landing squarely in the middle of the porch of a grand, two-story white house, with yellow shutters. An American flag graces the pole attached to the verandah, and the lawn is perfectly manicured, and just the right shade of green.

"Good morning, Mr. Johnson," the paperboy calls, and he waves, as a tall handsome man, dressed in a dazzling silk robe, reaches for the morning paper.

"Good morning, Marty," the man answers, and glides gracefully back into his house.

Marty continues whistling, landing the papers on other front porches, along this perfect street of this perfect American town.

I fall into a deep sleep, and my thoughts meld into a dream, perfect in every way; one where I want to stay, never to wake up to the harsh reality of this wicked world. When reality startles me awake on Sunday morning, I quietly get ready for Mass.

On the walk over, Pauline seems to be dragging behind, so Irene and I slow down as well.

"You wouldn't believe the evening I had last night with His Lordship, Pedro," Pauline says, and her eyes roll up to heaven.

"Where did you go?" Irene asks, and I watch Pauline's eyes with interest.

"We went to a drive-in movie," she says. "and I honestly couldn't tell you what it was about."

"Why is that?" I ask.

"That good Catholic fella had his hands all over the place. I spent the whole time fighting him off. When I finally got up the courage to tell him I wanted to leave, he got upset. He started the car and took off with that wee speaker thing-a-ma-jig still attached to the window. He didn't even give me a chance to unhook the bloody thing – just drove off in a rage, and ripped the cord right off the speaker in his haste. He's a lucky bugger he didn't break the side window of his beautiful Thunderbird."

"You're coddin' us, aren't you, Pauline?" Irene says.

"I am not. It's the bloody truth, his tongue was roaming out of his mouth as well, darn near choked the life out of me, so he did!" Showers of spittle hit us as she vents her frustration. "I had this strange feeling, when he brought me over to his house before the movie. There were nude statues and pictures everywhere. It gave me the bloomin' willies."

We tell Pauline about our interesting evening with the baseball player, and she's amazed.

We've reached the front doors of the church now. Mammy and Daddy look back at us with sharp eyes. They're probably hoping we're not going to keep talking all the way up the aisle.

"I hope he's not at this Mass," I whisper.

Pauline gives me a look of horror. "God forbid," she whispers, and we genuflect and move into the pew beside the rest of the family.

We can see Aunt Mari up ahead with Kevin, her oldest child. Her husband, Al, isn't Catholic. He really doesn't have any religion, but he doesn't mind Mari raising the kids in her own faith.

They walk home with us, and I tell her how grateful I am that she found the right school for me. It has changed my whole outlook on life. While we're walking, Kevin calls out the name of every car that passes. He seems to have a photographic memory or something, so he does. The different vehicles all look the same to us, but this wee tot can tell them apart.

Back home, while Mammy is putting a chicken in the oven and Pauline is peeling the spuds, Daddy calls Pauline into the living room.

"How was your date last night?"

"It wasn't any fun, Daddy. Your man had his hands all over me. I had to fight him off the whole time, so I did."

Daddy looks shocked and embarrassed. He seemed so sure that this was the one for Pauline, the one to take her mind off Sean, waiting patiently for her back home. He's at a loss for words, and when he finally gets over the shock he just says, "Sorry, I never thought he'd be like that."

Shrugging her shoulders, her indignation showing, she goes back to the kitchen to finish peeling the spuds.

As we three lie in bed in the evening, we talk about how the perfect man should be. Irene and I agree with Pauline; they should keep their hands off when requested the first time.

***

We've been in California for six months now, and our Pauline has saved almost enough for her passage home.

We had a memorable first Christmas here, with temperatures in the eighties. Granny couldn't believe it. She wrote that their winter was wetter than usual, and they even had a few days of snow.

She and Marjorie have received permission from the American Embassy to emigrate, and will arrive here shortly before Pauline leaves for home. They'll stay at Mari's until Marjorie finds work and a place for them to live.

I'm just reading the letter from Granny when my friend Deanna comes to the door wearing her roller skates. I run to get mine. The skates were a pleasant surprise for Christmas, something I didn't expect. We open the garage door and skate round and round inside so we can get some badly needed practice.

Daddy has been driving us down to the roller rink next to the Redondo Pier on Saturday evenings. I just love the sound of the organ and the throng of kids swirling round the floor with such precision. They sway from side to side in perfect time to the music. My problem has been the corners, and I spend a lot of time slamming into the railings.

Pauline comes out to the garage to have a wee peek at our skating. She watches with interest and listens to our conversation.

"You should try this, Pauline," I say, "it's loads of fun."

Pauline rolls her eyes and says, "My, oh my and wow, Patricia! don't we have the perfect American accent already, and only here six months."

I'm embarrassed, but I can't help it if Deanna's words rub off on me, and I sit in school every day listening to the same accent.

When we've had enough, Deanna, who came to California with her family just before we did, asks me to walk down to the telephone booth with her. She had to leave her boyfriend in Kalamazoo, Michigan, just like Pauline left hers in Belfast. Deanna's been calling him, person-to-person, several times a week, and is having difficulty lately catching him at home. We reach the phone booth and she puts in a great deal of change. She then gives the operator the number.

"I'd like to make a person-to-person call to Joe Vigo, please."

It costs less to do it this way if he's not home. She waits several minutes, and I can see her look of utter disappointment. She lets the mouthpiece dangle from her hand, and it hits the side of the glass phone booth. Then with a forlorn look she slowly replaces the mouthpiece.

"He's not there for the tenth time this week, and I haven't had an answer to the letter I sent two weeks ago either. I have a feeling he's found someone else. What do you think, Pat?"

"I think it's probably impossible to keep your romance going from such a distance, with both of you still in school and everything. You'll find someone else before you know it."

A week later, I call Deanna to see if she wants to come over.

"I can't, Pat, I'm in big trouble. My mom found my neighbor Bill and me in her car, in our closed garage. We were just necking, but I'm restricted for a week."

"I *thought* he was making eyes at you, the last time I was at your house," I say. "It looks like he won out over the distant Joe Vigo."

She laughs. "He's much cuter than Joe, too, and I find myself falling for him a little more every day."

Instead of falling for another, like Deanna, our Pauline is determined to go back to Sean.

Every morning I lie in bed listening to Pauline and Irene getting ready for work. They have to catch the bus at seven o'clock to get to Los Angeles by eight-thirty. When I smell the toast burning, it's time for me to get up. It never fails, every day Pauline puts toast under the grill and forgets to watch it.

I laugh when Irene tells me about what happened Yesterday. She had to go on ahead to the bus stop because

Pauline was running late. She got on the bus alone when it came because Pauline was nowhere in sight. Pauline ran like a harrier down the street, trying to get there on time, but realized it was too late.

A kindly neighbor who knew they waited at the same stop every morning, pulled his car over and spoke to her. "I can chase them down for you, if you'd like to get in," he said.

He drove her about a mile, right past Irene who was sitting on the bus, unaware, worrying herself sick about what would happen when Pauline arrived late for work.

At the next stop, Irene watched Pauline step onto the bus acting cool and collected, and drop her money in the container.

"How did you get here so fast?" Irene asked when Pauline sat next to her.

"I ran all the way, so I did," Pauline replied and Irene looked at her in bewilderment.

"It was so funny, Patricia," Irene says "I thought Pauline had turned into a sprinter."

"It won't happen again," Pauline says. "I was just lucky that Mr. Nelson saw me."

They've decided to wake up fifteen minutes earlier from now on, to avoid a repeat of yesterday's near miss.

Every morning, since the first morning I started St. Mary's Academy, Daddy's car door flies open as we turn the corner at the end of our street on the way to the school bus. He just grabs it shut, like it's part of the way things are done, kind of like Pauline's daily burned toast.

Chapter Twenty Six

It's a balmy day when Granny and Marjorie arrive at Los Angeles International Airport. Our parents have gone to meet them, and we sit watching for their return.

When they arrive there's great excitement, and everyone wants to show them everything. They're happy to see Mari again. She left home such a long time ago. Granny is infatuated with her Swedish-Irish-American grandchildren, and pleased with the warm weather at this time of year. It's nice that Mari and Al have the room to put them up for a while.

Aunt Mari's little girl, Terry, is eight months old now and a real handful. Mari will be forty soon, and has nearly as many children as she hoped for. One more and she'll be in seventh heaven. I do believe she's pregnant again, for there's a wee bump in just the right place. If she is expecting another, she'll have four children under four years of age. Mari is such a happy-go-lucky person, and the personality bubbles out of her, I know she loves every minute of being a mother.

It feels great to still have so many family members around us in a foreign land. We now have a grand total of sixteen. It looks like we'll be gaining another cousin soon but losing a sister.

Pauline is leaving next month. She's already booked passage with a Greek line, and will sail from New York to Cobh, in County Cork. First she'll fly to New Jersey and stay with Paul O'Hare, Mammy's cousin, who came to America with his wife several years ago. He'll drive Pauline to the New York Harbor. I don't know how we'll get along here without her.

Pauline gives notice to the telephone company, and will be leaving in a few weeks. She's betwixt and between about leaving. She wants to be with Sean, but she'll miss our family.

When the day comes, she's overcome and can't say goodbye to Michael and Denis. She walks out the door with her head turned in the other direction so as not to have to look at them. She says not being there to see them grow will be the hardest part about leaving.

Marjorie moves into our house and will sleep in Pauline's bed. Her first job quest is a success. She'll be a key punch operator at the Occidental Insurance Company in Los Angeles. It's said to be the tallest building in the city skyline.

She confesses to an indiscretion. On her job application she made up the name of a high school in Ireland, that she supposedly attended. Now she's in fear of her boss writing to the imaginary school and catching her in the fib. Mammy, who seems to be incapable of telling a lie, is amazed that Marjorie could take such a chance.

"But what would my chances be of getting the position, without a secondary school education, Bessie?" Marjorie says. "As long as I can do the job well, there shouldn't be any repercussions."

After a month Pauline's first letter arrives. She's staying with Lucy and Tom until she gets married, then she and Sean will move into Granny's house on the Springfield Road. She can take care of the house in case Granny ever wants to return.

At Granny's age it may be difficult adjusting to a place like this. To lead a normal life here, you have to drive a car. She could get homesick as well.

13 May 1957
Dear Family,
Hope you all are well. I am. It's strange to be

in Belfast and not have the lot of you around. I had
quite a trip back here. It was nothing like the H.M.S.
Saxonia though. The food was very strange and
all they served was peppermint tea, which I had to
drink for lack of anything else. The ship was so slow
that it took ten days to travel from New York to Cobh.
I suppose I can't complain though, because it was so
much cheaper. We were really spoiled on the British
Line, weren't we?
I spent ages looking for the chapel where Mass was
to be held on Sunday, and couldn't find it for the
life of me. Later in the day, I saw a priest out on
deck, and explained my predicament. He just laughed
at me for being upset, and told me not to worry.
In this case it wasn't a sin at all. What a relief.
There was a fellow on the ship who followed
me around, and made me awful nervous. When he
finally spoke, it was in Italian. He must have thought
I was too. As he didn't speak any English
the conversation didn't progress too well.
The weather here is rainy as usual, but
It's up to 68 degrees during the day.
Sean sends his love. I miss you all.
Please give Denis and Michael a big hug for me.
                    Love, Pauline xoxo

Pauline has only been gone a few weeks, when notices
are passed out in my school about our junior prom.

"Are you going, Pat?" Deanna asks.

"Who would I go with? I don't know any boys; I just
turned fifteen."

"Oh, come on, we can double date. I'm going with
Bill."

"I can't see me going, Deanna. I don't have a dress or
anything, and I'd have to get my parents' permission."

When I ask Mammy and Daddy about the prom, I'm
told, after several days of deliberation, that as long as it's a
double date there shouldn't be a problem. I have a feeling

that Aunt Mari was consulted and had some influence on their decision.

The dance is being held at the Hollywood Roosevelt Hotel, which sounds very posh. The only problem for me is finding a boy to go with.

"Bill has lots of friends," Deanna says. "You could go out once with one of them to get acquainted first." She finds a boy who is willing to go with me. After consulting with my parents again, they say that as long as there are four of us going, it'll be all right. But they want to meet the boy first.

"He's got an Irish name, Mr. Owens," Deanna says with confidence. "His name is Michael Milligan." They seem happy enough with this revelation.

On the evening of the "get-to-know-each-other" date, Mike comes in his car, with Deanna and Bill in the back seat. He knocks on the door, and when I see him I'm slightly disappointed. He has a haircut like a duck's behind. It's all greased up, and he's wearing a leather jacket and tight blue jeans. He could pass for a Teddy Boy any day. I'm nervous about how my parents are going to react, but they don't seem to have any objections.

We take off in Mike's car to get some hamburgers in Redondo Beach. On the way back he decides to show off his driving skills, and burns rubber several times. I'm a wee bit scared now, but Deanna and Bill seem to be enjoying the exhibition and not worrying at all. The third demonstration, however, goes a bit awry, and we end up doing what they call a one-eighty, right in the middle of a busy street. The car careens round and round and when it finally straightens up, my head is spinning. Mike acts like it's something he does often, and even on purpose. Deanna and Bill are laughing nervously. I don't think they enjoyed the spin any more than I did. Maybe Mike even scared himself, because the rest of the drive home is more relaxed, as we discuss our plans for the junior prom.

When Aunt Eileen finds out that I need a formal dress she suggests her wedding dress. It's white, but not too elaborate, and comes just below the knee. Mammy makes a few alterations, and now all I need is a pair of white shoes.

On the afternoon of the prom, Deanna calls and says that Mike Milligan is in jail.

"It isn't any wonder," I say. "His driving is wild, so Lord knows what else he's capable of. Now what are we going to do?"

"Don't worry, Pat, another friend of Bill's has offered to take Mike's place. Your parents will probably like him a lot better. He's more clean-cut, even sophisticated looking."

Mammy says it's all right, since I've got the dress and shoes and purchased the tickets. Deanna and Bill need another couple to double with anyhow.

I meet Paul for the first time when he arrives on prom night. He's very tall, and dressed nicely in a black suit and red tie. He's carrying a small white box and opens it for me. Inside is a beautiful white gardenia with dark green leaves. The aroma is beautiful, and he gently places it on my dress with a long pin that has a pearl at one end. I take the red carnation I purchased and pin it to his lapel. It goes nicely with his red tie.

We talk a bit on the way to the prom, and I notice that only a few subjects interest him. He talks on and on about car engines. His conversation is also sprinkled with discussions of Christian Dior fashions. I've never even heard of this Dior person, so I'm at a loss for words.

The Hollywood Roosevelt Hotel is up the street from Grauman's Chinese Theater. We're very impressed with its velvet curtains and tables set neatly around the gleaming dance floor. A large glittering ball hangs from the ceiling and is elegance at its best–so much so, that I feel uncomfortable and out of place, kind of like an impostor enjoying the grandeur of it all.

We meet up with Sharon, one of the girls who rides our school bus. She's dressed in a sleek, strapless red dress, that follows the contours of her bosom, revealing a fair amount of cleavage. Her bleached blonde hair is pageboy style, and bright red lipstick gleams on her full lips. Tonight she looks like a petite version of Rosemary Clooney. Her date happens to be her much older brother.

After several dances with Paul, I notice that he's making little side remarks to Sharon when we pass her on the dance floor. She seems to be flirting with him as well. Her brother is pale and thin and has a noticeable nervous tic. I don't think she's exactly enjoying his company.

Suddenly, at the end of a song, as the band starts up again and we're standing right next to Sharon and her brother, Paul says loudly, "Let's change partners!" He swoops over and grabs Sharon, and her brother walks shyly toward me. I'm slightly perturbed, even though Paul and I have nothing in common. I do feel sorry for Sharon's brother, however, and wonder what has caused him to be so nervous and bewildered.

The bandleader is taking requests, and after several more tunes, he smiles down at the dancers then speaks into the microphone.

"This song has been requested by the young lady in the red dress and the handsome man who's breathing down her neck. Cool down, Buddy, the night has just begun."

I'm so embarrassed, I could just crawl away and die. I've been hoodwinked. My date is dancing cheek-to-cheek with Miss Over-Sexed Sharon, and she has pawned her nervous brother off on me. His hand is visibly shaking in mine.

When I make an excuse to go to the restroom, Deanna is there primping her hair. I ask if she knows why Sharon's brother is such a bundle of nerves.

"He was in the Korean war and is suffering from shell shock," Deanna says. "I notice he's ended up with you."

"Yes, and Sharon and Paul are smooching on the dance floor now. It wouldn't have been so bad if they hadn't announced it over the loudspeaker," I say. "Oh well, I wasn't crazy about him anyhow." I sit down and try to enjoy the wonderful music, but I'll be happy when this dance is over. I didn't mind having my date fall for another, but it sort of stinks, the way it was done. Sharon's poor shell-shocked brother must be feeling just as bad as I am.

This prom was a disaster for me from day one, with Michael Milligan and his shenanigans, and then being dumped when the dance had hardly begun. I think I'll sit out the senior prom next year.

Anyhow, I'd rather be climbing trees.

***

I miss the smell of burning toast in the morning. Irene eats her bread cold with butter and jam. She misses Pauline's company terribly, both on the bus to and from work and on weekends as well. They enjoyed going down to Robert Hall's on Crenshaw Boulevard to see what bargains they could pick up.

This country has the cheapest food in the world, and you don't have to save for months to buy a shirt or shoes like you do everywhere else. Last week I got one of those crinoline petticoats for three dollars. It has four layers of netting and is very pouffy. Mammy said it doesn't behoove her to sew our clothes anymore. They're so much cheaper to buy.

I've got a box of really *American* things to send to Rachel. There's a jacket made of blue jean material, a lovely diary with a lock and key, some very classy ankle socks, and a hair brush with Elvis Presley's picture on it, and of course lots of bubble gum. I'm sure she'll love everything because I do. I just hope she knows who Elvis Presley is by now.

The people who own the house we rent sometimes come and pick me up on a Saturday night to baby-sit their three children. The best part is, the kids are usually asleep when I get there. Making fifty cents an hour, I can buy a new blouse with one evening of minding kids while watching television!

***

Michael and Denis have lost their Belfast accents like I have. I just hope they can remember Ireland. Although Denis should; he was nine when we left last year, Michael was just five and I'm not sure how much he will be able to recall.

New apartments are being built around the corner from our house, near the park. It's Saturday, and our boys are out playing with the neighborhood kids. Mammy and I are planting a border of flowers along the edge of our walkway when Michael comes racing across the park looking very scared.

"What's the matter?" Mammy asks. "You look like you've seen a ghost."

"It's...it's...our Du...Denis. He fell from upstairs...the new buildings," he says. Michael's chest is heaving, his voice making little choking sounds, and his eyes are filled with fear.

Mammy yells for Daddy and he comes out of the house looking alarmed. They run as fast as their legs can take them and I follow. There's a crowd of kids gathered around Denis, who's lying flat on his back on the ground. Up above him is a balcony. It's part of the new building, and the floor is constructed temporarily out of some kind of soft board. There's a gaping hole where Denis has fallen through.

Daddy carries him back to the house and he's moaning in pain.

"It hurts really bad," he says.

Now they have him in the back seat of the car and are off to the hospital. I say a prayer that he'll be okay.

We later learn that he fractured a few bones in his back, but luckily it didn't affect his spinal cord. I feel like we have received another blessing. Things could have been so much worse.

The next day, we go to the hospital to visit him, and he's lying on a bed out in the corridor. In fact the whole hallway is lined up with patients waiting for rooms. Denis looks a bit glum.

"The doctor said I have to wear this brace for four to six months, Patricia."

"There goes all your fun, Denis," I say. "You'll have to be more careful after this."

The brace reaches all the way from the top of his legs to his underarms. It's similar to the heavy corsets that Granny wore in the old days, although this one is much heavier and looks extremely cumbersome. I imagine he'll be walking around with a stiff gait, unable to bend or anything. I bet he won't be playing in construction sites after this, and I'm sure his mischievous friends have been taught a lesson as well.

Now when we go to the beach, Denis can't go out into the waves like the rest of us, but has to be content to paddle in shallow water.

***

Aunt Eileen left her abusive alcoholic husband for good. She and Marjorie have been saving every penny and are living in an apartment with Granny until they have enough for a down payment on a house. It's on Artesia Boulevard across from the park, so we can almost see it from our house. Eileen says she will remain unmarried for the rest of her life, and Marjorie doesn't seem to have any aspirations toward marriage either.

Aunt Mari and Uncle Al now have their fourth child, a son, named Owen. Mari said she's happy to have the family she always wanted, and her children mean the world to her.

Today when I come home from school, I learn that our landlord wants to build an extension on to our house and move his own family in. That means we'll have to move. Why did they have to make that decision, I wonder. We were so happy in this house by the park. It's the reason they want to move here, I suppose. The park being so handy for their growing family and all.

Mammy looks through the classified section of the paper every day now, searching for a house to rent. They don't have quite enough money yet to put down in order to buy one.

We find a place on Madrona Avenue right next to the City Hall complex, and we can see the Torrance Plunge from our front windows.

Deanna's upset that we've moved to a different part of Torrance. We won't be able to hang around together after school anymore.

Now that it's summer again, the boys and I can go swimming often at the plunge. I love my new bathing suit. It's black but has a large light pink panel in front. If you look at it quickly it makes you think I'm the size of the pink area, even though I'm much bigger. I've learned to dive off the edge and swim underwater, coming up at the other side of the pool. Denis, who's ten now, is so happy to have that awful brace removed, that he's being a wee bit rambunctious, and scares me the way he dive-bombs into the water. Michael just plays around in the shallow end as he's only six. It's great on the hot summer days to be able to cool off right across the street from home.

Our house is Spanish style and has a lovely big front window rounded at the top. Inside, curved arches divide some of the rooms. We've never been in a home like this before and really enjoy it. The only problem is the Italian people next door. During the day it's nice and quiet, but the minute Mr. Farino comes home from work, the yelling begins.

"Are all Italian people like that, Mammy?" I ask.

"I don't think so, Patricia," she says. "Although they do seem to have a more gregarious nature, I think the majority get along well. Our neighbours just seem to be mismatched."

"I would be really upset with all that shouting," I say, "but Mrs. Farino doesn't seem to mind it at all."

"Well, Patricia, she's probably so used to it, that it doesn't bother her. Don't forget, *she's* doing her fair share of yelling as well, isn't she? It seems like it's part of their daily routine, kind of like us having a normal conversation."

Our neighbours on the other side, the Watanabes, are Japanese and have two lovely little girls. The family usually keeps very much to itself.

Right across the road from our house, on this side of the plunge, is a railroad track. Every once in a while, a train goes by and makes a lot of racket. Lately there's been a car parked behind the cluster of Eucalyptus trees on this side of the track. Today, Mrs. Watanabe walks over to investigate, and when she comes back, her face is even whiter than it was before.

A short time later, several police cars arrive and drive up to the dirt area by the tree. Mrs. Watanabe comes out of her house and explains to Mammy that she saw a man in the car, who had a shotgun pointed under his chin. The car window was splattered with blood.

When Mrs. Watanabe speaks with the policemen, she's extremely upset. I would be too, if I'd seen such a gruesome sight. Several hours later, the coroner's van arrives, and the body is taken away. Everyone is wondering why no one heard the shot.

Days later, we read in the newspaper that the man, who was only in his forties, had financial problems and took his own life. He had probably waited for a noisy train to go by and then pulled the trigger with his toe.

Life is so fragile. We only have one chance on this earth. I wish people who are very depressed would speak up. If only he'd told someone how bad he felt, the horror across the street might have been avoided. I pray for the family of that poor desperate man.

This is not the kind of summer we expected, there's a pall of sadness hanging over it, and when it's time for school to start again, it's a kind of relief.

Chapter Twenty Seven

Mammy is driving now and has a big red 1953 Buick. It's powerful, sturdy and has a nice smooth ride. She drives Denis and Michael down to Nativity Catholic School every day. When the parish priest, Father Glynn, from County Roscommon, found out we were from Ireland, he made sure to keep two spaces open at the school for our boys. They started last week after summer vacation and seem to be happy there.

Irene just earned her license, and she's an excellent driver. In a few months I'll be finished learning, if Daddy can put up with me that long. Today I'm behind the wheel, and when I pull up behind another car at the stop sign on Maple Avenue, I start to go out onto the main road behind the car ahead of us.

"Stop!" Daddy shouts. I slam on the brakes and we both bounce forward.

"But I stopped behind the car in front and now the road is clear," I say impatiently.

"*Each* car must stop," he says, "even if the road is clear." He looks like he wants to hit me. I just can't understand why, when there wasn't any traffic, couldn't we just follow the car in front without stopping again. We go into an empty parking lot, and I practice backing into a space between two boxes that we brought along. The boxes are only slightly damaged by the time I'm finally successful.

When we get home, Daddy seems tired, and he's sound asleep and snoring loudly three minutes after he sits on the sofa. Mammy looks at him and smiles. I think she must realize how hard it is on him, being the driving instructor for all the females in the family.

***

Tonight, as our family watches the evening news, we are horrified to see crowds of people demonstrating in the streets of Little Rock, Arkansas. They chant things about whites only and segregation being the answer. We watch full grown men, policemen at that, standing in front of a high school, blocking the door and preventing five or six young colored girls from entering.

"My God," Daddy says, "Those girls are brave to stand up to that crowd."

"It sort of brings to mind the bigotry in Northern Ireland," I say. "Mari was right about this country not being a bed of roses, I suppose. It certainly isn't for those kids."

"Aye," Mammy says. "And nothing we went through can compare to this."

The phone in the kitchen rings and Mammy goes to answer it. The rest of us watch the scene unfolding before us on the TV.

"You'd think those grown-up people would be ashamed to treat other human beings like that," Irene says. "After all, the colored people were forced here against their will."

Mammy comes back into the living room. "That was my cousin who came out her after we did. Remember him?" she asks, and we nod. "I told him what we saw on the news and he mentioned something that happened to him in Georgia, only yesterday."

"Is that where he's stationed?" I ask.

"Yes, he was drafted as soon as he arrived and hardly got used to things up here before being sent down South," Mammy says. "He was on a crowded bus yesterday, and a pregnant woman got on, so he stood up right away and gave her his seat. Well, he couldn't believe it when people started yelling at him, and the driver even stopped the bus, and wouldn't go until the woman moved back to the rear."

"Why was that?" Irene asks. "Men always give up their seats to women in Ireland."

"Well, he was shocked when his army buddy explained it to him," Mammy says. "The woman was colored, and in the South they have to go to the back of the bus. They even have to use separate drinking fountains, toilets and restaurants from the whites."

"I can understand what they're going through," Irene says.

"The bigots from Northern Ireland, must have crossed the ocean and settled in the South," I say.

I think our whole family can feel an empathy with the colored people in the southern states. We suffered because of our religion, but *they* are discriminated against because of their race. We were not so obvious because we looked the same, but with their skin color, it's impossible for them to hide from the prejudice.

I just hope someday, things will change in both countries, and every man and woman can stand proud and have the same rights as the majority.

***

Irene and I are ecstatic. We've found out about an Irish club that holds Saturday night dances in the Sokol Hall in the Hollywood area.

She drives and she's so nervous about going in to a crowd of strangers, that when we finally do she rushes to the lady's room. I follow her, and can hear her throwing up in the toilet. I wonder why she has such a nervous stomach? After we get used to being checked over like a row of race-horses we have a great time, and especially enjoy the set dances that are interspersed throughout the evening between the waltzes and fox-trots. This way we don't have to talk to any one boy, we're so busy swinging and moving through the paces of a group of eight.

On our second visit, Irene throws up in the car on the way to the dance. It's just a small amount and I'm glad I brought a towel along for such emergencies, or we'd have to turn around and go home. We put the towel in the trunk and hope the smell doesn't come through to the rest of the car.

Irene is a bit shy, and I am too. But tonight, after attending the dances for several months, we meet two nice boys who are friends and roommates. They're from Ballymena, a small town not far from Belfast. John is nineteen, and Liam is about twenty-five. We dance with them several times, and by the end of the evening they ask if we'd like to go out the following Saturday.

We double date to a movie, and I think Irene really likes Liam. I like John, but no sparks fly or anything like that. I'm only sixteen after all. When we kiss, fireworks don't explode like I imagined they would, although I must admit it's a pleasant experience.

Now, every Thursday on the stroke of eight, the phone rings. Irene answers, and it's Liam calling to set up a date for the four of us the following Saturday. They take us all the way to Riverside one Saturday afternoon to see car races. The guys seem to enjoy the loud noise, as the cars speed by, but it's hot and dusty, and Irene and I don't know one car from the other. So when the winner comes in, it doesn't make much difference to us.

Week after week, for several months, the phone rings like clockwork on Thursday night. It's always Liam, never John. Always the four of us. The fellows are awful nice but the dating routine has become very boring altogether. So predictable. After about five months of this, we find reasons not to be home on Thursday nights when the inevitable call will come. We lay low, and don't even go to the Irish dances for a few weeks, in hopes that the fellows will get the message.

In the meantime I'm almost finished with my last year of high school.

A new girl has joined our home room. I'm delighted when she introduces herself to the class with a real Irish

293

brogue and says she's from Limerick. Her name is Dorothy, and she's a gold tie like I am. When I talk to her between classes, I learn that her younger sister, Dolores, also attends the school and is a red tie, or junior.

At lunch, the girls tell me all about themselves. Their father and mother are in their sixties and retired. Their mother was an Irish-American who went to visit Ireland on holiday. There she met and fell in love with their father. He even made a wild promise to buy her a castle if she would stay and marry him.

"Your dad must be really something," I say. "Offering a castle to win your mother's hand. You mean to say she really took him up on it?"

"Yes, would you believe it?" Dorothy says, "She's never returned to America until this year."

The sisters say they were born in the castle. It was slightly smaller than the usual size castle, but had turrets and abutments and looked grand enough for any princess.

"Pat, we darn near near froze to death in that place," Dolores says. "We could only heat a small portion of it, so the rest was closed off and unusable. It was an interesting life though, and we had a fair-sized plot of land to gallivant around."

The next Saturday after my visit to the dermatologist in Los Angeles, I take a bus to the girls' house and meet their parents. Paddy, their father, is a lanky man with a long bony nose and wavy, white hair. Even though I never see him stand, I can tell he's tall because his head sits so high in his easy chair, and his legs are long and skinny. On the small table at his elbow sits a glass of whiskey. He sips a little and holds it up to me. "This is *uisce beatha*, Pat. The water of life." He pronounces it "ish-k-baha," and I can tell by the red veins on his nose that it's his constant companion. After several hours of chatter and laughter with his daughters doing most of the talking, their dad looks at me strangely.

"Still waters run deep, Pat," he says. I feel a blush coming on, but can't really agree with him. I'm not that deep, I only wish I was. I'm just quiet by nature. I think he's amazed to meet someone with so little to say, after living with such chatty daughters.

When I leave, Dorothy and Dolores walk me to the bus stop.

"Do you think you could both come with Irene and me to the Irish dances on Saturdays?" I ask.

"I'll ask my parents, but Mom is very strict," Dorothy replies. She raises her eyes and crosses her fingers.

In the end, they can't go dancing, and I don't know why. Irene and I could pick them up; it's on our way. Oh well, maybe the old folks will change their minds before long. The dances are harmless, and great fun to boot.

***

It takes two tries before I get my license. The first time, I'm asked to drive through some quiet residential streets in Torrance. I come to an intersection that doesn't have a stop sign on either side. After I go through, the examiner tells me to pull over and stop, which I do right away.

"You failed right there, young lady," the man says sternly. "You should have slowed down a lot more than you actually did back there. What if another car reached the intersection at the same time going at the same speed?" He writes something on the paper. "Think about what you did wrong and reschedule."

I drive him back to the Department of Motor Vehicles in silence, unable to impress him with my newfound safer method of driving. I feel just like I do in confession when the priest raises his voice.

The next week I'm very mindful of my previous error, and pass the test.

Irene says I can drive to the Irish dance on Saturday to celebrate my accomplishment. After we're there for a while, I notice she's dancing with a fantastic-looking fellow I've never seen before. We pass on the dance floor, and she looks like she's in heaven. I'm dancing with one of the older fellows who reminds me of a leprechaun, and he's almost old enough to be my father. He's really great at the "Stack of Barley," though. That's a dance that requires some special footwork. We sing and laugh as we dance.

It's a little past midnight when the dance ends and Irene and I leave the Sokol Hall. She looks at me with a little sadness showing. "That fellow I was dancing with asked if he could take me home," she says.

"Oh, Irene, why didn't you let him?" I'm wondering why she didn't take the opportunity to go with him. He was a great dancer and extremely handsome as well.

I told him I couldn't let you go all the way home alone, Patricia. After all, you've only just gotten your driver's license."

"Oh, I'm sorry Irene. Maybe in a few months, you'll feel like I'm ready to drive alone."

"Maybe I will, but I doubt Mammy or Daddy will."

I drive home for practice. We just need to go up Western Avenue from the Hollywood area to Torrance. But when we get to Imperial Highway, we run into a fog that's so thick we can't see three feet in front of the car.

Irene and I are extremely nervous, and I drive at a crawl as we peer through the fog for any sign of a car ahead of us. My driving speed is down to about five miles an hour.

Soon people are getting out of their vehicles trying to figure what color the traffic lights are. We can hear them calling to each other that the light has changed, and it's all right to go ahead. This goes on through many intersections. We listen for voices through the thick soup of eerie fog, hoping they will say the light is green. At one point it's so bad that we can't tell if we're even on the right road. I pull over and Irene steps out of the car but can't see anything. I then open my door to get out and I'm shocked when my foot bumps into the curb to my left. *Sweet Jesus, it just can't be. We're not in Ireland, this is California.* "Irene," I whine, "if the curb is on my left, that means we're on the wrong side of the road!"

"Dear God in heaven," Irene says. "There must have been a curve to the right back there and we just kept going straight."

"What are we going to do, Irene?" I moan. The air is so cold it chills to the bone.

"Keep your windows open, Patricia. I'll walk beside the car and tell you if I hear any other vehicles," Irene says. "Start turning to the right, and when I feel the curb at the other side I'll let you know."

Thank God there's very little traffic on the road tonight. No one in his right mind would venture out in conditions like these. The only people around need to get home no matter what, just like us. Two hours later, we're finally on Crenshaw Boulevard. The fog has lifted enough that we can see the traffic lights faintly.

When we finally get in, Mammy is standing in the living room.

"Jesus, Mary and Joseph. I thought you'd been in an accident." She plops onto the sofa. "Thanks be to God you're all right." We plop down beside her.

"It was a nightmare, Mammy," Irene says. "You couldn't even see the signal lights."

We don't mention about driving on the wrong side of the road. After all, we still want to go to the Irish dances, don't we? I can just imagine the reaction from Dorothy and Dolores's mother if they'd gone to the dance with us tonight and been two hours late getting home. Maybe after graduation, when Dorothy is working, her mother will feel like she's ready to step out in the evening.

Practice for my graduation ceremony goes on for days. As the time approaches, Mammy gives me money to buy a new dress to wear beneath the cap and gown. I have enough to buy a pretty muted-turquoise chemise dress, a style that has become popular lately. Sack dresses are also popular. The shirtwaist dress seems to have fallen by the wayside.

It's hot when the big Sunday arrives. The whole family comes to watch the ceremony and have a look St. Mary's.

Mammy is the only one besides myself who has ever been here before.

I'm nervous when my name is called, all eyes seem to be upon me and I can feel my face get hot. But I don't trip like I feared, in my long white gown. The music and speeches are very moving, and, although I'm happy to be out of school, I'm going to feel lost next week, not being able to see Dorothy and Dolores every day.

Pauline's dream has come true and she and Sean are married. They live in Granny's house, which has stood empty since Granny came to America. Sean is a school teacher, and Pauline is pregnant with their first child. It's too bad we weren't able to be at the wedding and won't be there when their baby is born.

Chapter Twenty Eight

During the school year, every day after our homework was finished, Denis, Michael and I enjoyed watching the Mickey Mouse Club. Now that I've graduated, I'll have to grow up and start thinking about my future. Especially since this was emphasized by the girl who gave the valedictorian speech at graduation.

I've been hoping to sign up at El Camino College and take courses toward a teaching credential, but this morning Mammy takes that little dream and flings it out the window. She comes into the living room while I'm watching television.

"Patricia, I've been going through the ads and found the perfect job for you." She hands me the paper and I read the ad she has circled. It's an insurance company, and they want high school graduates as trainees.

I think Mammy and Daddy miss Pauline's salary since she left. They're paying tuition for Denis and Michael in the Catholic school. It's expensive, and Mammy isn't working. Irene has been contributing for almost two years now, so I suppose it's time I pitched in as well. I call the number to get the address of the company.

The next morning I take the bus to Eighth and Grand in Los Angeles and walk past a park called Pershing Square. The Biltmore Hotel overlooks the park, and the insurance company is on the same block. I go to the personnel department with a dry mouth and my heart doing a drum roll.

After filling out the necessary papers, I sit thumbing through a magazine, not really taking in what I'm reading. I just hope I'll be accepted.

A handsome man comes out of the office and takes me aside. "I'm sorry, but you're just too young for the job." He looks like he's feeling bad about the rejection and what effect it may be having on me.

Trying not to show my disappointment, I leave the building. Halfway down the block, I'm dragging along, through the moving mass of people when I hear someone calling, "Miss Owens, Miss Owens!" I turn slowly, wondering who would know my name in this big city.

"I'm sorry I sent you away earlier," the same young man says as he catches up with me. "I spoke to my supervisor, Mrs. Taylor..." He's out of breath from running after me. "She's from England and says she understands the education system over there. She wants you to come back and have a word with her." I smile, and follow him back to the building.

"Oh, Patricia, I'm glad Steve was able to find you. Have a seat, dear." Mrs. Taylor speaks kindly, and I already like this woman very much.

We talk about my schooling for a few minutes, and she tells me I can start tomorrow, if it's all right with me. I nod and she smiles. "You'll start as a mail dispatcher," she says. "It'll help you learn the ropes." She tells me the beginning salary is a whopping $250 a month.

I'm dumbfounded. She explains the lunch program to me and shakes my hand. I find myself humming all the way home on the bus.

"Now you can ride with me in the morning," Irene says, when she gets home from work. She's beaming and dancing in circles around me. No more lonely bus trips for her.

Mammy is very happy about the earnings, and when I tell her that for three dollars a week the company provides a daily hot cafeteria meal with dessert and a drink, she's really impressed.

"Mrs. Taylor told me they have much happier, wide-awake employees, by providing them with good nutrition every day," I say proudly. "They'll just deduct the money from my salary every other week."

"What a generous company," Mammy says. "I'm amazed, and such great earnings too."

There's a physical exam to pass, and I certainly don't enjoy this part of the process. The doctor who examines me gives me the creeps. He takes far too long checking my breast area. I must be healthy though, because they don't ask me to leave or anything. I'm just glad my psoriasis is almost gone. It might have created problems.

My job is to push a four-wheeled cart through the building, delivering mail to different departments. It also entails collecting for the football pools, and to my delight I pick some numbers out of the blue and win $20 my first week on the job. I just hope they don't think it was a setup.

After several months of this, I'm put in the policy records department in the basement.

The insurance policies are all lined up, aisle after aisle of them on ceiling-high shelves. There must be thousands of them. Employees in the building call our department and ask for the files by number, and I rush to find the right ones before they appear at the desk for their order. It certainly makes the day go faster, although we do have slow periods once in a while.

During the quiet times, I meet some of the other people doing the same job. One handsome fellow reminds me of my Uncle Frank, except he's younger. His name is Martin, and he tells me he's from South America. To look at him, you'd never think it. His skin is paler than mine and he has blue eyes.

He starts talking religion, and I tell him I'm Catholic, thinking he probably is as well, being from a Latin country and all. But he frowns.

"I belong to the Mormon faith," he says. "I'd like you to come to one of the meetings and learn about our church."

"I'm sorry, but I'm happy with my own faith. Thank you anyhow," I say. I'm hoping I haven't hurt his feelings. He goes on to tell me that if you're a Mormon you'll be assured a place in the highest heaven and have all your departed relatives around you when you die, and the Catholic religion is wrong.

He invites me to go with him to the movies someday after work, and I do go with him once. I can see him out of the corner of my eye staring at me in the dark while I watch the screen. But he's a real gentleman. He kisses me gently on the cheek and keeps his hands to himself. Thank God for small favors.

When I ask Daddy about the Mormon religion, he looks very stern. "You tell your man that the Mormon Church was *established* by Joseph Smith, a mere man, but the Catholic Church was *founded by Christ, and passed on to Peter, the first Pope.*"

The next day, I meet Martin in the policy aisles and tell him what my father said about Joseph Smith and all. He gets really red in the face and stomps off. I don't think there's much chance we'll be going out on any more dates together. The religion thing is just too important in his eyes. I'd probably do better to stay with my own, anyhow.

Once in a while, Irene and I stop at a movie downtown before going home. Today we're watching a scary feature. The theatre is almost empty this time of day, but before we realize it, there's a man sitting right next to us. Irene whispers to me to get up and move to another part of the theatre. When we're moving she tells me that he was putting his hand up her skirt. Before long, the same man is back beside her again and doing the same thing as before.

We end up having to leave the theater, our money wasted, because the feature had only been on about twenty minutes.

"Maybe we should have reported him, Patricia," Irene says. But I know we'd both be too embarrassed to bring up such a subject to the man in the wee ticket booth.

"I think we're getting a good education on creepy people," I say. "It seems like they're all over the world, doesn't it?"

Irene nods, and looks sad. She must have been shocked to feel a complete stranger's hand under her skirt.

On the bus to work in the morning, Irene and I wish we could talk quietly, but when the Mexican women get on around Normandie Avenue, they speak loudly to each other in Spanish. If you're surrounded by eight or ten people chattering rapidly away, and you don't understand a single word they say, it can be really frustrating. Now I wish we had been able to take Spanish in school instead of Latin. Then, at least we would understand what exciting stories they are telling each other.

Tonight when we get home Mammy meets us at the door. "Hello Aunt Irene and Aunt Patricia," she says, with a big grin.

"What did she have?" we both ask together.

"A little girl, they called her Paula." She hands us the telegram. I just wish we could have been with Pauline to share in her happiness. Maybe someday...

***

Today, I get a wonderful surprise. I'm in the Pacific Mutual cafeteria eating lunch, when I suddenly spy Dorothy from Limerick and St. Mary's Academy, standing in the food line.

"Dor!" I wave at her as she searches for a table. She comes over and sets her tray down.

"Imagine meeting you here, Pat. How long have you had this job?"

"Around six months," I say. "What department are you in, Dor?"

"I'm in claims. It's strange we haven't run into each other before this," She says. "I've been here a week already. Isn't it a bargain, all this lunch for three dollars a week?"

We chat between bites, and Dorothy asks me if I needed to have a medical exam for the job like she did. I nod, and she goes on to tell me about the doctor who checked her out. She had the same reaction to him as I did, so I'm sure now I wasn't imagining things.

"I heard there's a company glee club that practices once a week after work. How would you like to join, Pat?" She tells me they even participate in competitions. I'm all for it and make arrangements to meet her after work so I can try out. It turns out to be loads of fun, and practice is the same night as Irene's Telephone Company bowling league, so Irene and I can still go home on a later bus together. The fact that someone I like so much is working in the same building adds to my overall contentment.

Several weeks later, I drive Dorothy and Dolores, and another St. Mary's girl, Patsy, to Disneyland. It's a relief that their parents let them go out in the daytime, and we "have a ball," as the locals say. Walt Disney is blessed with a great imagination and he has done so much to share his dreams with other people.

After about eight months in the records department, I'm moved up to the beneficiary change department. All we do is type in the names of new beneficiaries on the life policies. It's not as easy as it sounds, however. I find that sitting at a desk all day is more tiring than running up and down aisles searching for policies.

Dorothy's sister, Dolores has graduated from St. Mary's Academy and landed a job with Pacific Mutual as well. We're like the Three Lovely Lassies from Banion that Daddy used to sing about. We're all in the glee club and love the feeling of contributing to such beautiful music. Sometimes at lunchtime we go for a walk around the block, and during summer, find the smog is so bad that it makes our eyes burn.

The glee club enters several competitons where we have to wear semi-formal dresses, and although we never come in first, we enjoy the experience.

Dorothy and Dolores's mom wants to get rid of a piano that is taking up too much room in their house, and Mammy gets a good deal on it. She said she feels like she's back in Ireland again and playing the songs she enjoyed there. I seem to have forgotten how to read music, and content myself with playing by ear. But I'll never be as good as Mammy.

I've been in the typist position for more than a year now. Judith, who also lives in Torrance, sits next to me. One morning she catches me at break time and asks if I'd be interested in working in a savings and loan company in Redondo Beach, just two blocks from the ocean.

"They need an escrow trainee, and my dad is the manager, so I can't be hired," she says. "You'd like it, Pat. They're friendly there, and you wouldn't have to travel so far."

"If you think I'd have a chance," I say. "It would be handy being close to home, and I wouldn't have to get up so early in the morning."

If I change jobs now, I'm going to really miss my friends, the glee club, and the hot meals served daily at the insurance company. But I'm still hoping Dorothy and Dolores will be able to come to the dances with Irene and me.

I apply for and get the job, assisting the escrow officer. I type the notes, trust deeds and other papers necessary for the transfer of property from one person to the other. The company is in a small building, and they have purchased a motel next door for future expansion.

"I think you could afford to buy a car of your own, now, Patricia," Mammy suggests.

"But I don't have anything saved for a down payment," I say.

"Let me talk to your daddy when he comes home," she says.

After dinner, we visit several car dealerships. The first one has a cute wee Metropolitan that only holds two people. The price is right, but it's a stick shift. When we pull into the next lot, we see a lovely looking 1958 Chevy. It's light blue and white and a real beauty. After a short test drive, Mammy and Daddy put up the money for the down payment. I will make the monthly payments. As I drive home in this smooth, roomy, two-year-old-car, I can't believe it's really mine.

Mammy and Daddy have been discussing a vacation to Yosemite and San Francisco in the summer. I'll be very proud as we can use my snazzy car for the trip.

Since I'm working close to home, I've lots of extra time, and I've been driving Denis and Michael down to the beach these warm evenings.

We have a new blow-up mattress about four-feet square. We're floating out by the big waves, and it's amazing how the raft can take you right over waves that would normally knock you down and throw you around like a rag doll toward the beach.

Michael is pointing out boats that are just outside the harbor; both sail-boats and fancy yachts. The sun is low in the sky and has been hiding behind fluffy clouds on the horizon. When it peeks through we have to turn our heads because of the intense glare.

When I focus on the shore, I'm shocked and frightened. The beach has suddenly become miles away. People at the edge of the water are just tiny specks in the distance.

Michael looks alarmed and I speak calmly. "We're going to have to get back. Both of you hold on to the raft, and kick your feet as hard as you can." Thank God there's a rope looped around its outside edges for the boys to grab onto. I put my arm through the loop at the end of the rope, stretch my body out and start swimming toward land with all my might, pulling the air-mattress with my brothers hanging on behind. I'm using the breast stroke, the only one I feel comfortable with.

Minutes later the shore seems just as far away, we're getting nowhere and beginning to panic. "Just keep pushing," I say, "and hold on for goodness sake."

The second attempt is no better than the first. We only seem to be slipping farther and farther away as time passes.

We're so intent on getting back to land, we haven't noticed a red plastic float coming toward us. On the other end of the float is a lifeguard. "Thank God," I say. "What would we have done if you hadn't come?"

"Everyone hold on to the raft," he says with a strong confident voice. He grabs the rope and swims with powerful strokes parallel to the land. After a short time he changes direction and swims toward the shore with the three of us in tow, making it look downright easy. When we're in shallow water he explains that we were caught in a rip-tide.

"Thank you," I say, and Denis and Michael, repeat my words, but the lifeguard has already headed back to perform his lifesaving duty on other people like us who have been swept out by the undertow.

On the beach, a crowd of people are watching the rescues, and we are told undercurrents can happen suddenly, and you are helpless against them. The reason the lifeguard swam sideways though, was to get us beyond that particular current and back into safe water.

I think I'll stick to the beach side of the waves from now on.

Back on the job, I watch with my fellow employees as the motel next door is torn down and the land cleared and graded for the beautiful new building. There's a picture of the architect's concept on an easel in our small lobby. People stop and admire it, and I try to imagine what the inside will be like.

The brand new Harbor Savings and Loan springs up quickly out of the dust, while we slave away in our tiny building, anticipating the move. There's an open house celebration, and someone takes a picture of the female employees standing on the wide staircase looking elegant. On Monday we'll walk through the beautiful glass doors and sit at our brand new desks.

Chapter Twenty Nine

Our family has finally been able to save enough money for a down payment on a house of our own. This time we move closer to the downtown Torrance area, only two blocks from Nativity Church and one block from the school that Denis and Michael attend. It will also mean a much shorter walk to the bus stop for Irene.

It's a small frame house with only two bedrooms. Mammy said they just couldn't afford to pay the prices being asked for three bedrooms. The back yard is big enough, and they hope to add on a bedroom and bathroom someday. We're only two blocks from Marjorie and Eileen's house. Every street has sidewalks and the neighbourhood is great for taking a stroll.

Mammy and Daddy are trying to pay a little extra on their monthly payment, so that they'll have the house paid off sooner. That could take forever to accomplish since it cost thirteen thousand dollars.

***

Irene has been talking about entering the convent. I don't know what's come over her, and I question her about it.

"I always wanted to be a nun, Patricia. I've finally gathered up the nerve to act on my feelings."

She's been spending a lot of time in church lately, praying about it and wondering if she really does have a vocation. I'll miss her if she goes. I know she misses me on the bus to Los Angeles now that I'm working in Redondo Beach.

It takes months of prayer and pondering, and when Irene finally makes her decision, Daddy is happy. Having a nun or priest in an Irish family is a feather in your cap, and being as staunch as he is, he should be in seventh heaven.

Irene decides on the Poor Clare Convent in Santa Barbara. It's less than a block from the beautiful Santa Barbara Mission. When she lets me read the brochure they sent her, I'm shocked.

"This order is completely cloistered, Irene. They don't even speak, for heaven's sake, except for an hour at recreation time every day." I look at Irene, trying to understand her desire to make such a radical change in her life. "Their schedule is strict," I go on. "They rise for matins at midnight." I'm hoping she'll change her mind.

"Prayer and solitude is their whole life," Irene replies calmly, looking content with her decision.

I can't imagine spending the rest of my life in a place like that, but she looks serene and happy and seems ready to dedicate her life to God through prayer.

On an April morning in 1960, I hug Irene goodbye. She'll be twenty-one later this year and seems to know what she wants. Mammy and Daddy will drive her up to join the novitiate. She's left me her cookbook. I don't think she'll be needing it. I'm only eighteen and don't know when I'll ever need it, but you never can tell. Someday, Mr. Right may come along.

They don't eat meat in the convent, and they drink only water, milk, and Ovaltine. I can't imagine eating only fruit and vegetables, bread and cereal. Mammy is a bit concerned about her health on such a diet, but only time will tell.

Irene and I had a lot of fun together throughout our lives, and she was someone I could always talk to. Now I'll be the only daughter left in the house.

When our parents return from Santa Barbara, they inform the rest of us that Irene was given her novitiate habit to wear and assigned a tiny cell with only a bed and a side table. They waited while she changed, then said their goodbyes. They were told that the family can see her once a month.

For our first visit, we use my car. It can hold six comfortably, and Granny wants to come this time. Next month it'll be Marjorie.

When we reach Santa Barbara, we stop for lunch at a family restaurant on State Street. The town is absolutely fabulous with its Spanish-style structures and pretty parks, and the main street is buzzing with people.

As we file into the front hallway of the Poor Clare Convent, we notice that the nun who unlocked the door for us is nowhere to be seen. She's moved to another room behind a little round-about business. Anything that we wish to leave for Irene or the convent must be left on our side of the circular shelf that works like a turnstile. We place the items on the shelf and give it a push. It spins around and everything ends up on the other side. This way there is no contact. I knew they were cloistered, but this seems so extreme.

We have been told to walk down a corridor with gleaming wooden floors and enter a little room off to the side. Once there, we are shocked to see a metal grilled window on the wall with a black net curtain behind it. In front of this opening are straight-back chairs in a semi-circle. When Irene comes into the room on the other side of the grill, we can see her through the grill and netting but can't touch her. I was hoping to give her a hug, but this way it's impossible.

We sit quietly listening, as she describes her day. It's just like the brochure: no speaking, except for an hour a day, and no contact with the outside world. One great thing they do have is a dog. Irene says he's a real sweetheart. She's been put in charge of a section of the garden where they

310

grow vegetables. She also helps scrub and shine the convent floors. The nuns take turns doing dishes and cooking. She tells us the thing she misses most is a good cup of tea. She's willing to give it up, however, for the good of her soul. But to me, drinking hot water seems too much of a sacrifice. When she finishes her novitiate she'll receive a long brown habit, like St. Francis of Assisi, and will be give the name Sister Mary Catherine, a name she has chosen for herself.

I'm afraid Irene's good example is rubbing off on Denis, who is thirteen and thinking of going to the junior seminary instead of regular high school. If Daddy was proud before, he can be doubly so after this announcement.

***

In late summer our family, including Granny, makes the trip to Yosemite, for which we have finally learned the correct pronunciation. Getting closer to the valley after seven tedious hours of driving, we find ourselves in a long tunnel. When we reach the other end and emerge into the sunlight, the scene before us is almost too much to absorb.

High granite cliffs enclose the green valley below, and to the right a waterfall, long and graceful, seems to spout from the mountain like magic. In the distance we see Half Dome, the famous landmark that everyone talks about. The scenery is so beautiful and gloriously peaceful that we are awestruck for the first time since the aurora borealis.

"This was worth coming all the way from Ireland for, wasn't it?" Granny whispers.

We all nod in agreement, and Michael lets out a little squeal. He has found some tiny little creatures with stripes that don't seem to mind humans at all. We ask one of the tourists if he knows what the animals are, since they're too small to be squirrels.

"Oh, those are chipmunks," the man says, and he can't believe we've never seen one.

"In Ireland, we have hedgehogs," Michael says.

311

"I've never seen one of those," the man says. "What do they look like"

"They have sharp quills all over their bodies," Michael says proudly.

I remember seeing his excitement after a walk with Daddy, telling us about his encounter with one of the prickly creatures.

"Well, that makes us even then," the man says. "Although I do believe we have something similar here. They're called porcupines."

Michael and Denis laugh at the funny name and go back to watching the chipmunks.

Down in Yosemite Valley, we stop at several cascading waterfalls and gaze at the sheer cliffs that rise high above us. The first fall is called Bridalveil, and that describes it perfectly. It's the one we could see from the scenic point above the valley.

Before reaching the cabins at the Lodge we notice a line of cars stopped up ahead. As we get closer we see the reason for the holdup. Several bears have walked right up to car windows, and people are busy taking snapshots. We stop and wait for the line to move and keep our windows closed. Uncle Al warned us that the bears may seem tame, but they're wild animals and dangerous.

Our cabins at the Lodge are little square huts. Four beds are already made up in one, and two in the other. The boys and I will share with Granny, and our parents will have a room of their own. The cafeteria is right across the parking lot, so we can eat our meals there.

After several days, we're told by some other vacationers that if we drive to the Yosemite dump after dark we'll see lots of bears. We try it and see them scrounging through the piles of trash. The car headlights give them an eerie look. They look at us with ghostly phosphorescent eyes, and go on rummaging.

"They'll always know where their next meal is coming from," Daddy says, "and look how well they're training their wee'uns."

Other campers tell us that every night bears walk through the campsites and wake them up by rattling trash cans looking for human food. I'm glad we have our little wooden cabins with doors to protect us from these lumbering night creatures.

We stroll the peaceful valley by day, enjoying the winding river and flat green meadows. At twilight, we watch the deer grazing in the meadows, then gather at the community campfire for a lesson in nature. Later, around nine o'clock we stand in the valley with hundreds of other spectators looking up with anticipation. Glacier Point is thousands of feet above us and that's where the excitement lies. It's know as the ritual of the Fire Fall.

Everyone remains quiet when instructed, and we can hear the park ranger in the valley calling to the ranger on the cliff high above. They seem to be sending signals. Suddenly we see fire dropping from the cliff. Bright red embers glow in the pitch black night, shining against the cliff as they fall thousands of feet to the valley below. Cheers ring out and feeling like the little specks that we are, we watch in awe as this glimmering fire fades and dies just before reaching the valley floor.

It's one of the thrills of Yosemite, but by no means the greatest. The rushing waters of the giant waterfalls, spewing forth cooling mists, thundering claps, and resounding rumbles, are by far the most amazing sights and sounds to us.

The first day after we've seen the Fire Fall, Daddy suggests we drive up the mountain to Glacier Point where the fire originates. The journey is a pleasant one lasting about forty minutes, and the scene at the end is spectacular. As we stand at the railing on the edge, we can see the peaceful valley below, with the shimmering river snaking through green meadows. Looking straight across, we see a vast landscape covered with mountaintops as far as the eye can see. The silence is overpowering. Taking a picture of this splendid scene is almost impossible; there's just too much to cover.

"To think that Irene will never get to see all this beauty makes me sad," I say.

"Irene is seeing her own kind of beauty in what she's doing," Daddy replies.

But I'm thinking this would do her heart and soul a world of good. Maybe someday... And maybe someday Pauline can visit us and see this wonderful place as well.

What a great country this America is. Such a variety of scenery, all beautiful and so different from what we're used to. But for me majestic Yosemite reigns over it all.

***

Back to the old routine of my job, I sometimes go down to St. Lawrence Martyr Church during lunch and just sit in the empty sanctuary feeling the presence of God in the stillness. It's so comforting to watch the flickering light from hundreds of candles and wonder what the person who lit each one, was praying for, or offering up to God.

At other times, when I need to get away from the chatter and noise of the office kitchen, I enjoy walking to the bluff above the ocean where I sit on a bench to eat my sandwich. The beach is usually not very crowded at this time of day during the week. You only see an occasional housewife with her toddlers, or in summer, a few surfers. I love the sound of the waves, and today it brings back happy memories of Ballyhornan. It's been four years since we left, and I feel a sudden pang of longing for home. I miss the wild buttercups and daisies that we gathered throughout our childhood, and the country lanes where we meandered so many times. I think of the fun we had just doing simple things. We knew the names of everyone on our street, and the neighbors looked out for us. Today after sitting on my bench, I walk quickly back to the office and write down some of the thoughts that spilled from my mind above the blue Pacific.

At home and while driving, the images crowd my mind. During my lunch hour for about a week, I sit on the patio at

Harbor Savings under the shade of a table umbrella and work on the memories that have come to the forefront of my thoughts. Just putting it down on paper helps to relieve my longing, and gives me solace.

DREAMS OF HOME

By Patricia Owens

I still can hear the fragrant heather rustling in the breeze
Its royal hues of purple more colorful than trees.
And down below the heather, are fields of golden corn
Swaying gently to and fro on such a beautiful morn.

The little stone walls that for centuries have stood
Though crumbled in spots here and there.
Still act like shepherds protecting their flocks
From the wind and the moist salty air.

And if I close my eyes once more
I can feel the gentle spray.
As waves beat against the rugged cliffs
And are drawn back out on their way.

There are spots I remember where crabs used to play
When the waves withdrew much too soon.
In warm little rocky tidepools they'd stay
Till the tide turned again with the moon.

The seaweed that popped when you squeezed very hard
The dulse that tasted so good.
Are some of the things that are brought to my mind
When I'm lost in a pensive mood.

The dear winding lanes where wild woodbine grew
The blackberries, juicy and sweet.
Ready for plucking by eager young lads
On the way to the fields with their sheep.

Bright little cottages set here and there
With rain-water barrels so neat.
And occasional clucking from busy hens
When the chicks strayed too far from their feet.

And though I'm many miles from my dreams
My heart will never forget.
The beautiful home I've left far behind
But I'll never have any regrets.

For times were, when washing was done on a board
And water was pumped from a well.
And children went barefoot in cold winter rain
Till their small feet with chilblains would swell.

And though I grow pensive and homesick at times
I'm thankful to God up above.
For giving me what not everyone has
To be near the people I love.

Chapter Thirty

Ever since our Irene left, I'm lost on Saturday nights. I don't want to go to the dances alone, so I'm relieved when I find out about a small group called the Ulster Gael's Social Club. As Belfast is in the province of Ulster, I figure this club should be perfect for me.

They have picnics, beach parties and other weekend social events along with their Sunday evening dances. Dorothy and Dolores are able to talk their parents into letting them go to the afternoon activities with me. I have the car, and I'm happy to do the driving.

After a few months of the daytime activities with the club, their parents break down and allow them to go to the Sunday dances, since they end at nine o'clock.

A cute wee man called Harry McDermott runs the club. He's probably in his sixties, about five feet tall, with a roly-poly body. He's from the Republic of Ireland, so I don't know why the club is called the Ulster Gaels. I end up being the one and only member from the North.

Harry lives in a basement apartment of the large Jewish Temple on Wilshire Boulevard. He's the caretaker, and I always wonder why they hired an Irish-Catholic fellow for the position and not someone of their own persuasion. But Harry is happy with the job and isn't thinking of asking them any questions of that type.

One Saturday evening, when we go to visit Harry in his basement hideaway, he lets us peek inside the synagogue while the service is in progress. We can see the Rabbi taking the Torah from its resting place and reading in Hebrew. It's very different from a Catholic Church, and thank God no one notices us peering through the crack in the door. The faithful are lost in the fervor of their impassioned prayers.

It's strange to think that I passed that building so many times and had no reason to think I'd ever see inside the place. Now, every time I drive by I think of Harry's cozy apartment in the basement–his special pieces of Belleek china, his teapot with the crocheted tea cozy made by a member, and the pictures of club gatherings adorning the walls. Up above, I can imagine the large hall, holding the congregation, and the bearded rabbi reading from the Torah.

The social club is in dire need of musicians to play at the dances. They have a wonderful pianist, Sheila McGrath, who can play any Irish piece by ear. Dorothy tries out with her accordion and is accepted on the spot. Her fine talent will be greatly appreciated. I'm surprised she never told me she could play. It looks like she'll have a good excuse from now on for both herself and Dolores not to miss any of the dances.

The Ulster Gael's club meets in a church hall not far from MacArthur Park. When Dorothy takes a break from her accordion, Sheila plays the piano. Then Dorothy will play alone and let Sheila have a dance or two. The rest of the time they play together and keep the place hopping with their great Irish waltzes and quick-steps.

There's an occasional Saturday night dance in the Blarney Castle on Western Avenue. Dorothy and Dolores have finally graduated to the evening dances there, which usually last until midnight. Since I'm their transportation, I have been invited to sleep at their house to avoid having to drive alone all the way from their house to Torrance.

When we come in from our night out, we usually sit at their dining room table and talk about the different young men at the dances. Since we've gone well beyond our sleep we usually end up in a state of hysterical laughing and giddiness. We discuss how so many of the men stand by the bar all night and won't ever dance. Others, even the absolutely gorgeous ones, still need a few strong drinks to summon up the courage to ask. So many young girls sit there hoping for a miracle and many have been disappointed. We've come to the conclusion that Irishmen are basically shy.

In the middle of the night when we're all dead to the world, it never fails. Dolores will wake up groaning with horrible cramps in her legs. It's the result of a mild case of polio she suffered as a child. Dorothy runs in and massages her younger sister's legs until the pain subsides. I really admire her for this. Few people would wake nightly from a deep sleep and crawl out of a warm bed without complaining. To me it's a great example of Dorothy's kindness and her sisterly love.

Chapter Thirty One

Sean and Pauline have two children, now. A baby boy named John has recently been added to their family.

Pauline writes in the summer of 1960 telling us about the great unrest in Belfast and the rest of the North. The unemployment rate among Catholics is worse than ever, and a fundamentalist minister named Ian Paisley has been preaching bigotry and hatred against Catholics from his pulpit.

I'm saddened by the news. You'd think a man of the cloth would follow in the footsteps of a loving, caring God and preach tolerance. But he somehow imagines there's a conspiracy from Rome itself to take control of Northern Ireland. How can the Catholics take control, when their votes don't even count and so many of them depend on the government for their bread and butter.

Pauline also says that Catholics who live on the border streets near Protestant areas are beginning to feel threatened in their own homes, and the hostility is more open and vocal.

Daddy shakes his head when he reads the letter. "We were darn lucky I had a job while we lived in Belfast," he says, "because so many others were hopelessly unemployed. It's been four years already since we left there, and things only seem to be getting worse. That young Reverend Paisley is nothing but a blatherskite, if you ask me."

Michael looks up from his homework. "Blatherskite?"

Daddy smiles. "The Americans would call him someone who runs off at the mouth."

"Like Father O'Rourke," Denis blurts out, and everyone laughs.

Maybe someday we can visit Pauline and Ireland again. Or if things get bad over there, she could come back here again with her family.

***

Irene is quite content with her convent life, and Denis has signed up for the junior seminary in Dominguez Hills. The school is run by the Claretian order, and he'll begin in September. Michael has loads of friends since his school is just down the street, so having his older brother gone shouldn't be so difficult for him.

Mammy and Daddy are happy that I've found the dances and they hope I will meet a nice Irish fellow. At eighteen, I'm sort of hoping for the same thing.

The Ulster Gael's Social Club is having a beach party, and the three of us girls have been counting the days. There's always a chance that some different fellows will be there, aside from the usual crowd.

On the Saturday night before the beach party, I pick up Dorothy and Dolores for the Ancient Order of Hibernian's dance. It's also on Western Avenue, but this club uses the Blarney Castle, a much bigger hall. The usual fellows are there holding down the bar with their elbows, while keeping a sharp eye on the dance floor for any new beauties. I can't see how they could listen to all this lively music and just stand there drinking. They should be downright itching to get out on the floor and participate.

I notice a new fellow waltzing around the hall with Moira Duffy and he's keeping her laughing with his sharp wit. He has great dancing style and doesn't seem to depend on liquor to build up his confidence.

I'm wearing a brand-new navy blue shirtwaist dress with white polka-dots. Underneath I have my new petticoat, with three layers of red netting that really make it pouf out.

A fellow called Paul, who's fiancée is finishing up college in Canada, asks me up. They're playing "The Stacks of Barley," and we sing along as we whirl around:

Put your little foot,
Put your little foot
Put your little foot right down!

We face each other, and each slap our right foot twice like a tap dancer, and drag the left foot behind. This is repeated three times then repeated in the opposite direction with the other foot. When we say "right down," we lift our leading foot high and stomp it on the floor. This is followed by a one-two-three, one-two-three waltz around the floor. We whirl until I feel dizzy. Paul laughs, and when I ask, he tells me his fiancée should be arriving soon for a visit.

When the music ends Paul leaves, and Mike McMorrow walks slowly over from the bar. He's a good dancer but very shy and always has to drink up his courage. We dance an Irish waltz and Mike's height gives him lots of strength on the floor. We spin smoothly and almost bump into Moira and the new fellow.

After the music stops, Mike returns to the bar, and I go to the ladies room to freshen up. When I return, I notice Dorothy and Dolores doing the quick-step with several of the regulars. I don't quite make it back to my seat, however.

The jovial fellow who was dancing earlier with Moira, walks toward me with a sparkle in his eye. Looking like he has a bit of the devil in him, he holds out his hand and beckons me to the dance floor. We take our positions and wind our way into the swirling crowd just as the music ends.

A polka begins, and it's impossible to speak, but we laugh and twirl as the band beats out the lively tempo. When it's over we stand in place breathing deeply, waiting for the music to start again.

"I'm Neil," he says, and looks at me for my contribution.

"I'm Pat, or Patricia, as my family calls me."

"What part of the Auld Sod are you from?"

"Belfast," I answer, hoping this will not eliminate me as a possible interest.

"I'm from Cork City," Neil answers. "My sister, Tess, married a Belfast man by the name of Crilly."

This gives me a feeling of hope. "One of the Crillys from Cavendish Street?" I ask with interest.

"Yes indeed, the very ones. Do you know them?"

"My granny was a midwife, and she often spoke of their large family, and I know Cavendish Street well."

"What a coincidence, Pat or Patricia. How long have you been in the States?"

"Since 1956, and you?"

"Since 1957," he says, his eyes sparkling--lovely blue, mischievous eyes.

"Where have you been hiding yourself if you've been here for three years?" I ask.

"I was only here in California about three months when I was drafted. So I spent the last two years in the army. In fact I was just recently discharged and drove across the States with an army buddy to get back here. Before moving to California, I lived in New York for several months. I was in Toronto for four years and England for two."

"That explains why I haven't seen you around then," I say. I'm feeling attracted to him already. "Are you going to the Ulster Gael's beach party tomorrow?" I ask.

"It's the first I heard of it, but if you'll be there, I will too," he says, his eyes twinkling.

Suddenly I'm feeling all warm and wonderful inside. The hall looks brighter, the crowd more friendly, and the music sweeter. I wonder what is coming over me?

The band has started to play a slow romantic ballad, and we move closer.

"What's your surname?" he asks, moving me around the floor with a strength I wouldn't expect from a fellow not much taller than myself.

"It's Owens. Not very Irish, is it?" I almost apologize.

"Well, you'd be surprised," he says. He holds me tightly round the waist, and I don't mind a bit. "The Gaelic equivalent to your name would be McKeown." He's amused at my surprised reaction.

Dorothy dances by and raises her eyebrows at me. I try to ignore her. Neil whirls me and dips me back for the final rousing notes of the Irish rebel song, then whips me toward him. I have to hold on tight to keep from losing my balance. Heaven seems to be pouring forth a fair measure of jubilation and delight.

"What's *your* last name?" I ask.

"Sheehan," he says "It means peace-keeper."

"It's so Irish," I say. "I'd *love* to have that name, so I would."

And so I did.

Lightning Source UK Ltd.
Milton Keynes UK
UKHW021143060820
367802UK00008B/1884

9 780741 417251